Shattered Dreams
The story of a historic ICE raid in the words of the detainees

Compiled, edited and translated
by
Virginia Gibbs and Luz María Hernández

FLORICANTO PRESS

Copyright © 2014 by Virginia Gibbs and Luz María Hernández
Copyright © 2014 of this edition by Floricanto and Berkeley Press

All rights reserved. No part of this publication may be stored in a retrieval system, transmitted or reproduced in any way, including but not limited to photocopy, photograph, magnetic, laser or other type of record, without prior agreement and written permission of the publisher. Floricanto is a trademark of Floricanto Press. Berkeley Press is an imprint of Inter American Development, Inc.

Floricanto Press
7177 Walnut Canyon Rd.
Moorpark, California 93021
(415) 793-2662

www. FloricantoPress. com

ISBN:13: 978-1491086377
"Por nuestra cultura hablarán nuestros libros. Our books shall speak for our culture."
Roberto Cabello-Argandoña, Editor

*To Earnie —
a friend in the
struggle for human
rights.*
Virgi Stehr

Shattered Dreams

We dedicate this book to the women and men who generously shared their testimonies of the Postville ICE raid. We thank them for their willingness to talk about their experiences even though the telling was often painful. We also wish to dedicate the book to the many families in the United States, Guatemala, and Mexico who lives were forever impacted by the raid.

"It was both my privilege and challenge to serve as the Pastoral Administrator of St. Bridget's Parish in Postville, Iowa at the time of the notorious and disgraceful immigration raid at Agriprocessors on May 12, 2008. This experience convinced me that the "Postville Story" needed to be told and retold, for the sharing of a story can have a profound impact on our lives. Stories shape our lives. Stories inspire. Stories bring to life our deepest held values and beliefs. Stories inform and stories have the potential to transform. My hope is that the stories within this sacred text will have the power, not only to transform individual hearts, but ultimately to transform our current immigration policy."

Sister Mary McCauley, BVM

"An earthquake would not have been able to plunge Postville into a greater sense of loss and confusion than the federal government did that day. I remember the stories of the parents and the children who could not find each other, a community simply devastated by the raid, and the religious community stepping up to help, provide shelter, and provide information in the vacuum. Postville instantly became iconic in the American Latino community for why we need immigration reform and it is still an image that haunts and inspires me. And it is a story that must be told and remembered."

Rep. Luis V. Gutiérrez,
U.S. House of Representatives (IL-04)

Introduction

Postville, Agriprocessors and I.C.E.:

The Background

At ten in the morning Monday, May 12, 2008, the small town of Postville, Iowa, population 2,300, was the site of one of the largest immigration raids in the history of the United States. Some 389 undocumented workers who had made Postville their home—contributing to the economy, enrolling their children in school, participating in local faith communities—were detained by Immigration and Customs Enforcement (ICE) agents while at work at Agriprocessors, the nation's largest kosher meat processing plant. As two black helicopters flew overhead, a force of 900 heavily armed operatives plus personnel from eleven other agencies detained close to a fifth of the town's population. The raid gained national and international attention for its devastating economic and social impact on the community, and, especially, for the unprecedented use of the threat of aggravated identity theft charges that followed, and which the Supreme Court has since ruled unconstitutional.

In the years prior to that date Postville, once a rather typically homogeneous community of European heritage in the Midwest, went through enormous economic and social changes. The long-term residents of Postville, generally of German or Scandinavian background, provided services to the surrounding agricultural majority. Like many small rural towns it had begun to decline and the town's meat-packing plant had closed. In 1987 Aaron Rubashkin purchased the plant and turned it into one of the most important kosher slaughter houses in the country. Another company, Iowa Turkey Processors, also opened a plant in Postville, but it was destroyed by fire in 2003. With the arrival of major butchering facilities, Postville experienced an economic boom. Several quite different ethnic groups began to take up residence in the town. With the arrival of the kosher plant, a community of Lubavitchers, a highly orthodox Jewish sect, came to town to work at Agriprocessors, particularly to carry out the butchering requisites for kosher meat. At the same time, low-wage plant workers arrived. These unskilled laborers were made up of mostly Spanish-speaking immigrants from Guatemala and Mexico. In addition, there were workers from Russia, from El Salvador, and other ethnic groups.

Postville became an experiment in diversity. There were some conflicts and misunderstandings. Since the Lubavitchers have such strict dietary rules and have traditionally maintained a unique and separate identity, they were viewed as unwilling to become part of the wider Postville community. The mostly young and poorly educated Latinos were also viewed with suspicion, and the workers in the plants, most of whom had little education, were slow to learn English. On the other hand, attempts were made to celebrate this diversity with events such as the September gathering called *A Taste of Postville* which included foods and music from different heritages. People drove from other towns in the area to go to the Mexican or Jewish restaurants and grocery stores. Although the Lubavitch children went to their own school, in the Postville public schools the children of long-time residents and the sons and daughters of recent immigrants mixed. This second generation of Latinos learned English well and began to produce high school scholars and sports stars. Had the I.C.E. raid of Agriprocessors never occurred, who knows what the eventual result of the Postville experiment would have been?

Sadly, in the five years since the I.C.E. raid, the town of Postville, Iowa, went from proudly calling itself *Hometown to the World* to becoming an international symbol of the broken

Introduction

immigration policy. Directly after the events of May 12 the town found itself filled with broken and needy families. Most of the men who had been detained, and some of the women, were charged with aggravated identity theft—the first and last time the Justice Department used the threat of this charge for a large group of undocumented workers. Those arrested were given the choice of pleading guilty to lesser charges or facing more severe penalties for identity theft. They were tried in groups of ten, found guilty of the lesser charges and sent to prison for five and one-half months. The loss of these breadwinners left many families without food, rent, and other necessities. Some of the women who were arrested were allowed to return to their homes in Postville to care for children who otherwise would have been left with no parental support. Each one was fitted with an electronic monitoring device and told she could not leave the state of Iowa or she would be sent to prison and her children would be put into foster care. They were also told that it was forbidden for them to work.

These women, over 40 of them, found themselves unable to earn a cent and yet were expected to feed and house themselves and their small children. They also found themselves in legal limbo, having no idea if they would eventually be jailed, deported or when the electronic monitoring devices would be removed. After more than a year, some of the women returned to Guatemala under voluntary deportation, but not before spending many months depending on the Postville and Decorah churches and communities for material and emotional support. Others, who were victims of crimes while in the U.S., were eligible to apply for what is called a U visa. Part of that process is an agreement by the victim to collaborate with the authorities in prosecuting those crimes. The earliest recipients of the U visa waited almost a year, while others waited many more months for their legal situation to be clarified. Some still ended up being deported. On the second year anniversary of the raid, some women were still waiting to know their legal status. As for Agriprocessors, months after the raid, the company declared bankruptcy and was eventually purchased at auction to be run under the name Agristar. Agristar continues to produce kosher meat products but at a much reduced quantity than Agriprocessors.

Meanwhile, both state and federal offices prepared and prosecuted several cases against the Agriprocessors slaughterhouse. The first of these began in October 2009. Sholom Rubashkin, manager of the plant, was accused in federal court of cheating a bank, money laundering, and fraud. In November 2009 he was found guilty on 86 of 91 counts. On June 22, 2010 he was sentenced to 27 years in prison for the financial crimes for which he had been found guilty.

As part of a second planned trial against Rubashkin, this one for immigration felonies, the U.S. Department of Justice had brought back to northeast Iowa some of the Central American and Mexican workers who had been jailed for five and a half months. While most were deported directly after fulfilling their sentences, 30 men and four women were brought to Decorah and other towns to wait to serve as witnesses in this case. They were also fitted with electronic monitoring devices and remained in northeast Iowa as virtual prisoners until the completion of the first trial. The government had planned to try Rubashkin in December of the same year for 72 federal immigration-related charges but dropped the case after the guilty verdicts in the fraud case in the interest of judicial economy.

Unlike the women who had been returned to their homes to care for children, the men held as witnesses were eventually given work permits. Another story in itself was the response of the many Decorah families and individuals who took these men into their hearts and provided them with places to stay, clothing (they were returned to Iowa in November in nothing but shirts and slacks), food and employment, none of which were provided by the government that was holding them. One of the results of the community support for these men is a play the ex-prisoners wrote

Introduction

and presented called *The Story of Our Lives*. Once the immigration charges against Rubashkin had been dropped, these men were deported without the chance to tell their stories in court as they had waited almost a year to do.

The Attorney General of the State of Iowa also tried plant manager Rubashkin on 67 misdemeanor child labor charges. The trial took place in Waterloo during May 2010. The state alleged he had knowingly employed children in a packing plant (illegal in the state of Iowa) and that he also allowed these children to work around dangerous chemicals and machinery and for an excessive number of hours. On May 13 Rubashkin was personally acquitted of all these charges. The company he managed, Agriprocessors, pleaded guilty to 83 child labor charges. For Rubashkin's trial, six young Guatemalans who had been deported returned to Iowa voluntarily to testify, but the jury indicated that since they had originally entered the United States illegally and had lied about their ages to get employment at Agriprocessors they were not credible witnesses. After the trial they were sent back to Guatemala.

The Push and the Pull: The Situations in Mexico and Guatemala

In order to fully understand the testimonials in this book we believe it is necessary to have some grasp of the situations faced by Hispanic immigrants before they decide to come to the United States. We will concentrate on Guatemala and Mexico since these countries provided by far the greatest number of immigrants who arrived in Postville and all of the immigrants interviewed for this book.

Guatemala is a nation plagued by exploitation, poverty and natural disaster. According to the U.S. Department of State's statistics, "50% of the population engages in some form of agriculture, often at the subsistence level outside the monetized economy." At the same time, the Department of State recognizes that "more than half of Guatemalans are descendants of indigenous Mayan peoples." Some 24 indigenous languages are spoken in the country. Guatemala is a nation with a deep separation between the rural indigenous community and the "ladino" population that is of European descent and also includes mestizos who have abandoned indigenous languages and customs. These facts are important in the lives of the people who tell their stories here, from the young man who is unable to speak his native Kaqchikel after the trauma of prison, to the woman who wears traditional Mayan clothes in small town Iowa with pride. In most of these stories the scars of prejudice and abuse in Guatemala's strict hierarchical society are evident.

Key to understanding the narratives in this book is some recognition of the brutal civil war that decimated the Guatemalan Mayan population from 1960 to 1996. This war, the longest in the history of Central America, resulted in over 200,000 deaths over 36 years, largely among the rural indigenous population. Because of its general targeting of indigenous communities, the Guatemalan government's actions during those years have been termed genocide. Civil rights abuses that have unfortunately become commonplace in Central and Latin America typified the civil war years—torture, disappearances, death squads, the destruction of villages and crops, and mass assassinations. Nearly every one of the Guatemalans whose stories appear in these pages lost relatives during the civil war. Many remember raids on their villages or the disappearances of loved ones. The I.C.E. raid of Agriprocessors awoke memories of these terrible times for those who had lived through the Guatemalan civil war.

Since the 1996 Peace Accords that, with the help of the United Nations, restored some sense of democracy, political violence has lessened somewhat, only to be replaced by ever-increasing

Introduction

criminality. According to the Overseas Security Advisory Council, "the number of homicides [...] increased almost 45% from 4,507 in 2004 to 6,498 homicides in 2009. The prosecution rate for murder has remained between two percent and three percent." Although the number of homicides in Guatemala has fallen for three consecutive years to 5,174 in 2012, the murder rate of 35 per 100,000 inhabitants is still one of the highest in the world, according to Claire O'Neill McCleskey at *Insight Crime*. Gangs now pose a serious threat not only in large cities but in rural areas as well. Among other criminal activities commonly reported are armed robbery (even in daylight), narcotics and human trafficking, kidnapping and extortion, and rape.

The problem of impunity in Guatemala—the fact that criminals are very rarely held accountable for their actions—led to the establishment in January 2008 of a U.N.-backed International Commission Against Impunity in Guatemala (CICIG). However, in June 2010, the head of the U.N. panel, Spanish attorney Carlos Castresana, resigned from his post, stating that he could do nothing more to improve the situation because the government of Guatemala had been unwilling or unable to reform the justice system. The workers who have been forcibly deported back to Guatemala have expressed great fear for themselves and their families. Of particular concern to those who are or have been in the United States is the practice of targeting for kidnapping family members of people who have emigrated. The kidnappers ask for ransoms based on the idea that those with ties in the U.S. will be able to pressure family or friends to send money for the release of the child or spouse who has been taken. Extortion by threats of violence against family members who may be receiving remittances from the U.S. is also not uncommon.

Of particular concern is the situation of women in Guatemala. The CICIG reported that "687 women were the victims of homicide in 2008; their bodies frequently showed signs of rape and other torture." Amnesty International's 2009 Annual Report for Guatemala states that "The Office of the U.N. High Commissioner for Human Rights reported [...] that discriminatory practices by the authorities persisted, resulting in a failure to investigate killings of women, and a tendency to blame the victim." In 2012, Amnesty reported 631 female homicides despite a new law against femicide and other forms of violence against women. An article by Ezra Fieser in the *Christian Science Monitor* traces violence against women throughout Guatemalan history:

> From the patriarchal days of the Spanish conquistadores to the military's systematic torture of women during its 36-year civil war, the country has long cultivated a reputation as one of the Western hemisphere's most brutal places for women [...] The government estimated that 10,000 women were raped [in 2008], about 77 for every 100,000 residents. The real numbers are likely higher, organizations said. [Fieser 2009, para. 4]

The article goes on to state that only about 2% of rapes are ever brought to trial, again indicative of the problem of impunity. It isn't strange then that parents are willing to face the long trip and the difficult situation of living undocumented in the United States for the sake of their daughters. Some of the women we have spoken with before their deportation were convinced they faced a strong possibility of rape.

There is some hope that the United States government is beginning to take into account the situation facing the thousands of deported Guatemalan women. On July 12, 2010 a federal appeals court in San Francisco ruled on the case of Lesly Yajayra Perdomo, who was fighting deportation and requesting asylum in the U.S. based on her native Guatemala's record of violence against women. Perdomo said that she feared for her life if she was forced to return to Guatemala. The 9th U.S. Court of Appeals found in

Introduction

her favor and ordered that her deportation order be reconsidered by the U.S. Department of Justice. The court also ordered the U.S. Department of Justice to determine whether all Guatemalan women might qualify for asylum as a special class of persons at risk.

Guatemala is also a nation beset by natural disasters and poverty. Earthquakes, hurricanes, volcanic eruptions define the area inhabited by the Guatemalan people. In July 2010 tropical storm Agatha killed at least 152 people in the country and some 74,000 lost their homes and were living in shelters. At the very same time, the Pacaya volcano erupted, spewing ash over broad areas, causing the airport to close, and killing at least three who were crushed by rocks and debris. Mudslides destroyed buildings and buried some people in or near their homes. Thirteen bridges were washed away, and classes throughout the nation were cancelled. Heavy flooding, mudslides and winds affected some 136,000 in 2012. Natural disasters like these further lead Guatemalans to look towards *El Norte* as one of the only options for survival.

Some of the people who tell their stories in this book were prompted to immigrate following the massive destruction of Hurricane Mitch in 1998. As a matter of fact, during that time the U.S. had a special immigration policy regarding Guatemalans in response to the storm's devastation—they could not be summarily deported if caught crossing the border. They were given permission to stay in the United States pending a hearing approximately one month after their capture at which they could clarify their situation. Many didn't understand the procedure and thought they had crossed legally, oblivious, often due to language issues or the inability to give a permanent address for receipt of documents, that when they did not present themselves in court they immediately re-entered the status of undocumented.

Finally, and sadly, a problem that faces children in particular is extreme poverty and hunger. Much of Guatemala's population has engaged in subsistence farming throughout history. This has created a consistent struggle to sustain families. The situation has worsened in recent years. In July 2010 CNN reported that Guatemalan President Alvaro Colom had declared a state of national calamity because of the vast number of citizens who did not have enough food. Blaming that year's food problems on global warming, drought, and the effects of the international economic crisis, he sought help from international aid groups and other countries. The World Bank states that the nation has the fourth highest rate of chronic malnutrition in the world and the highest in Latin America and the Caribbean. Some 75% of Guatemalans live below the poverty level and some 58% have incomes below the extreme poverty level. Chronic malnutrition affects about 50% of Guatemalan children under five. The Guatemalans who tell their stories on these pages are mainly indigenous people from the highlands, where seven of ten children are malnourished. The children who are deported along with their parents, many of whom were born in the U.S. and are therefore American citizens, return to these conditions of malnourishment.

Extreme poverty, violence, abuse of basic human rights, hunger, and hopelessness are what push Guatemalans to immigrate to *El Norte* no matter what dangers they face on the way. The same conditions await them if they return and convince them to do whatever it takes to stay in the U.S., enduring abuse, exploitation, and constant fear for the sake of their families.

In many ways Mexico is quite different from Guatemala, having the thirteenth largest economy in the world and prospering on many levels. Its immigrants, however, are driven by many of the same problems—violence, poverty, and hopelessness. In the case of Mexico these chronic problems have been worsened by the "colombianization" of the country—the term used to describe the increasing role of the illegal drug trade and its effects on every sector of society.

Introduction

The Encyclopedia of Nations describes the present-day social stratification of Mexico, pointing out that despite the land-reform goals of the Mexican Revolution of 1910, 60% of Mexicans remain poor and income is very unevenly distributed. In some respects, however, Mexico has done quite well. In the field of health, from 1940 to 2000 life expectancy had risen from 42 to 75.3 years, and infant mortality has lowered from 125 to 25 per 1,000 live infant births. Mexico has an extensive educational system and 89% of the population is literate. Nevertheless, only 60% of Mexicans finish primary school. Housing illustrates the disparity between classes with over one million poorer Mexicans living in shanty towns around Mexico City while the wealthy enjoy life in the city's elegant areas. The Encyclopedia of Nations summarizes the situation as follows:

> In the modern era, persistent poverty has been one of the abiding problems of the Mexican economy. The economy has few safety nets; there is no unemployment compensation and the poor do not receive welfare payments. [Encyclopedia of Nations, 2010, para. 5]

As in Guatemala, poverty and lack of education are concentrated in rural areas, particularly those with a largely indigenous population.

David Bacon, in his excellent book *Illegal People* [p. 24], presents a series of illuminating statistics:

- With a total population in 2010 of over 111 million, 30 million Mexicans live on less than thirty pesos (less than $3) a day.

- According to the government of Mexico, some 37% of the population lives in poverty, and 23.6% in extreme poverty.

- Income in Mexico is falling faster than in any other country in Latin America.

- Rates of poverty vary a great deal from region to region. The state of Oaxaca, with a large indigenous population, has an extreme poverty rate of 75%.

A major event affecting the Mexican economy for the last several decades has been the establishment of the North American Free Trade Agreement (NAFTA) in 1994. This treaty eliminated most commercial and investment barriers among its trading partners: Mexico, Canada, and the U.S. While the overall effects of NAFTA on the Mexican economy are a matter of dispute, few ignore the uneven impact this policy has had on certain sectors of society. A 2008 U.S. Congressional Research Service Report on NAFTA and the Mexican Economy recognizes that "the overall effects of NAFTA on the Mexican economy might have been positive, [but] the effects have been unequal across regions and sectors."

In the conversations we have had with some Mexican immigrants they have tended to agree with the many scholars who present NAFTA as harmful to the working poor. A 2006 report by Roger Bybee and Carolyn Winter for CommonDreams.org, *Immigration Flood Unleashed by NAFTA's Disastrous Impact on Mexican Economy*, cites several aspects of NAFTA that have increased poverty, especially in rural areas. First, since U.S. subsidized corn and other products began to compete with agricultural products grown by Mexican farmers, especially those with limited amounts of land and technology, about two million Mexicans have been forced out of agriculture. At the same time, the cost of corn flour to make tortillas grew some 400% by 2007, causing thousands of Mexicans to take to the streets to demonstrate in the so-called "tortilla riots." Factors that have intensified the difficulties for the Mexican poor include product hoarding by suppliers to increase scarcity and the increased use of corn for biofuels in the U.S., both causing a steep rise in prices. Some of the immigrants from Mexico in this book left their homes because of the crisis in Mexican farming.

Introduction

The system of agricultural *ranchos* is itself an endemic problem that leads to exploitation, particularly for marginalized indigenous groups. In a sense, they function like company towns in the United States. These large extensions of agricultural land whose products include tomatoes, chilies, artichokes, and beef, to mention just a few, are owned by wealthy, frequently absent landlords. Men, women, and children often work from dawn to dusk in the fields, and then are charged for food (a plate of beans and tortillas) and a cot to sleep on. The children are unable to go to school. An article by César Salgado in the Mexican newspaper *La Jornada*, explains how workers, often brought from poorer areas of the country to the more fertile zones, are contracted for months at a time and are held at the *ranchos* semi-captive [*semicautivos*] and in subhuman conditions [*condiciones infrahumanas*]. It is not unheard of for workers to literally flee these conditions. The Human Rights Commission of the municipality of Jiménez in the state of Chihuahua reported on a group of 68 workers who had fled a *rancho* after being beaten and threatened. NAFTA has only exacerbated the situation since a large proportion of *rancho* products are now exported to the United States.

Big-box stores from U.S. companies have also been able to enter Mexico because of NAFTA, bringing with them low-priced goods made in China and other cheap labor markets, displacing local manufacturers of clothing, toys, snacks and other items. Bybee and Winter estimate that 28,000 small and medium-sized businesses have had to close because of the competition. It is ironic to watch the Mexican and Guatemalan immigrants from Postville flock to Walmart to buy nearly everything they need not only because the prices are low but also because many are used to shopping in Walmart in their countries of origin. It is also ironic to note that while NAFTA has opened the borders for a freer exchange of goods and investment opportunities, the borders have remained closed to the Mexican workers who have been affected most negatively by NAFTA policies.

Another factor important for the Mexican economy in the last several decades has been the initial growth and the subsequent decline of *maquiladoras*, cheap labor assembly factories, located directly south of the border between Mexico and the United States. This phenomenon began before NAFTA. Since the 1980s, Mexican workers have been drawn to the industrial belt located on the Mexican side of the border that has provided lower labor costs and fewer environmental and other regulations to mainly U.S. companies. This area of industrial development offered employment lacking elsewhere in Mexico. One interesting by-product of the *maquiladoras* is a shift in male-female relations since the *maquiladoras* tend to hire women more than men, thus turning women into the primary bread-winners for families who have come to the border to work in the new industries there. Competition from Asia is now causing some *maquiladoras* to close, leading to more unemployed workers who find that immigration seems to be the only option. Though not a rigid pattern, it is possible to see in Mexico a tendency for a displaced rural population to move from *rancho* to larger town, from there to urban areas and (increasingly) the U.S.-Mexico border *maquiladora* area, and then, finally, to the U.S. to become cheap undocumented labor.

Any discussion of the Mexican-North American border leads to issues of violence (especially violence against women) and to drug cartels and human trafficking. On July 25, 2010 at least 51 bodies were found in unmarked graves in a suburb of Monterrey, a major Mexican city near the border that is a battleground in the drug wars among competing cartels which also battle with Mexican and U.S. authorities. In June 2010 the remains of 55 recently deceased human bodies were found in a mine shaft in the state of Guerrero. In both cases the bodies showed signs of torture and mutilation. Recently drug violence has begun to affect tourist areas. On April 12, 2013, six people, believed to be independent drug dealers, were strangled and one decapitated in a home in Cancún.

Introduction

A special report from the Trans-border Institute of the University of San Diego states there have been more than 50,000 organized crime murders in Mexico from 2006 through 2011: "On average, for every day of 2011, 77 people were killed, three of whom were tortured, one of whom was decapitated, two of whom were women, and ten of whom were young people whose lives were cut short by violence."

To help gain perspective on the power and finances of the Mexican drug cartels, we note that in 2009 Forbes magazine included on its list of the world's wealthiest people Joaquín Guzmán Loera. Guzmán 'El Chapo' Loera, who escaped from prison in 2001, heads one of Mexico's largest drug cartels, and has earned his estimated $1 billion fortune supplying cocaine to U.S. consumers.

Connected with this violence is the case of Ciudad Juárez, another border city, which has become internationally infamous for the hundreds of women murdered in what is referred to as "the femicides of Juárez." There are over 400 cases of unsolved murders, mostly of young female workers in the *maquiladoras*. Bodies that have been recovered generally show signs of torture and mutilation. As in the case of Guatemala, impunity characterizes these crimes which most authors attribute to gang violence, corruption of local law enforcement, exploitation in the *maquiladoras*, and, finally, to a generalized collapse of systems of justice and human rights.

For many of Mexico's poorest, increased loss of the ability to make a living in agriculture or industry, added to the spiraling lawlessness brought on by the aforementioned colombianization of Mexico, has left them with few options other than the attempt to cross the border, in itself a most dangerous proposition given that the Mexico-U.S. border could currently be likened to a war-zone.

Lest we assume that the problem of violence stems entirely from conditions on the Mexican side of the border, it is important to recognize that since gun-possession laws are far stricter in Mexico, the United States has become, to quote the title of a New York Times article, an "Arms Bazaar for Mexican Cartels." The article states that there are more than 6,600 licensed arms dealers operating along the U.S. side of the border, many who sell directly out of their homes. In addition, the entire drug trafficking activity along the border is based on supplying the vast demand of North American drug consumers. The more the need grows for Mexicans and other Latin Americans to illegally cross the border for the work they need to feed, house, and clothe their families, the more drug trafficking and human trafficking become intertwined in a web of violence. In the Postville narratives, it is interesting to watch how the border-crossing experiences of those who crossed years ago, in the '90s, differ from those who crossed more recently, when kidnapping, for example, begins to appear in the stories.

The Voices from Postville

Before the 2008 raid, Postville had already been the subject of a book about its diverse community—Stephen G. Bloom's *Postville: A Clash of Cultures in Heartland America*. The book concentrates on the relations between the community of Orthodox Jews who arrived in Postville in the early 1990s to work in the kosher packing plant, and those non-Jews whose families had lived in Postville for several generations, mostly descendants of Germans, Swedes, or Norwegians. The book has since led to a documentary film produced by Iowa Public Television called *Postville: When Cultures Collide*. A major concern of critics of the book is that the Mexican and Central American workers who flocked to Postville to work in the plant were largely ignored in Bloom's book. In the year following the raid a new book on Postville appeared: *Postville U.S.A.: Surviving Diversity in Small Town America*. Authors Mark Grey

Introduction

and Michelle Devlin, professors at the University of Northern Iowa, and Aaron Goldsmith, former mayor of Postville, do a particularly good job describing the raid and its effects on the region. Here again, however, the perspectives of the Spanish-speaking workers most affected by the raid were almost entirely absent. Their voices have yet to be heard.

Since the raid Postville has also earned the attention of several documentary film makers. Luis Argueta, prestigious Guatemalan-born director-producer and Academy Award nominee for his 1994 film *The Silence of Neto*, came to Postville a few weeks after the raid with the idea of doing a short documentary.

Almost instantly captivated by the human drama and its implications for justice and immigration reform, he began working tirelessly to complete a feature length documentary, *AbUSed: The Postville Raid*. The film was released in 2010. A short film that is part of Argueta's project and can be found on the AbUSed website: *De Facto Deportee*, highlights a little girl who is a U.S. citizen but was deported along with her mother and now faces malnutrition. Greg Brosnan and Jennifer Szymaszek created another independent documentary film called *In the Shadow of the Raid* which shows the effects of the raid both in Postville and in Guatemala.

These documentaries are the only real opportunities the Guatemalan and Mexican victims of the raid have had to tell their own stories. Anxious to speak on their own behalf about the situations they faced in their countries of origin and the working conditions inside Agriprocessors, they were in the end denied that opportunity when the federal government dropped the immigration-related case against Sholom Rubashkin. More than anything they wanted to communicate to anyone who would listen that despite arrests, months in jail, and deportation they were not common criminals, they were not thieves or murderers. Their crime had been to work; their crime had been to fill jobs that allowed them to feed their families.

Shattered Dreams

The purpose of this book is to allow those most affected by the May 12, 2008 I.C.E. raid of Agriprocessors in Postville, Iowa, to speak at length about their lives, why and how they crossed the border, the conditions they faced at the plant, what they experienced during the raid, and what has happened to their families since.

The Making of this Book

The two of us who gathered the stories and edited this volume were among the many from nearby communities who began to work with the Guatemalan and Mexican families who needed immediate help to survive after the May 12, 2008 raid. The raid had turned Postville into the scene of a massive humanitarian crisis as hundreds of families were left without breadwinners, parents were separated from children, and entire families suffered psychological trauma. Volunteers arrived from all over the Midwest and journalists arrived from all over the world. As professors of Spanish at Luther College, half an hour away from Postville, we have language skills that were needed to help the families affected by the raid. Luz María Hernandez, who had already been working with Postville's immigrant community, arrived while the raid was still in progress, and soon became one of the members of the Postville Response Team as media liaison. Virginia Gibbs became active in the effort a few days later, serving throughout the summer as a volunteer interpreter/translator for attorneys, public officials, medical personnel and social workers. She also began helping a group of Guatemalan weavers distribute their textiles.

After several months of close contact with families we became convinced that many of them had important stories to tell about how and why they came to the United States, the working conditions they endured (particularly in the meat packing industry

Introduction

in Postville), and the raid itself and its aftermath. We also found that the workers and their families, many from indigenous communities and coming from primarily oral cultures, had a real gift for story-telling and are very anxious for people of the United States to understand their lives and experiences. By the end of the summer of 2008, we began conducting and recording lengthy interviews with a variety of informants.

One of the things we quickly discovered was that many of the people caught up in the events of the raid and its consequences were extremely anxious to have their voices heard, to have their stories told. Some had spontaneously started to write down their memories of working at the plant and of the raid, which seemed to trigger in them a need to cease being silent victims and to begin to speak out. The fact that the second trial which had to do with working conditions was cancelled, and that the state trial over child labor focused only on the issues of age, has left us and our immigrant friends feeling an urgent need to present their side of the story, their experiences, their emotions and the results of the whole immigration experience on their families. With the current debates over immigration reform in the United States it is also important to let the immigrants themselves explain their lives. The stories we have gathered include stories of childhood and family life in the home country, the decision to come north, the journey and the border crossing, life in Postville pre-raid, the raid itself, the months after the raid, and visions of the future.

As editors, we have tried to let our friends speak for themselves, avoiding any manipulation of the texts. At the same time we recognize that spoken language is different from language written to be read, and we have done some editing to make the accounts more readable, but this has been minor. We began and continued our project based on the idea that language is power and a recognition that the Hispanic immigrants of Postville have been systematically denied the opportunity to tell their stories.

This book attempts to undo that silencing and to give them that opportunity to speak for themselves.

The story of Postville belongs, more than to anyone else, to the people who lived through the raid and have suffered its most extreme and long-lasting consequences. The real story of Postville is part of the history of Guatemala, Mexico, and the United States, and it is the story of generations of indigenous people. It is our hope that these testimonials provide a partial remedy to the barriers that have kept our friends from fully using the power of their own language. These men and women individually tell of their lives in their own words but in doing so help empower the millions of Hispanics who have come north because they believed it was their only option. At this point in U.S. history, anti-immigrant sentiment has led some to want to eliminate the 14th Amendment of the U.S. Constitution, the amendment that makes all of us who were born in this country automatically citizens of the United States. Given this trend, it is time for as many of us as possible to get to know the voices of our Hispanic immigrants.

Virginia Gibbs

Luz María Hernandez

Julia

My name is Julia, and I'm from Guatemala. I was born on a farm called Finca Concepción. I'm thirty four years old. My mother's name is Lola, and my father's name is Luis. I'm from a poor family. There were eleven of us siblings, six boys and five girls. I'm the fifth child. Three of the children went to school on the farm. The farm belonged to a man who had a lot of land, and he grew fruit and vegetables, apples, pears, peaches. The farm workers worked half the month for him, and half the month for themselves. Half the month was paid, the other half wasn't.

The workers who were on the farm lived in houses made of corn stalks. The roofs were straw, and the floors were dirt. The workers lived there with their families. There were about 150 to 200 houses because there were a lot of people working there. They paid everyone the same, 40 *centavos* a day. That was 31 years ago. My father worked on that farm for many years, but then they took away his job, and we went to the town of Rosario.

My three older brothers left school, and they went to the capital when they were still small in order to work and help my parents, but there were still eight of us at home. My parents put us in school there in Rosario, but we only studied for two or three years. When we got a little bigger we started to work in the fields, and that's how we were raised.

I got married when I was 17 years old. I had four daughters and one son. We were very poor, but happy. Then all of a sudden my husband decided to come to the United States. He came for the first time in 1996. For a while he would come to the U.S. for two years, save some money, and then go back to Guatemala, and then come back here again to the U.S. for two more years.

Shattered Dreams

In 2004 we decided that all of us should come. We brought the kids. On the border they arrested my husband, but they let me and the children stay. They held my husband for 45 days, and then they deported him.

I came to Postville and lived with my brothers because they were already here. They were working and had encouraged us to come. That's why we brought the whole family, because they said there was work at Agriprocessors. They said that they would hire us and give us jobs.

After they deported my husband, he tried to come back across the border, but they caught him again. That time he was in jail for almost seven months. I was very unhappy and wanted badly to go back to my country, but our debt made me withstand the suffering. We owed so much money that I had to work for the children, and I had to think about the future and keep on struggling for them. I waited until my husband decided whether to stay in Guatemala or try to come here again, but he put his faith in God and was able to join us eleven months later.

The days and months went by and we were so happy to be in Postville. We were here for three years and five months. Our family was full of dreams until one Sunday when, as usual on a weekend, the whole family got together. But that day was different because none of my brothers wanted to drink, nobody even drank one beer. We made dinner, and we were very happy as we ate together, and had a good time on that blessed Sunday.

Then we all said goodbye. I went home with my children and night fell. That was the day before the raid; it was May 11th. I think now that it was as if we could sense something, because that day we were all together and so happy.

That Monday I got up early like every other morning to go back to work. I went into the plant and punched in at about 6:45 a.m. I put on the work clothes they gave us: a coat, a plastic apron, plastic

Julia

sleeves, rubber gloves, rubber boots to go over shoes, and a hair net. I started to work just like always.

At about 9:45 another worker ran past shouting, "The *migra* is coming!"

I couldn't believe it because people always said that Immigration couldn't come into the plant because the owners gave the *migra* a lot of money from us the workers so that they wouldn't come. I was terrified, but I didn't think about running away because the only thing I could think about was my children—four of them were at school. Another daughter was at home with my husband, and the littlest one was six months old and was with one of my sisters.

It was a very sad day because by the time I looked they were already coming for us. They arrested me at about 10:15. My mind just went blank, and I couldn't move from where I was. I could only watch as they took away my friends, how the agents treated them, how they swore and called them filthy names.

When two of my friends ran off trying to get away, a woman agent shouted "Stop, you bitches! Stop, you whores!"

They said so many things to us. I just stood there without moving. Suddenly I saw my brother, the one who was living with us. I felt that the blood had gone out of my veins on that May 12th.

That was a day that marked us forever. It changed all of us in different ways, psychologically and mentally. It forever marked the lives of the children because they were in some ways affected more than anyone else. For example, my children saw how other parents had chains on their hands and feet. They saw this because when they got home, my second daughter went on the internet. She started to show her sisters and brothers what was on the internet and how all the Hispanics who worked in the plant were being taken away.

Shattered Dreams

My brother was at the head of one of the two lines of all the men. He was in the line when they started leading them out of the plant. There he was on the internet, and my children saw him. They also saw how we mothers were confronted with the humiliation of having to wear an electronic shackle on our ankles. In my case, if I don't plug it in for just one night, an immigration officer calls, and since I don't speak much English I'm forced to put my son on the line.

This is how my kids are most affected because they ask me, "*mamá*, why don't they take that thing off your foot?"

I try to find a way to explain so that they can understand. I have a five-year-old daughter, and she asks me "*mamá*, did you kill somebody? Is that why you have to wear that thing?"

I tell her that of course that isn't true, but she can't understand. I brought her here when she was only five months old so she has no idea of how we came and how we crossed the border without documents. She asked me if the electronic shackle was a toy, or if I had stolen something, if I had done something bad in someone else's house. She asked if the shackle hurt my foot, and why it was so heavy. She would touch the shackle while it was plugged in to feel what it was like.

She's spending her childhood here in Postville where a lot of the kids dream about having a better future. This is a dream that in most cases has gone unfulfilled because many of the children have been deported together with their parents. Some of them were born here. Postville was the cradle of a lot of families in Guatemala as well as here. This is the reason why the lives of most of the men were destroyed when they were deported. Their dreams of giving a better life to their children were destroyed.

May 12th was a very sad day, a very dark day, a day that will mark my life forever, a day that made me remember the massacre in

Julia

the village of Aguacate where we were humiliated and abused and where we thought we were going to die. I remember the massacre because when I was a little girl, maybe six years old, we lived on a farm. The owner paid us very little, about 25 cents, because the workers were also given a place to live and a little area to farm. So the workers went on strike. They marched to the capital city to the presidential palace to ask for help but they were given nothing. In the strike one person died and several others disappeared and then turned up later severely beaten. The one who died was tortured, and then they killed him.

Just after the strike, we went a long time without eating because our parents were afraid to make a cooking fire with wood because if there was smoke then the soldiers would know there were people living on the farm. A short time after that, the massacre took place in that village of Aguacate. Our parents hid all of us under the beds. Some men took my uncle on my mother's side, and he never was found. That was twenty years ago. Another man that they took did reappear, wrapped in black plastic. Half his tongue was gone, he was missing the tips of his fingers, and there was wire wrapped around his neck. I saw that because we lived on the farm, and they took him there, and like any curious little girl I went to look. They had taken three men away because of the strike. Some said it was the government, some said it was the Guatemalan guerrillas, we never knew who had done this. They just showed up and asked to speak with someone, called his or her name, and put them in a car. The men who took them were dressed in civilian clothing.

Then we could hear how the helicopters were flying overhead dropping bombs, and we could hear shooting in the village. So the day of the raid in Postville we lived through the same thing because they carried off the men and the women, and we never saw them again. I was more afraid that day in Agriprocessors. It was worse for me because they pointed their guns at us, they screamed at us to give up our "guns" and knives because to them we were dangerous people. They yelled at us to hand over the drugs and tell them where the lab was with the drugs they were looking for. I was terrified. When we were kids I saw my uncle being taken away, but here it was worse for me because we experienced it ourselves. The agents swore and yelled and pointed their guns at us.

When I left the plant it was 2:00 in the afternoon. I went home. The whole town was like dead, there were no people in the streets, just police patrols. When I went to the school, all the Hispanic children had been separated from the American kids. They were all crying, some for their mothers and some for their fathers.

Thank God for bringing us Luz María, Father Pablo, and *Don* Pablo, Pastor David, Sister Mary, and Violeta [people who worked with the Postville Response Team]. They were like a glass of water that calmed our thirst and a cloth to wipe away the tears of all of us who were released for so-called humanitarian reasons. I don't think it's at all humane to have to wear an electronic shackle on your ankle—it hurts! And the way people look at you when you are wearing it hurts, and it hurts, too, when your children ask why you have to wear it.

Meanwhile, in the plant, all the terror and humiliation of mothers who were mistreated by immigration agents continued. The agents were heartless, they viewed us with racism. The officers treated people very badly. There were about eight or ten officers for each person who was detained. They would talk together in English and laugh at us. From the look in their eyes when they watched us and the expression on their faces, we realized that it was pure racism. They laughed at us a lot. But a few of them told us they were very sorry, it was their job, and they had to do it. For example, I was standing just outside the area I worked in watching how everyone was running. I wanted to see my brother, but a female agent grabbed me from behind and pulled me down by the hair. When I asked her why she was hitting me since I wasn't even trying to get away, she told me to shut up and said I had no right to say anything at all, and anything I said could be used against me. She said if I talked it would make things even worse for me.

The agents were hitting a lot of the men. They grabbed them anyway they could and forced them to sit. I saw how they were pulling one of my husband's cousins by the hair, they made him sit, they pulled him back up, and then they pulled him back down again, always by the hair. They were kicking another one of my friends, who was restrained by plastic ties, because he was trying to get away. I also saw how another young man from my town had an iron spike go through his calf—it went all the way through from one side to the other—and they wouldn't let him clean the blood. The blood was squirting out and they just had him tied up. This is something you never forget; it marks your life forever. Even if they end up giving you papers to legalize your situation, this is never going to go away.

Every time they caught someone they would applaud and shout with happiness. They didn't seem to be okay in the head. When we were in the bus they were laughing at us. They would say, "Are you hungry? Do want something to eat? Well too bad, you aren't going to eat anything until tomorrow at this time."

When they were questioning us at the computers they mistreated us and yelled at us. For example, they told a woman friend of mine that she had crossed the border before, and she said no, no she hadn't. But a woman said to her that she had better tell the truth or the agent was going to lose her patience. We couldn't even remember things because we were so frightened. All we can do now is ask God to help us forget, but the more we try to forget, the more we remember.

They put us in two lines, one for the women, and one for the men. They would tell us to sit, and then when we were barely seated, they would tell us to stand up again. They tied the men's hands with plastic [ties] which was what they used to detain people inside the plant. When they took them out to the bus, they put them in chains from their waists to their hands and ankles. They separated the women who had said they had children, and put paper bands on our wrists with our names, a detention number, and the number of children we had in school. There were red bands, pink ones, and green ones with the number of kids who went to school.

They took my brother to Waterloo, and then they put him in jail. When we were talking on the phone he told me that at noon on May 13 the agents sent out for pizza, and they were celebrating their success at detaining so many people. They had a big party and were throwing beer at each other because they were so happy that everyone had been caught.

I will never forget that day. We had never thought that something like that would happen. It was a day that shredded all my dreams because everything collapsed, and we will never again be able to pull ourselves up because we will never be able to come back to the U.S. either legally or illegally because they presented us before the law and the government as terrible criminals. We know we have violated the law, but we aren't criminals. It's so humiliating. If I see a policeman or an agent I still feel very afraid, like the same thing is going to happen to me again because that day we were feeling so confident and happy as we worked and joked together when all of a sudden we heard our friends shouting behind us the *migra* was coming.

I'd like to tell you a little more about my childhood. I worked on the farm harvesting green beans and peaches, and cleaning carrots and *frijoles*. Kids there would start to work at about eight or nine years old. All I did was work in the fields. I didn't go to school because we would start working at 7:00 in the morning and finish at 5:00 in the afternoon. Then we would have to haul water from the river to our house. We did that every day. Twice a week we would go to the river to wash at 4:00 in the morning and I would

Julia

wash my younger brothers' diapers. Then at about 6:30 we would have to go back to work in the co-op. It was a company formed by five brothers. They planted different kinds of vegetables—peas, string beans, carrots. They were planting crops all the time. They gave work to the other people. There were also peach and pear trees that we harvested from once a year. But it was only the vegetables that gave us jobs all year round.

When I started to work I was earning 2.5 *quetzales* an hour. That would be about 35 cents [actually 54 cents] because back then there were 4.5 *quetzales* per dollar. The head of the coop traveled to the United States to show the products and then started sending them there. So then we were the ones who packaged the crops. There were about 15 girls; the oldest were 16 or 17. They used us girls to put the peaches or the peas in plastic trays. We packaged five peaches or a pound of peas in each pack. There was a packaging machine, and it had a roll of plastic wrap. We would put in the five peaches and pull out the plastic, wrap it around the tray of fruit and pack it all in boxes.

We did that work for about four years. My brothers helped my Dad plant corn. Only one of my brothers, the one who was deported because of the raid, worked with me. He was eleven years old, and I was nine. We were the smallest ones there. After me there were just the youngest ones in the family. It was their clothes that we had to wash in the river. My brother and I got along really well. My Mom would get a bath ready for me, and my brother would pour the water over my head. He would help me with everything. When there was no work in the cooperative, they would give us a day or two off. Then we would pasture the animals or work in the corn fields. That's why sometimes I don't understand my youngest sister, Lola, at all.

Lola is the youngest, and she says a lot of things. I tell her that she and my little brothers didn't suffer what we suffered. Day after day we had to carry water in big jars that held four or five gallons. We would carry one jar on our heads and hold another in our hands and we were always bringing water. My brother would put a rope through each of the handles so that it was like a big *macapal* [forehead harness] so that we could carry the water. This brother who helped me so much is named Antonio.

We worked in several different places. For example, when we finished harvesting carrots we would go to pick coffee with my mother. All of us would go—all eleven brothers and sisters. She took us, and we would go on a Sunday and return on Saturday, every one or two months. During that time we could only manage to pick fifteen or twenty pounds of coffee, which was the most we could do since we were so young. The coffee harvest ended in December, and then we would go home in January or February and start digging carrots. I remember once we went to pick coffee, and we had to cross a big river, jumping from rock to rock. That day I dropped my *caite* [sandal] in the water. I had to walk without it—it was like walking from Postville to Decorah [22 miles]. But that's how it was. There was a lot of suffering.

I really liked studying, but we couldn't go to school because there were so many of us. None of my brothers or sisters went to school and graduated. We each just studied for two years. My youngest sister was able to study more because the rest of us didn't complete our schooling. We helped pay for her studies, but after the raid here in Postville she had to drop out because we couldn't send any more money. Now the only ones who are going to school are some nieces and nephews who are living with my mother. They are one of my sister's children, but she forgot all about them and left them with my mother. When we can, we send them some money so that they can eat better, and when they don't have anything, they just have to put up with it.

When we decided that all of us should go to the United States,

Luisa

I was born on September 22, 1977. I have a sister and two brothers. Since I can remember we have always lived in extreme poverty. When my fourth sibling was born I was sent to sleep at my grandfather's house with my aunts, who were single. I had to sleep with them because there weren't enough beds in my house.

I remember that my father drank a lot, and sometimes he would hit my mother. She would hide us in the bed and cover us up with a poncho. I would lift up the poncho to see how my mother defended herself. He would hit the wall when she protected herself. Sometimes my mother would try to get him out of the room and leave us there so we wouldn't see him beating her. He also abused her with a lot of foul language. He humiliated her, and he did the same thing with us.

Once he tried to hit my *mamá* with a machete. She defended herself and tried to talk with him. It was as if he was looking at someone else, and then he tried to hit himself with the machete like he wanted to cut himself. I got out from under the poncho and started to scream. My father stopped hitting himself and left.

He often said when he was drunk that he was going to leave the house. He would tell my mother and then put some clothes in a flour bag and go away, who knows where? When he had finished his binge he would come back. Then he wouldn't talk to my *mamá*, but I would take him food out in the fields. There was a place in the road that was like a "Y," and I would stop there and call to him. He would whistle back and say "Here I am," so I would take that road and go to meet him so I could give him the food.

They sent me to kindergarten for a year and then to first grade. I was living with my paternal grandfather and my aunts. I only came home to leave my school books, and then I would go out into the fields to weed and plant carrots. My father also grew natural medicinal herbs, and I helped him with that. He knew a person who lived in Santo Tomás Antigua, Guatemala, and he would take the herbs to him. We never got the chance to visit that man's house because my Dad was ashamed to say he was our father. He was very abusive to me in the fields. He would put a furrow in the ground, and I had to watch him very carefully because if I didn't pay attention he would call me a piece of shit and things like that if I didn't do a good job.

After a time my mother started selling vegetables like radishes, cauliflower, spinach and other things, so everyone went to the fields to work. With everyone so busy working the land, I had to start making the tortillas for the family when I was only eight years old. I would make them by hand, put them on the *comal* and cook them over a wood stove. When I was doing that task they would leave me all alone. Nobody lived near our house, and I felt lonely. I would cry and ask "*mamá*, why did you leave me?" When they came back from the fields I felt better.

I was still a little girl when I realized my mother was taking *Sal Andrés* with mineral water. Sal Andrés was a remedy for stomach troubles that came in little green envelopes. She said she was taking it because she often felt nauseated. One day my mother started to vomit, as if she were pregnant. She was always sick to her stomach. She couldn't eat because she couldn't keep anything down. Little by little she kept getting worse. Finally she couldn't get out of bed. My father and my grandfather went to the *brujos* [healers] but instead of feeling better she got worse. They wouldn't allow me to go to school anymore because I had to take care of my mother. It all took a long time. I would make dirt baths for her to help her with her vomit. Dirt baths are when you fill a bucket with dirt and put it beside the bed so that the person can vomit and then cover it with soil. When she had no more dirt left she would

Luisa

call to me, "*M'ija.*" Then I would drag the bucket out and bring in another one.

My father became very upset and on edge. He scolded me and hit me. *Mamá* would try to defend me in spite of being in bed. She told him not to hit me, not to beat me. She would get out of bed and stand between my father and me so that he couldn't hurt me. Then one day her death agony began, and she was screaming. Her chest and her neck were all purple as if she didn't bathe. Now, from what I've seen and learned from television, I guess that she died of cancer. When I was a little girl I didn't know about those things.

People gathered round. They said she was going. I didn't know she was dying. She tried to speak with us, but she no longer could. They took us to see her. Then they sent me to a store that was pretty far away, it was about eight or ten minutes on foot. When I was coming back one of my aunts called to me from the door of her house, "Luisa! Luisa!"

When I stopped to talk to her she said, "Your *mamá* just died."

I don't know what else she said, I could see that she was still talking, but my mind wasn't making any sense of what she was saying. I just kept hearing "Your *mamá* died." When I got home there were a lot of people, and they wouldn't let me into the room. I knocked and knocked, and then I ran inside. I talked to her. I tried to move her. I took the covers off of her. It was as if she were asleep. I told her not to leave me. One of my aunts realized [what I was doing] and told me not to look at her, and they took me out of the room.

"Don't cry. don't cry," they told me. My father said, "We'll be okay."

I didn't react. What came next was the worst for us. It was so hard because my mother was gone. My father told me he was going to teach me how to cook just once, no more than that, just once. I had to cook. I had to make the tortillas. I had to wash the clothes. I would go by myself to do the laundry.

No one ever helped me or said, "This girl needs help with the washing." I always did a bad job because I was so little.

After a while my father got together with another woman. He asked us if we thought it was all right. I told him, "I don't know." She was what we call *una mujer de vida alegre*, a loose woman. She hooked up with my father. She didn't give us anything to eat. Only when my father was looking would she give us eggs, tortillas and coffee. When he wasn't watching she tried not to feed us. A long time went by like this. She tried to turn my father against us, saying that we were disobedient, that we didn't pay any attention to her.

One day she tried to hit my youngest brother, and I tried to stop her but I couldn't find a way to defend him. She was screaming at him, and there was a hatchet that someone had left from cutting wood so I grabbed it and I said to her, "Let's see. Come on over. Try to hit us now."

When she saw I was serious, she thought I was going to hit her with what I had in my hand. My brother was very small, like six or seven years old, and he couldn't defend himself. I think I grew up and became a woman when I was very young because not even my aunts and uncles would defend us. So that day I told that woman to beat the two of us, and she backed down. She shut herself up in a room, and when my father returned she was crying. She told him I tried to hit her and that I wanted to kill her. She thought I was really going to attack her with the hatchet. That day they threw me out of the house.

They exchanged me for my sister who was living with my paternal grandfather. She took my place, and I went to live with him. My *Papá* lied to my grandfather about me. He said I was

Luisa

seeing a married man—that I had a boyfriend. But *Papá* said he didn't want to punish me in front of his new woman because I was only 13 or 14 years old. He told my grandfather that if I ever got pregnant he should throw me out in the street with my clothes and that he should beat me. My father said he couldn't beat me himself because the woman would see and laugh at me. He said it would be better if my grandfather took me to live with him.

My father told me to go to my grandfather's house, and he told my brother to take me there right away. I told him, no, that it was better to wait because I had heard stories and was scared. When we set out anyway, I told my brother to go back home and say that he had left me at grandfather's house. I was afraid because I had heard that people in the coffee trucks that passed through abducted little boys. Some who had asked for rides on the trucks told us that when they got on they saw that there were dead people under the canvas or covered by leaves. So they always said they stole children and that we had to be very careful.

When I got to my grandfather's house he asked me, "What happened? What did you do?"

I was afraid of my grandfather. He was a very strict man. Then I started to cry.

"You must have done something for them to throw you out."

I told him that woman had tried to beat Santiago, my brother, and that I got involved trying to defend him.

"That stupid woman," he said. "She isn't even your mother."

After grandfather went to sleep, my aunts asked me what I had done. I told them, and they said I did exactly what I should have because she wasn't my mother.

They had thrown me out with just the clothes on my back. I

spent several days like that. I always wore traditional Guatemalan clothing. Then my grandfather decided to change that and had me wear a dress that was hemmed at the knee and I stopped wearing the typical dress that went all the way down to the eye of the foot, in other words, to the ankle.

After a while they began to mistreat my brother, and he had to leave my father's house, too. Then my father became gravely ill from nose-bleeds. The blood was gushing out. They sent for my grandfather who took him to the hospital. When he was in the hospital they told us he was ill. I went to see him in the hospital, and he looked very sick. That day he told us to take my little brother to live with us, too, since he thought he was going to die. Then only the third brother was living at my father's house. Three of us were living with my grandfather.

They sent me to work. I didn't want to work because I was afraid. I went to work at a house in Antigua. My father had managed to find me that job. I took care of a little American girl. Two grandchildren were living in the house. The little boy was Hispanic and the little girl was American. I was hired to take care of the boy, but the one who really became fond of me was the American girl, so they decided I should look after her because she always wanted to be with me. While she was asleep I was also supposed to clean the house. Then my father got scared because he found out that the American girl wanted to bring me to the United States. They were going to send me to school to learn English. Everything sounded really nice, but he was afraid so he took me back to my grandfather's house.

Then I went to work for a *Señora*—housecleaning, cooking, everything. My aunts were the ones who got that job for me. I was very angry, and I refused to go see them. Afterwards, they would say, "Come on. Come see your father." I didn't want to go back to them. I was so mad. I was only 14 or 15 and I thought, "Why did they send me away?"

Luisa

I refused to visit them. Finally the woman I was working for went to Italy with her daughters and then I went back to my grandfather's house. That's when I met my husband. I was sixteen. I had a lot of boyfriends because I wanted to be able to choose. I decided that I wanted a young man who was older than me by two or three years. I wanted a husband who didn't drink because I had seen how my mother had suffered. I would tell the boys that I would be their girlfriend but that if I found out they had another girl, I would never speak to them again. That's what I did with several of them, and then I dumped them.

My husband and I were sweethearts for only six months. When we got together I didn't go out with anyone else, just him. I met him through a cousin of mine. When we decided to be together we went to ask for permission to marry. Well, it wasn't exactly like that—we went to tell them we were going to get married. Not many people came to the wedding because my father didn't want us to spend a lot of money and have us go into debt because then we wouldn't have enough money to buy food.

We went to live with my mother-in-law. I suffered a lot in her house because she had a lot of children. I had to do all the housework. One of my husband's sisters-in-law was angry that he had married me and that we were happy and doing just fine. My husband has never beaten me, at least up to now.

Everything went well until my second child was born. When he was a year and three months old he got sick, and after two months he died. I became very depressed, and I got sick. The day he died I slipped and twisted my ankle, and then I couldn't walk. Since I'm an Evangelical Christian we practice the custom that when a male child dies he is carried out of the house by other boys in the family. When I saw that they took my little boy out of the house, and he disappeared from my sight, I fainted. I was pregnant with my third child who was born with hydrocephalus or spina bifida, and he died three days after he was born. I became despondent and disappointed with life. I asked myself why my mother had died, why my children had died. How could I be strong enough to bear all that?

At that time my brother Juan and I became very close. He would visit me a lot. Once when I was very sad he said, "Go buy a chicken and let's eat together" as if he were wishing my mother was there.

He said, "I have no one to visit." I told him not to be sad because, "I'm here. You can visit me."

He helped me a lot. He was already a young man. He helped me with my first child. The one who suffered the most was the brother who stayed living with my father and the *Señora*. He had to cook for my father. He had to find noodles to feed them because that woman would always leave them alone, being a loose woman.

After my third baby died—his name was also Juan like my brother—they took me home from the hospital, and I was in bad shape because they had to operate to get the baby out. My brother kept on visiting me and encouraging me. In those days my sugar increased and since then I've been a diabetic. I continued to live with my husband. I was sick because I couldn't get pregnant because of the operation. I was sad because I didn't want another baby. I wanted the one I already had. And then, suddenly, I was pregnant again. I was six months pregnant when I realized. I was very skinny, I had no belly at all. From that pregnancy Luis was born. Then I got seriously ill from the sugar, and while I was sick that was when my husband decided to come to the United States. He tried to come across the border, but it took him eight months to travel all the way through Mexico.

In those months he left me in his mother's house, but she threw me out because she said that since Carlos, my husband, was gone I had to leave. I took my two children, and I left. My brother Juan was living with us, and we took everything we had and left without money and without food. I returned to a small plot of land that was my mother's; it was her inheritance. When they deported my husband from Mexico back to Guatemala, I was no longer at his parent's home.

My sister-in-law cried when he asked for me, and she said to him, "Carlos, you don't need to come here anymore because Luisa is in Calderas." He asked why.

She answered, "*mamá* threw her out. You shouldn't stay here with your mother because she despises your wife and children."

She told her brother to take my husband to where I was living, and her brother said, "I'll take you to Luisa."

When he arrived, I was working with the people, doing laundry, making tortillas, working in the fields, and I was working in a house. That day when I went out to go to work I saw two men who looked familiar.

Another woman who was with me said, "That's your husband."

I was stunned, so I ran inside. I didn't know what to do. When my husband saw me he began to cry because I was so poorly dressed and dirty. I didn't have time to take care of myself because I was working so much. He just hugged me and said, "What have they done to you?"

This kind of thing happened pretty often. He came back from Mexico a lot because he kept trying and failing to travel all the way through Mexico to reach the U.S. border. Meanwhile, I was working in the fields waiting for him to be able to make it through Mexico and one day get to the United States so that we could live better. So I wouldn't be so alone, I went to live with an aunt, and we sold *tostadas* and *atole* and that was what we lived on.

Shattered Dreams

One Sunday I was heating *tostadas* when my aunt came and said to me, "Someone is looking for you." Eight months had passed since I had last seen my husband.

It was a young girl, and she said to me, "Luisa, Esperanza says that Carlos has arrived in the United States."

I didn't know whether to cry from joy or scream. That day he was in the United States! It had been such a long time, and he had been traveling for eight months. He got lost and had spent time on a ranch in Mexico, but I didn't know that. I had expected him to be brought back to Guatemala or to return on his own because that is what had happened the other times.

The girl told me to go down to Esperanza's house the next day. On the way there I ran into my husband's other sister-in-law, Juana.

She said, "Sister Luisa, haven't you heard?" "What?" I said. I pretended I didn't know.

"They say that Brother Carlos is in the U.S. Yesterday he called his brother and said he had finally made it."

I just said, "Ah," and I said good-bye and headed to Esperanza's house.

Esperanza was waiting for me, but I couldn't believe it. It was like a dream. I asked her if it was true. My aunt hugged me and said, "Yes. Now it's true. Now it's real. Everything has finally worked out."

She also told me that my husband had sent $50 for food. We were very happy. She said he was going to call me. When I went to take the call on a Tuesday, I didn't know how to react because he was so far away. My two-year-old son had been sick and I had gone through a very difficult time because we didn't have anything to eat. I could only buy two loaves of bread, and sometimes the

Luisa

smallest child would leave a little of his, and then my oldest would eat it.

After that things started to improve. My husband began to send money. We went on like that for four years until one day he decided the children and I should all come to the United States. It had taken him such a long time to get here, he didn't want to go through the same thing again. That's when we found out that they were letting people in who came with children.

The *coyotes* are people from there in Guatemala. They are people from our village, and we know them. So Carlos called and told me people could come across with permission. That's when I found out I could come with the children. I tried to come legally but I couldn't.

Then I decided to come over land. I crossed Mexico with my children without documents. The *coyotes* put us in taxis, and they put us up in hotels, and we got to the border that way. We crossed the border with the children and with another man. Immigration caught us but then gave us permission to stay for a month, and after that we were supposed to go to court.

I got on a bus, and we arrived in Dallas. My husband had a friend who knew the way from Postville to Dallas, and he went to pick us up. When I saw my husband there was joy but also sadness because my sister had stayed behind and had no one to turn to. I was happy, too, because I was with my children and my husband after four years apart. From that point on I concentrated on working so that I could help my sister and my maternal grandmother.

I arrived here in Postville on a Saturday at about 1:00 in the morning. It was in April of 2005. I was very sick with my diabetes, and it looked like I might die. This was because we had taken so long to cross all of Mexico. They put us in hotels for a day or two to throw the police off our track and sometimes for even eight days. I

Shattered Dreams

only ate twice a day, and I ate very little because I preferred to feed the children.

I waited two months in Postville, and then I started to work in June. I worked at night for two years. While I was still working at night I found out I was pregnant. When I discovered I was expecting, I was already pregnant by five and a half months. At the plant they wouldn't let us eat or go to the bathroom. They didn't give us permission. The baby wasn't doing well. Since I'm diabetic I need a lot of care.

I was having a lot of problems with my husband so he decided I should work during the day. He changed me from the night shift to the day shift. He changed my Social Security number. He found the people who take care of the papers. One day when I got home he told me that he had sent for the new papers, so I went to re-apply for the job and that's when I started to work during the day. The supervisor, Filomena, threatened to take me and make me go back to working on the night shift. Then I had to stop working because the pregnancy had become high-risk. On August 14, 2007 the doctor examined me because I was very sick and had a headache and nausea. They found out that the baby had died during the seventh month of pregnancy.

When they told me the baby was dead I wanted to disappear, I wanted the earth to swallow me up. I was supposed to see the doctor three times a week—Monday, Wednesday and Friday—I had an appointment to go to La Crosse on Monday. That's why I was waiting to go, but on Sunday I spent the day with a tremendous headache and sick to my stomach. I felt that I wasn't going to make it alive to the next morning. So my husband told me we should see the doctor here in Postville. When the doctor saw me the baby was already dead. I asked him what was happening. He told me to go to the emergency room in West Union. My husband took me. He didn't want to believe that the baby was dead. I could see that we

Luisa

couldn't hear the baby's heartbeat when they did the ultrasound. The doctor didn't want to say anything to me because he knew the baby was dead. The child was already dead on Monday.

They put me in the hospital at 1:45 p.m. The doctor said it would take a long time for me to give birth. They did a caesarean delivery and the baby was born at 4:00 a.m. When he was born I thought I would go crazy, seeing him as if he were asleep. Then they brought me home. He was sent to a funeral home in La Crosse. We buried him on Friday. I could hardly walk because of the delivery. When they were going to bury him and I saw the earth where they were going to put him my knees turned to water. My sister grabbed me and took me away so that I couldn't see what they were going to do with my baby.

They fired me from my job because I couldn't go right back. The doctor had told me not to work. I had stopped going to work before the baby was born, and after he was born I couldn't go back because they had changed the color of the ID you needed to work at the plant. I couldn't go back to work until I found a way to get papers in the color they wanted. They made me change papers twice. First were the papers I used when I started work. Then I had new papers when my husband changed my schedule for the day shift. Those were pink. And then I had to get white ones when I went back to work the last time.

After losing my child I went into a depression. They gave me medicine. I started back to work on December 7th, 2007, but on the 5th of January I had been very sick and on the 6th I had so much pain that I left. I went to the doctor, but they wouldn't let my husband out of work to take me to the hospital. The doctor told me I had to go to the hospital to have an operation on one of my ovaries. They took me to West Union, and they did the surgery there. I spent six weeks recovering, and then I went back to work. Six weeks later was when Immigration entered the plant.

Shattered Dreams

I only went back to work so that *la migra* could catch me.

On the day of the raid I got up and got dressed even though I didn't feel like working. Since they had taken away my husband's job I thought that if I didn't go to work the paycheck would be smaller. I started at 7:00 in the morning and at 9:25 we went downstairs for our break. The women were saying that Immigration was coming. People had been warning about this for a year, saying that Immigration was coming, and then they didn't come. The people in town were telling everyone not to go out because Immigration was setting up roadblocks. There was always this rumor, but nothing ever happened. The workers in the plant were there talking about how Immigration was coming, but I thought it was a joke as usual. We went back upstairs, and after putting on our work clothes again, started working. There weren't a lot of people because they had fired many just before the raid. All of a sudden people were running every which way.

I asked, "Why are they running?" and the supervisor told me to run, "Luisa! Luisa! Let's go!"

My supervisor was an American. When I turned around there was no one left. I went behind the packaging area. Everyone was really upset. People from all the different departments were there—sausage makers, chicken processors, butchering. Everyone was running.

A young man told me "It's Immigration. Run!" But I said to myself, where will I run?

I knew there was no place to hide. A Mexican lady told us to escape through the garbage chute. When we opened it the Immigration people were running in telling us to stop. They raised something they had in their hands. We shut ourselves in the garbage room and left another way, but everywhere was full of Immigration. It was incredible. I couldn't believe it. It was as if I

Luisa

was dreaming. Then they began to yell at us and shove us. The first agents I saw were really big. They stared at you as if they wanted to intimidate you. I had my cell phone because I was always in contact with my son. I thought I had better call my husband and tell him not to leave the house because he was planning to come and re-apply. They didn't let me make the call.

A female agent told me "No calls allowed," and grabbed the phone right out of my hands.

I felt shaky and faint because of my diabetes. When I came to my senses I saw that there were a lot of women I knew.

They were saying, "Our children are out there. What are we going to do?"

They were bitterly crying. You wished you had wings to fly away in that moment of terror. They treated us like criminals. There were three people from Immigration for every one of the people in the plant. There were more Immigration agents than us. They held us there, and I didn't have any sense of time because I was so full of anxiety for my children and thinking about my brothers-in-law who were also working in the plant. I didn't know if they had been able to escape.

It was awhile, some time, and I don't have the words to express how I felt. They told us to start walking, and they took our aprons and other things we had from the company. The owners had been making new dining rooms in the plant, and the agents took us there. As we moved along we were falling and getting back up. My body didn't want to hold me upright. When I got to the dining room many people were crying. The women were crying, and as I looked from one side to the other everyone was in tears. The women were the first to be questioned by Immigration. The people from Immigration were laughing, they were looking at us and joking. I didn't cry because at that moment I went into shock.

I was with Margarita Pérez, and she said to me "We aren't going to cry because it makes them laugh. Don't cry. It just helps them make fun of us."

A young Hispanic man like us questioned me. He spoke Spanish well. He asked me where I was from, where I was born, and they took a picture. Then it occurred to me to say that I have two children. He said it didn't matter to him, it wasn't his problem; it was mine. That really hurt. Wanting to cry I kept looking at him. "You're a bad person," I said. He just turned around and walked away.

An older man was going around taking pictures. He was wearing civilian clothing. I told him I had two children that were in school and that all the adults in the family were there inside the plant. He said he would go talk to his boss and that he was sure they would let me out. After a while they put a pink plastic bracelet on my wrist. They had already put on a green one. The agents wouldn't tell me what they were for, if they meant I had to stay or not. I didn't know what was going to happen to me. They began to separate me from the other women. My sister-in-law was crying but the Immigration officer didn't let me go to her. I wanted to console her, but he shoved me and told me to go back to where the others were, where they had separated me.

I went back. I don't know what time it was. They told us to form a line because they were going to take us out. They took us outside. The women were screaming. Amalia shouted to me, "My daughters!"

I told her "Tell them you have little girls. Then they'll let you go."

They made us get onto a bus. It was as if someone had died. The others were all saying, "What about our children? They're taking us away, this is really happening."

Luisa

Some of the women didn't want to get on the bus. We were lined up and they made us all get in. Once in the bus a woman started to search us. She looked inside our purses. I went to sit down, and then I don't know exactly what happened, if they called to her or not, but she left and someone came back and shouted at me that I needed to be searched. The person spoke Spanish well. I was searched twice. Who knows what they could have been looking for? Then I did sit down. The women were still crying.

One of the ICE agents came on the bus and with a big smile said to us, "If you're too cold, tell us, and if you're too hot, don't worry."

Then Sonia stood up and said, "Tell us the truth. Tell us what is going to happen to us. We saw that they were putting people on buses and driving away, but not us."

The man said, "You want the truth? Don't worry. They're going to let those who are on this bus go, for sure."

They had already taken some women off the bus. We could see that they had something in their hand and that they took the women out of the plant. We couldn't tell if they were letting them go or not, or if they were just taking them to another bus, until the man told us that.

From my perspective what he said really worried me. I had heard that after the raid in Marshalltown they had let the women with children born in the United States go. I thought that they would take me away, even if it took awhile, because my children were born in Guatemala. They asked that another woman get off the bus, but I refused because I said to myself that they were going to take me away. One of the people from Immigration shouted that one of us had to get off. Some of the bravest women did leave the bus.

Then they fed us, and we had to get on a different bus. They gave us a bag with a little cake, some potato chips, and a bottle of water. I didn't even feel like looking in the bag. All of us women who were still on a bus said, "Now for sure they're going to take us away because they changed buses."

I was seated in the second seat and one of the Immigration agents told us they wanted us to get off in the order we were seated. When they called my number I got off. I felt like I couldn't walk. Because my operation had been such a short time ago, I felt that the part they had cut was splitting. They took me to another bus where there were a lot of computers. An agent found my file on the computer and said they had my fingerprints from when I crossed the border. He told me to tell the truth because if I lied they would find out. I said that the only truth was that yes, Immigration had caught me. They asked me where I had crossed, and I said I didn't know except that I had ended up in Dallas. Then he told me that I had entered through the border with Texas. He told me to get off the bus, and I left by the back door.

Another officer took me to where they were putting ankle bracelets [Electronic Monitoring Devices] on the women they had decided to release. When I sat down to wait I saw that the other women were crying, and I wondered why. The people from Immigration were shouting. They asked me about my mother and father. I couldn't answer because my brain wasn't working in those moments. Then they took me to put on the ankle bracelet. When I saw it I wondered what it was. "What are they going to do to me?" When they put the shackle on my ankle I felt so humiliated because on television I had seen a woman who had to wear one, and she was crying because people stared at her and said she was a criminal.

I felt so bad, but at the same time I was glad I was going to return to my children. The other women were crying and I was trying to breathe so I wouldn't. I told them not to put the device on so tight because I was diabetic, and it could harm me. They put it on a little more loosely and told me that now I could go. I asked

Luisa

for my cell phone, and they said they would return it the next day. We were at the very back of the plant and had to come up near the entrance. There were three other señoras with me. They were very tired and were having trouble walking. I lead the way past Immigration because I was so nervous, and we left the plant. There were a lot of reporters, a lot of people up close to the plant and no one said anything to them. I turned around and went back so I could leave along the train tracks.

One of the Immigration men said to me, "*Adiós, Señora.* I wish you good luck."

I didn't say anything because I was so angry. At that moment I was thinking, "God is good because he didn't let them take me away." I knew that I was free. Only then could I cry. A car with some Russian ladies stopped next to me and they asked me if there were any more of their women detained inside. I told them there weren't. Then a man who had good papers because he had a clothing store and we knew that he was legal walked by. He told me to go up the street. I ran up and passed by the church. I saw a lot of people there, tons of people, but I didn't know what was happening. Then I saw that my son and my sister-in-law's son were coming to the church.

I yelled at my son, "Alfredo! Alfredo!" and I remember that I felt like crying when I saw him.

He said to me, "*mamá*, I went to the church to ask about you. I already filled out the forms for missing people, but they let you go." And he said, "Let's go to the church because *papá* is there."

I didn't want to go to the church because I didn't want people to see me so I went to my house. My son went to the church to get his father because he had the keys.

When my husband saw me he didn't want the reunion to be so

dramatic and sad. He only said *"Ay, hija.* They made you suffer, those people."

I arrived home with swollen feet. They gave me water for the pain. I asked if anyone had a phone card because I needed to call my sister. I spoke to her, and she burst out crying. She said she had been calling but no one answered. I was always trying to be strong, and I told her I was safe at home already. She wasn't even thinking about her husband but was thinking about me because she knew I would get sick.

After that I couldn't sleep, thinking about my people and where they had taken them. The next day I went to the church because they were going to explain to us how to charge the [GPS] "bracelets." Immigration was calling the women at home to remind us we had to charge them.

That was the beginning of five long months of painful experiences for my family as well as people I knew in Postville. I started to look for everyone on the lists [of the imprisoned people] that were [posted] in the church. There they began to help us find a way to write to them or talk to them. I visited the Eldora jail to see María, my sister-in-law, who has two daughters in Guatemala and one son here. I remember the first day I saw her in prison. I thought I would go crazy. I didn't have words to say to her. All she did was cry and ask about her children. I thought that my friends and family would be held a month or two before I.C.E. would let the people in jail and the women with "bracelets" go home. I visited María several times, and when I couldn't because they sent her to another jail, I wrote and wrote. I wrote to her, to my brother-in-law, and to several young men I knew. Sometimes they wrote back, sometimes not. The jailors wouldn't always give them paper to write on. I wrote all the time. Until the final two weeks of their imprisonment I was writing letters.

Luisa

Sometimes they sent me letters that were just too sad. I wrote words that would make them feel that I was helping them.

There was a letter from María where she said she wanted to die because she couldn't stand what the other women inmates were doing to her. She couldn't even stand one more day. I told her that God is so powerful that he wouldn't allow her to feel that way, that she shouldn't feel that way because of her children. I put a lot of encouraging words in my letters.

The hardest was to talk to people in Guatemala like when my nieces or nephews would answer and would ask where their father, my brother Jaime, was. I told them he was on his way, but it was a long way to Guatemala and that's why he wasn't there yet, why he would take a little longer to get home. They wanted him to call them, but I didn't have money to send him so that he could make a call from prison until one day I sent him twenty dollars and I wrote him a letter.

"Please, Jaime," I wrote, "talk to my nieces and nephews at least once."

One of Jaime's brothers had been pretending to be their father. He would call to send them greetings and chat with them on the phone as if he were Jaime. He made them believe he was their *papá*. The one who was talking was my cousin's husband, and he did it because their father was in jail and didn't have the courage to tell his children he was in prison and didn't have enough money for food.

My sister was terribly depressed sometimes, and when I talked with her she said she couldn't stand it anymore and asked God why they had done this to her. I tried to give her strength and not to cry and to tell her that many families were suffering and going through the same thing. Sometimes she just wanted to go away and leave the children. I wanted to run to her and help her, but I couldn't because she was so very far away.

Shattered Dreams

Then one day Jaime found the courage and called. His oldest son answered and asked why he hadn't made it home yet. The other children were running to hear their father on the phone. My sister told me that the kids were hugging each other and crying, and they couldn't even talk. She said that he was crying, too, and when he talked to my sister he told her he was so ashamed to be a prisoner and not be able to help his family. It was difficult to call family back in Guatemala because everyone wanted to know when we would arrive and what was happening. We had so little information.

Months passed, and we were waiting and hoping for a miracle, hoping that the hearts of those who were keeping us prisoner would be touched, but everyone who was in jail spent five months in prison, the longest five months of our lives. The people from Immigration celebrated the fact that they had caught us. I only believe that there is a God who judges and who knows who has done good and who has done evil.

I have survived on charity—the food pantry and help from the church. My oldest son is getting the help of a psychologist at school. He says he never again wants to remember how the teacher told him what had happened. The teachers were all together talking in secret. They didn't want to tell the children what was happening at the plant. Finally one of the teachers stood up and said, "I have to tell you something. Immigration has arrested your parents at the plant."

He says that he started to cry and was saying to himself, "My parents are both there. What am I going to do with my little brother?"

He called me on the phone, and I didn't answer. He called his father, and he didn't answer. He says he never again wants to remember that sad moment because all the kids were crying and asking to use the phone to call their parents. Because of this his grades have gone down, and he's had to get extra help at school.

Luisa

He doesn't want to go back to Guatemala. He's been here for four years. He asks why we should go back there. He says he wants to start working.

It's been hard for me to survive these months with the electronic shackle on my ankle. I haven't been able to work. We just want the chance to stay here, to help our relatives who were sent away, because they won't be able to come back and work to help their families. We are their only chances for a decent life.

My family had its share of tragedy in the past, too, while we were all still living in Guatemala. I was eight years old when things turned violent in the neighboring town of Chimachoy. The army killed a lot of people there, and the town almost completely disappeared. They buried people anyplace, sometimes stacking the bodies one on top of the other. They took some people away, and these people were never heard from again. They "disappeared" people.

The soldiers were staying in the village with us. There was a soccer field that they used as their camp. They were living in tents. The town was surrounded by soldiers. They had look-outs on the street corners. The soldiers stood there with their weapons, watching. They would go to people's houses to demand food, tortillas and beans. They stayed in the village a long time. They told us not to talk to other people in town because they were bad, they were guerrillas.

Because we were children we went out into the streets to see. Our parents told us not to leave the house. We were supposed to stay inside because there was a mountain right on the edge of town, and there were a lot of soldiers there. They were training, and there were bombs and gunshots where they were practicing. Sometimes they would bomb the other mountain because according to them the guerrillas were there.

Sometimes the troops would go away and then come back again, and when they came back they would walk through the village and ask people in their houses for food. Once there was another platoon, and they were up on the mountain watching the village, and they thought that the soldiers in the village were guerrillas. They wanted to take the village by surprise, and they ran into town and they almost opened fire on the other platoon. They were really scared because when they saw the other soldiers they realized they had almost shot their own men.

Sometimes the soldiers would make all the people in town gather together. They had meetings in which they told us not to be like the others who were rotten apples and had joined the guerrilla movement. They shouted and swore at the people from the other village. They made us come to meetings where they told us not to get together, not to form groups. I don't remember exactly, but it was something like that.

I had relatives in Techán, Guatemala, and they were "disappeared." My uncles searched for their children among the many dead. Wherever dead bodies showed up they would go and turn them over to see their faces, to see if those were the bodies of their sons. They looked for my cousins a long time, and we still don't have any idea of what happened to them. Three of my cousins disappeared. I heard they were told to come to court. One was taken from there and the other two were told to go to the encampment.

There was a fourth cousin who was told to turn himself in at the encampment. He said he went there about four or five o'clock one morning and everything was silent. He was going to go in, but he changed his mind. There was truck coming, and he got on it and went to Guatemala City. He disappeared for awhile, but he had escaped. He was living in the capital, but his family thought he was dead like the others. His family was searching for him, too. He had a sister who was working for some Americans, but he was afraid to look for her. He didn't want to put his children, his parents, and the rest of the family in danger.

Luisa

When the situation had calmed down a little he found his sister in the capital. He made her swear not to say anything to his parents until the danger had passed. He also asked his cousin to bring his wife to the city, but in secret. He told her to make up a story and say that his wife had fallen in love with someone else. So his wife went to Guatemala City to be with him, and she could hardly believe it. It took a long time for my aunt and uncle to know that my cousin was alive. They thought their daughter-in-law had deceived them by going away with another man. In the end there was a happy ending for those two but not for the families of three other cousins.

As I said before, as a family we already lived through a lot of tragedy because of events in Guatemala. I only hope that now I can help those who were deported and now depend on me. And finally I hope to be able to tell other people what happened to us during the raid and afterwards.

Shattered Dreams

Julio

My name is Julio Xol. I'm from the small town of Chimachoy San Andrés Itzapa, Chimaltenango, Guatemala. I was born on the third of December 1990. I'm the second of ten siblings, four brothers and five sisters.

I learned to speak Spanish when I started school. It was hard to learn Spanish because in the family we spoke only Kaqchikel, but at school we had to speak Spanish. I attended grade school from first to the sixth grade. When they gave me homework, I didn't do it because I had to help my father. He worked delivering vegetables and greens to Chimaltenango, and while I was in school I did trips with him. At school they never let me have recess because I didn't finish the assignments. I usually got home really late after working with my father and went to bed about 2:00 a.m. and there just wasn't time for homework. I got up at 6:00 a.m. to take our three animals, a gelding and two mares, out to pasture. At 7:00 I would have my coffee and I still couldn't do my homework. We were given a lot of school work and my teacher was always scolding me, and sometimes he would hit me, and then I had to do the assignments during recess.

When I was about ten years old my father had a pick-up truck that he used to transport the produce. I learned to drive by watching my older brother, Carlos. It took him a year to learn, but then he went to the United States and I had to help. With the truck, my father would transport loads of produce like lettuce, *huicoy* [chayote], carrots and cauliflower to Chimaltenango. I was his assistant, and I helped him do the driving. I had to sit on a folded up poncho to be able to see over the dashboard, but I really couldn't reach the clutch to change speeds. I was barely able to reach the brake pedal. Driving was really hard for me. You had to drive very slowly because the truck was so heavily loaded, and if

Julio

you weren't careful with the bumps in the road the truck felt like it was going to tip over. I did that for about four years. When we were driving along the roads there were police, but since the windows in the van were polarized they couldn't see me.

I was pretty small so I couldn't really help carry the big loads. I only helped with the driving and dragging some of the loads out of the truck. Sometimes we would do two night trips of two and a half hours each. We would go to Chimaltenango and then get back at 2 or 3 o'clock in the morning. Other times we would load up at 6:00 in the evening and finish at 5:00 in the morning. When it was raining we got soaking wet and just went on working.

When my *Papá* went to Chimaltenango I would sometimes take another pick-up to drive to places like Calderas or Rosario that were 15 or 20 minutes from my village. I was always the one who went to pick up the midwife to help my mother when she was going to have a baby in the village. They paid me 50 *quetzales* to bring her and then to take her home. Once I went to get the midwife at about midnight. She lived about half an hour from our house.

When she saw me she said, "Oh, you're driving? Then I'm not going." She was scared because I was so young.

I told her, "Let's just get going." There was another *Señora* with me and she said, "Yes, come on, let's go." The midwife was scared the whole trip!

Everybody at home had to help. When we went to school, my mother made *chicharrines* [fritters] and *pan pirujo* [homemade bread] that my sisters could sell during recess. My sisters would race out and get a table for the *chicharrines*, *pan pirujo* and oranges that they would sell every day. I helped my father and not my mother because I was the oldest boy at home.

My father's first truck was very old. Everybody in our village had to walk 25 minutes to catch a bus that would take us to other towns. So when my brother came to the U.S. he helped my father buy a van, and my father would drive people to Chimaltenango in it. He would honk his horn at 7:00 a.m. and people would begin to gather because the van left at 7:30.

In my town there is a high school that you can go to after grade school. I wanted to go there, but I couldn't because I was the oldest at home. I had to take the horses out to pasture and gather hay and help my father. There was no time for school, and by the time I was fourteen I had left school. My little brothers, seven and five years old, would also go out and watch the animals and cut and gather hay. I would go to the fields in the evening to carry it back because it was too heavy for them. They always made the hay, and I would lift and carry it. Life in Guatemala is very hard.

When my older brother came to the United States my father's situation improved because he was able to buy the van. He hired some kids to help me grow cauliflower, carrots and squash because he didn't have time to do it himself.

"If you work, it's yours," my *Papá* said to me.

I also took care of the animals, the horses, in addition to farming. While I was farming I opened an account and started to save money in the bank. My mother would go and sell my produce. If she sold 400 *quetzales* worth, she kept 100 and I saved the rest. I saved and saved. In three years I saved 12,000 *quetzales*.

My father loaned me 3,000 and I bought a car that cost me 15,000 *quetzales*. It was an Isuzu van. I used the van to fetch midwives because there were always a lot of women in my town who were having babies. I was sixteen years old, and I also drove people to the hospitals in Chimaltenango and Antigua. I had my license and was a good driver. Now I had my van and was saving more money. We would also transport people in the pick-up, but they preferred my van because it was covered. Sometimes I also

Julio

took people to the fair.

My father improved his situation and so did I because my brother was able to help him buy the van. When my brother did that I thought about going to the United States, too, because here you can do so much more. My *Papá* told me I couldn't go because I was the oldest at home and needed to help him do the driving. I told him that I was going to go because my brother had improved his life. At that time I was earning about 6,000 *quetzales* growing carrots and cauliflower, but suddenly the price went from 200 to 50 *quetzales* the kilo. I was desperate and I couldn't imagine trying to farm anymore and earning so little.

I talked with my brother and asked him to help me. He told me to get back to him in two weeks. Then he told me he could help by giving me 25,000 *quetzales*. I had my van which was worth 15,000, and my father bought it from me. So then I had 40,000 and I used that money to come. One of my brothers had a mare that had a filly, and my brother sold them to me for 1000 *quetzales*, and I resold them. That way we had only two horses because my two younger brothers couldn't take care of four animals.

My Mother told me not to come to the United States, but what could she do? *Mamá* struggled to make a living with a store. When I told her I was leaving, she stayed behind, crying, and couldn't see me off because she couldn't stand to see me go.

I came in January 2007. My father took me to Chimaltenango where the *coyote* was. We formed a group of 21 people, 19 men and two women. One of the women was pregnant. We waited for the bus. When it picked us up, there were 23 in all with the two *coyotes*. We got to the Mexico-Guatemala border. It was a direct trip through the highlands. The *coyote* took us to a hotel to sleep. Because there were 21 of us, he divided us into two groups. One group was to leave on Monday and the other on Tuesday.

65

Shattered Dreams

My group left on Monday, we walked about ten minutes, and then two taxis picked us up, five per taxi. We rode in the taxis for about 20 minutes. Then we had to walk again, and then we got into a van. It was the middle of the night. We were still in the van at about 4:00 a.m. when a police patrol started to follow us. The van sped up to lose the patrol car and as soon as it was out of sight the driver stopped and had us all get out. We started to run, and then we saw that the police stopped the van. But no one was inside so they let it go, and after the police disappeared the van driver came back for us. We drove for another three hours and arrived in Tuxtla Gutiérrez where we stayed in a hotel again. Then the *coyotes* went to get the other group, and we had to wait for two days because the Mexican police had caught them.

On Thursday our group of ten left again, and we were riding in a bus like the day before, and at the end of the day a taxi took us to a hotel. We were there for five days because the other group was still on its way to Monterrey, which is where I think we were resting. We were traveling like this for a week, and we were walking for about ten days. We kept getting on and off buses. The *coyote* would drive ahead of the bus, and if he saw there was a roadblock he would make us get off the bus and hide in the fields and trees for a few hours before he came and got us again. We arrived at the border with the U.S., and we were stuck there in a house for about ten days because we couldn't cross. Whenever we got close to the river, Immigration was always nearby.

I wasn't in the first group that tried to cross. Immigration saw them and chased them and caught two of the men who had already reached the other side, and they sent them back to Guatemala. They caught the women, too, but let them go on the bridge to Mexico because the women said they were Mexican.

My group left early in the morning; it was still dark. We walked for a while and then crossed the river in inner tubes and then

Julio

walked for eight hours. We had left at 6:00 in the morning and were still walking at 4:00 in the afternoon. We finally stopped walking in the evening. We got to San Antonio and spent the whole rest of the day hidden in the underbrush until about 1:00 in the morning. Helicopters were flying overhead searching, but we were well-hidden.

Then a truck picked us up, and we were lying down hiding in the truck until we arrived in Texas [sic]. We spent another week there. The group that had arrived before us left for Postville before we did. The *coyote* had brothers in Texas and he arranged to have us brought to Postville. We left Texas on a Friday, and arrived in Postville about 10:00 at night. When we got there I met my brother, and I was very happy. I had spent 28 days getting from Guatemala to Texas.

When I got to Postville we had my picture taken in Walmart, a man got me an ID, and I went to ask for work at Agriprocessors. I began to work that Wednesday. I was working in Department #3 where we packaged sausage, ham, turkey legs, and cow tongues. I worked fourteen hours a day. I would start work at 6:00 a.m. and leave at 8:00 p.m. First some women would put the sausages in packages, and then I would close them and put on the label. It was very tiring. I was still working in the same place on the day of the raid.

The first day the supervisor, Carlos, a guy from Guatemala, started having me put on labels. Then he had me carry boxes to the conveyor belt to send them someplace else. I was doing that work, and he was just watching me. On the third day, since I had figured out how to do everything, he treated me as if I had been there for two years, since I could do things okay. One day soon after he approached me and swore at me—"Chínguele!"— and I didn't pay any attention to him since I was working. Since I didn't answer him, he grabbed my sweater and jerked my arm. I was angry because he didn't seem to care that I was working.

After that, when he would pass by he would hit me on the back of the head. He hit hard enough to make my head jerk forward. I have a very short neck, that's the way I was born. I can't hold my head upright. It's a handicap. The supervisor Carlos would try to straighten my head.

"Hold your head up, you stupid ox," he would say.

He would hold my head with his two hands and pull it straight as hard as he could. That made me angry, and I felt ashamed because the men I worked with were watching.

The supervisor was always swearing at me—"*Chínguele! Chínguele!*" Sometimes he would shove the boxes, and I would have to struggle to keep them from falling, because if they did he was going to report me to a "yellow hardhat" [supervisor], and they could fire me. I felt angry and unhappy, and I thought that when I was in Guatemala with my father he would never swear at me or abuse me. When the supervisor was nearby I was always afraid. I held my head really tight because I knew he might hit me from behind. I couldn't say anything to anyone because he could take away my job for awhile or fire me, and I needed to work to help my family.

Once he grabbed my apron at my right shoulder, and he pushed me hard because he was reprimanding us. I fell backwards and tried not to fall completely, but I injured my back, and it hurt a lot. He continued to yell at me and my companions. He was threatening us and said if we didn't work hard we could lose our jobs. I was angry, and it seemed to me that I was the one he always picked on. The others were grown men, and he saw me as someone young he could mess with. It upset me because I didn't know how long I could take it.

Julio

The day of the raid I got to the plant at quarter to ten in the morning. While I was heading into the plant nothing was happening, everything was quiet. Suddenly I saw a helicopter flying overhead, and I wondered what it was doing and if I should go back home or go into the plant. And after thinking a little I decided it was best to go home. When I was heading out I saw two men who were wearing the same kind of coveralls that we used in the plant. They didn't look at all like policemen, nothing at all, and that's the way some of them came to check and be sure that no one escaped. Then other agents arrived, and they were talking together. They looked big and fat. They told me to come over to them and, while I was watching, a lot of patrol cars drove into the parking lot. I was at the security gate. More police were coming with weapons—rifles, big guns, pistols. I was afraid that they were going to do something to me. There they caught about ten of us who were just coming to work, and they took us inside where there is a big cafeteria. Once inside, I saw a lot of women who were crying.

When they caught us, a friend of mine tried to get away so they put chains on his feet, hands and around his waist, and they told us not to try to escape because, if we did, things would get worse. They also told us not to talk or we would be in more trouble. When they had all of us they put me in Area #1 which is right next to the dining room. The "yellow hardhats" told us they were just going to check our Social Security IDs and nothing was going to happen. I was afraid and I can't describe how I felt with all the police—and there were a lot of them—that were coming in by the handful.

When I went into the dining room the immigration people took pictures and then they gave me a bag for my belt, keys, cell phone, and watch. When I asked one of my work buddies what was going to happen to us, especially to me because I was a minor, he said they were going to put the underage workers in jail for two years. That really scared me so what was I supposed to do? Tell the truth, or say I was older than I was? That's why I told them I was 19, so that nothing bad would happen to me. But it made it much worse because they let most of the minors go at the plant and let some of them go in Waterloo. But not me.

Then they gave all of us a number, going row by row. They searched me, and they chained my hands to my waist and then my feet. They put me on a bus because they were loading everyone who was chained on buses right away. I was so frightened. It was as if I was dreaming that they were putting me in chains because I had never before been chained. At that time in the morning I hadn't eaten anything. On the bus they gave us food and bottled water. I was upset because I didn't know what was going to happen.

When I got off the bus they asked for my date of birth, and I told them I was born in 1988 even though I was born in 1990. This was because, as I said before, a man told us they were really going to screw those of us who were minors, and that they were going to put us in jail for two years before deporting us to Guatemala. That's why I said I was older. When we arrived in Waterloo they took my pants, and I only had my underwear on from the waist down. They gave me a pair of sandals. I was cold. There was a big enclosure, and they crowded all of us in, and while we were waiting others were arriving. They put us in groups of about 80, and took us to a place with cots to sleep on.

At 5:00 a.m. the next morning they took me to be interviewed where there were some computers. They asked me where I was from, where I got my ID, how I came, who brought me, if I was a minor, how long I had worked at Agriprocessors. They asked me about my family here in the United States and in Guatemala. I got back to the enclosure at about 11:00 at night.

During that time I had to walk with the chains on. It was hard for me to walk because the faster I walked the harder the chains pressed against my ankles. My companions were all taller and they

Julio

could walk faster, and I was smaller and my steps were shorter. I asked one of the officials if he could loosen the chains on my feet a little because they were very tight, and he said it wasn't his problem, so I was hurting all day. The officials were always telling us to walk faster and they kept pushing me. Then the chain would get tighter and hurt my ankles.

The next day, at about 3:00 in the morning, they took me to the computers again. I was chained the whole time. At something like 5:00 p.m. they told me that I wasn't the one whose files they had been checking; I was the wrong person. They had been confused. That's how I spent that whole day. They fed me just once.

On Wednesday night they took me out of the enclosure to transport me to jail. They took me to the jail in Vinton, Iowa. When I woke up on Thursday I spent the whole day locked up with my companions. We were all crying because we were locked in. I felt like I was going crazy, like I couldn't breathe, that I couldn't get enough air, all day shut up in one room. That's the way the days passed. You couldn't tell if it was day or night; there were no windows and you couldn't see a thing. We could only know what time it was because when they brought us food we would know it was morning, noon, or 5:00 in the evening.

While I was in that jail a lawyer came to talk to me and asked me to sign some papers. I didn't know what they were or why they needed my signature. I just signed them. They didn't explain anything to me. They told me that next Wednesday I was going to be in court. When Wednesday came they chained us again, they loaded us into a van, and they took us before the judge to receive the sentence.

When we were seated facing the judge and before he sentenced us he told us, "Thank you very much for coming to the United States to work, and I know that you are all working because of your families and out of need. For that reason I thank you for coming. I wish that tomorrow or the next day you could see your families again, but I can't do anything. They are compelling me to sentence you for violating the law with your IDs."

Then he sentenced us to five months in prison, and we stood up to leave.

Because we were in chains, traveling in the van was hard. Each time it turned we would all slide over to one side and pile on top of each other and sometimes get hurt because we couldn't control the movement. It was really ugly every time they drove us from one place to another.

The jail cell was very small and dark and had one bathroom. All we did was watch television. There were bright lights on all the time so like I said before, we couldn't tell what time it was. I slept during the day and not at night, because night time passes more quickly. When you are in jail you go crazy.

From Vinton they took me to Cedar Rapids. They got us up at 10:00 in the morning. My feet were hot from being in bed. They told us they were taking us someplace else because the jail was flooding. The water was very high, and I didn't want to wade through it. I was sleepy and toasty warm from bed. They made us go through, and then they put us in a boat, and then a bus took us to a school in Cedar Rapids. They took three more photos and then fingerprinted us again, and then we were in the Cedar Rapids jail. Then that flooded, too, and they took us to Kansas. I felt better there. It was a big prison and there was a yard. It was such a relief to see the sun and to walk. I was in Kansas for three months, and it was very bad.

When I got to the prison in Kansas a police officer asked me how old I was. Like always I told him I was 19. He said it wasn't true, but nothing happened. In that prison there were some very

Julio

big black guys. I only came up to their waists! They said to me that I was too young, that I was younger than 19. I also remember that when I would be taken to the cell, the Chicanos who were there would say, "You're a minor. Tell them you're underage, and they'll get you out of here fast."

One Chicano told me, "You have to tell them you're a minor because in your cell there are only older and bigger guys, and you're too young. There might be a fight, and you could get killed."

I was scared, and I didn't know what to do, so he translated for me and told the officer that I was a minor. The guard called some of his colleagues, and they asked me how old I was, and I said I was 17. They chained my hands behind my back, and one guard grabbed my left side and another my right side, as if I was a criminal.

"You son of a bitch." they said.

They took me to their boss and when he asked me how old I was I answered "Seventeen." So he said to me, "We're going to put you someplace else."

Then I saw they were taking me to a small, enclosed room. It was "the hole." There was no sunlight. Another official who spoke Spanish came, and I asked him, "What's going to happen to me? Are you going to let me out of prison? Can't I go back with the others?"

"Whether you are a minor or not doesn't matter to us because we aren't the ones who caught you," he said.

I asked him to let me go back to my companions, but he said that because I was a liar and had told them I was 17 years old I was going to stay in solitary for a week or two.

I felt like I was dying there in the hole. I didn't know what time it was, what time to go to sleep. It was dark. The only way I had any idea was the meal schedule—6:00 a.m., 11:00 a.m. and 4:00 p.m. After that I didn't get fed until the following morning. You go crazy in there. I couldn't sleep because the bed was made of metal and I was freezing. I didn't have a jacket or a poncho, just the prison clothes—pants and a short-sleeved t-shirt. I felt like I was losing my mind. As I was lying on my bed I always thought of Guatemala and my family.

While I was in the hole they would give me meals through a small metal window. It is impossible to sleep there because the black guys would bang on their cell doors. I was sorry I had told them I was a minor. I was much better off with the other prisoners that I knew.

There in the hole you find the worst people. Because of that when they took me out to take a shower they would chain me. They took me to shower with cold water, and they locked me in. They treated me like a criminal, the same way they treated the other criminals, as if I was a murderer. When they would take me back to my cell I would get so sad I would cry. They did whatever they wanted with me, as if I was some big macho guy, but I'm just a kid. They treated me like a killer.

So a week passed and then they told me to gather my things, and they took me to another cell. The same Chicano who told me to say I was a minor was there. Now he didn't say anything.

What a freaking mess.

While I was in prison I got the flu and I had a bad headache. There was a doctor, but I had to fill out some papers, and then a week later they brought me the medicine. I felt awful, like I was going to die. I didn't know how much longer I could stand it. Half a year in jail, and it seemed as if the days never ended because it was so hard to take. They fed us hard beans that gave me a stomach

Julio

ache, and I was always hungry. I cried every time I thought about my family, and I asked myself why this was happening to me. I cried and I cried in prison.

After a time they told me, "You have to go someplace else."

We got up at 3:00 in the morning, and we left at six o'clock. We were chained, and they took us to Cerro Gordo. There were three of us from Postville. We went to court. There were about 12 people on the jury. They asked me where I had gotten my ID and how I started working. Each of the three of us was brought before that court. We didn't know what was happening or why we were there. They never explained.

After that they had us shower and put us back in jail. About a week later, they took us back to Kansas. There we could go outside into the yard. We were back with the others, playing basketball and soccer. It felt so much better to be outside and in sunlight.

One day they got me up at 3:00 in the morning and told me I was going to take a plane someplace. I thought I was going to Guatemala. One of the prisoners translated and told me that the plane was taking off at 9:00 in the morning. I bundled my clothing and my poncho, and they took me to another cell. I saw that there were a lot of guys from Guatemala, maybe a hundred, and I knew them because they had all worked in Agriprocessors. There were a lot of us, and again they put chains on our hands, waist, and feet. It was 5:00 a.m. and we were on our feet the whole time. Breakfast arrived at 7:00 but they didn't take off the chains. We had to eat with the chains on. They gave us a little bag with a sandwich and bottled water. We couldn't sit down or stand up because of the chains, and we couldn't eat. It made me angry because how could they not see that we couldn't eat or drink water with the chains on? I think they were making fun of us.

They took us to the airport where we were supposed to wait

for the plane, and we thought we were going to Guatemala. There were two buses and six vans, and the plane was there when we got to the airport. The airplane already had some prisoners on it when it arrived. They took us out of the van, searched us, and took us to the plane.

I was so sad, because I didn't know when the nightmare would end, like when you're dreaming and don't know what is going to happen next. I didn't know where they were going to take me or for how long. It was before dawn when we took off, all one hundred of us who had been in Kansas. We arrived in Miami at about 2:00 in the afternoon. By then I knew we were going to Miami because one of the other guys asked an official in Kansas where we were going. In Miami they divided us up. There were two big buses, like tour buses, and six vans. One bus and three vans went to one prison and the other bus and three vans went to another.

We got to the prison, and they took blood to test for tuberculosis and other things. Every time we were moving from one jail to another they were taking blood, maybe fifteen times. They would give me a shot in one arm and take blood from the other one. Every time I arrived at new jail they didn't care if my arm was swollen, they just gave me a shot of who knows what. I asked them to look at how sore my skin was, and they said it didn't matter to them because that had happened in another prison.

In Miami they said they were going to give me a tetanus shot. I told them I had already been vaccinated for that, and they said that it was the rule in that prison that all prisoners had to receive a tetanus shot. My arm swelled up and it wouldn't stop bleeding. They put on a band-aid, and my upper arm was swollen for two days. It's terrible what they do to you in jail.

After that they called us from a list. The put me in a large cell, and there were four of us. I was a little sad because it was better

Julio

in Kansas where I was with some people that I knew. When they put me in the cell, they didn't turn the light on. They just told me that my bed was the top bunk. Then I could make out in the dark that there was a big, black guy. I was frightened and wondered who would protect me. I was so despondent wondering when all this was going to end.

The Mexican and the Colombian prisoners said that those of us from Postville shouldn't be there. It wasn't a place for people who were undocumented. Those prisons were for people who were murderers, drug traffickers and guilty of other really bad crimes. They thought that what we did wasn't such a big crime and that the prison we were in wasn't for people like us.

Then I saw that the prison in Miami was like the one in Kansas because there was space outside to walk around and play sports. The prison was very big.

The Mexicans and Colombians asked me if I had any money, and I told them I didn't, so they gave me soft drinks and soup. I collected about 12 sodas. They gave me shoes, too. Mexicans and Colombians are good people. Every Thursday I would give my serving of chicken to the black prisoners because they served it only once a week, and they would give me six packages of soup.

One of the Mexicans scolded me, saying, "No, you have to eat well. If you want soup, ask me for some."

In that prison, every Sunday a priest would come to say mass at about 5:00 in the afternoon. He told us to be patient and encouraged us.

After about a month, there were only two weeks left of the jail sentence. We were very happy, and then they called just me to the office. They told me that I wasn't going to Guatemala because my lawyer had sent my papers. I had to sign and say where I was going to stay.

I thought I must be dreaming. I didn't understand what was happening. I read the paper, but I couldn't understand it.

"Just sign it and say where you will be staying. You know that when you finish your sentence you're aren't going to Guatemala. You are going to stay here in the United States. When you go back upstairs, don't tell anyone," the official said.

Then I signed the paper and wrote that I would stay in Iowa.

When there were only three days left, they took all of the Guatemalans and one Mexican downstairs to meet with the Guatemalan consul. He told us to be patient since there were only three days in jail left.

I asked him, "Am I going back to Guatemala or not?"

The consul said, "Yes."

Then I signed a paper and they asked all of us for our family's phone number so the embassy could call them and tell them when we would be arriving so that they could pick us up in Guatemala. I gave my *Papá*'s number.

They took us back to the cells. It was Thursday, and on Friday they turned us over to Immigration. We were supposed to fly out on Saturday. I couldn't figure out what was going to happen with me. The consulate had the list of who was going to be deported, and I was on the list. I was very happy, and I gave away everything—my clothes, my shoes, soft drinks and soup, everything—because I was about to leave.

A woman came to see me. She spoke to me in English, and I couldn't understand a thing. Then they took me out. Who knows what she was telling me? As we passed by the other cells, I saw that the rest of my companions were still sleeping. I asked where they were taking me.

Julio

An official who spoke Spanish told me, "You're not leaving. You have to go to court."

"Why do I have to go to court?" I wondered. I was afraid, and then they took me to another cell where there were about 30 black guys. Oh, my God, it made me want to cry. Those black guys were so tall, and I felt so small. I only came up to their waists!

They were bringing more men down. There was a Mexican. It was Lalo, someone I knew from Postville. I told him I didn't know what the heck was happening. He told me that he had given all his things away, too, because we were going back to our countries.

Then another Guatemalan arrived and I asked him, "Are we going to Guatemala?"

"No. I received a permit and I'm going to stay in Iowa."

I didn't understand a thing. We went to the courthouse and got there about 7:00 a.m.

"Why do we have to do this if we're going back to our countries?"

"No. You all are staying here in the U.S."

So we were staying? What could we do? The consulate told us one thing and the U.S. officials told us something else. What a mess.

In court the judge told us that we couldn't leave yet.

"Someone wants to detain you because there are new charges against you. There is someone who says there are more charges since they interviewed you. For that reason, since you have already completed your sentence, if I put you back where you were and something happens to you they're going to blame us because you've served your time already. We're going to protect you."

79

Shattered Dreams

And they took us to the hole! There were three of us—[me]; the Mexican, Lalo; and another Guatemalan. We asked if only the three of us were staying.

The guard said, "There are ten of you. Seven are in the other prison. On Tuesday you have to come to court again."

They gave us orange coveralls to wear and put us in the hole with our hands chained behind our backs. The rooms have doors with little windows in them to deliver food, and once you are in the cell you have to turn around so they can take the chains off. They treated us worse than they treat criminals. They put me in a room by myself, and they put the Mexican and the Guatemalan together. I didn't want them to put me with a black prisoner. I would have preferred a fellow Guatemalan.

In the hole we only ate and slept. At 5:00 in the morning they brought breakfast, at 10:00 a.m. lunch, and at 3:00 p.m. dinner. So I ate my 5:00 a.m. food at 10:00 a.m., my lunch at 3:00 and then the food they brought me at 3:00 I would eat at night.

We were there for a week. I thought it would have been so much better to be in Guatemala, and I wished I hadn't signed that paper. I thought of the others who had already arrived in Guatemala and here I was, in the hole. Oh, my God, it can drive you crazy to be there.

At the end of that terrible week, they got us up at 4:00 or 5:00 a.m. and they took us in chains to a cell. We were on our way to court when the other seven Guatemalans arrived. We were happier because now there were ten of us.

The judge said, "You are supposed to return to Iowa, but I'm going to set a date, and if they don't come to get you by that date, I'm going to send you back to your countries. The date is October 28th."

Julio

But they came for us, and we left on October 27th. We knew we were on our way to Iowa. They took the clothes we were wearing and gave us other clothing, chained our hands and our feet, and loaded us onto a bus. A van drove behind the bus. A total of 80 prisoners were with us. In the airport they loaded us onto a plane. We asked where we were going, and they said we were headed to Oklahoma. We were there for two days. The prison was big, and we were a lot more at ease because we knew we were getting out.

When an official arrived he said that we had served our time. "They want you as witnesses. I'm going to search you, but if you say no, that's okay because I know you aren't criminals. If you give me authorization to search you I'll do it, but if not, I won't."

We said yes, and then they put us in jail for two days. If you say no, where are you going to stay and what are you going to do?

Then two days later they got us up early again and 60 of us got on a plane and flew to Kentucky. The plane landed and some prisoners got off and others got on. Then we took off and went to Virginia where again some prisoners left and other prisoners boarded the plane. It was about 2:00 in the afternoon and we were tired from being on the plane all day. When the plane landed again we recognized the Kansas airport.

We looked out and said, "Now we're in Kansas. It's true; we're going to get out."

We arrived. They interviewed us all again. They prepared some papers for us. They took blood again and into another jail we went. We asked how many days we were going to be there, and they said they didn't know. Then some friends called Postville to ask if there were any people there who had been let out of jail and had gone back to Postville. They learned that there were about 20 guys in that situation. Then we really thought we were going to get out. There were fifteen of us in Kansas.

Shattered Dreams

Again, at about 6:00 a.m. they took us out and chained us. We asked where we were going, and they said they were taking us to Des Moines. We got there, and they took us to an office and told us they were going to take pictures and fingerprint us, and then they were going to give us work permits. We felt pretty happy.

After they put us in the van, they asked, "Are you hungry? Do you want a hamburger and a soda" and, of course, we said yes. We were so happy to be eating a hamburger again. We ate right there in the van, in chains.

We got to Dubuque and had to spend another week there, but on a Monday when they put us in a van again it was the day we would be set free.

We appeared in court again that day, and I don't remember exactly what the judge said but it was something like, "From now on you are going to be free. You are going to be witnesses, and you will be fitted with a GPS monitoring device so that you don't go back to your homes. You are free now, and they will take off your chains."

Right there in the court room they removed our chains. We were so happy, jumping and jumping for joy. We never thought we would be free and in Iowa again. They took us to an office and put the GPS devices on our ankles. We thought that was fine, much better than being in prison. After that a woman in charge took us to get something to eat, and we were so glad. And then she brought us to Decorah and said that we were going to live there. We got to a little yellow house. Six of us stayed there, and the other four went to live in the church. It was all over.

When they took me out of prison I could hardly tell if it was true or a lie that I was really out. And I can't forget how hard it was, how I suffered, and sometimes when I sleep I wake up with a jerk, terrified because I feel like I'm still inside.

Julio

I don't understand exactly what happened to me during the raid and while I was in jail, but now I can't speak Kaqchikel, the language I grew up with and that my family speaks. Who knows what's wrong with me? I understand everything, but it's very hard for me to speak it. Maybe it's because I was so afraid when the Immigration police caught me and put me in jail. I kept thinking, "When am I ever going to see my family again?"

Look, I understand, I understand everything they say to me in Kaqchikel, but when I want to answer them, to talk to them, I can't. I can't. Oh, my God, I'm so screwed up. Who knows what my problem is?

Epilogue

Julio and the other men brought back to northeast Iowa were held as witnesses and kept in the area for 15 months. In a remarkable show of solidarity, the community of Decorah welcomed them with open arms and hearts, finding places for them to live, giving them jobs shoveling snow, working in the Luther College cafeteria, and inviting them into their homes for meals and holiday celebrations. A group representing several churches gathered thousands of dollars that were used first to pay off the debts that most of the men still had in Guatemala because of money borrowed to pay *coyotes* for the trip north. After that a fund was established to give loans to the men once they returned to their homelands to be used to start up small businesses. When they were finally deported in March 2010, they left many new friends and a community committed to immigration reform.

Shattered Dreams

Janet

Sixteen years ago my husband came here to the United States. I stayed back in Mexico with my four children. He came because we didn't have our own home. We were renting, and everything we earned went to pay the rent. My brother is a resident of the United States and once, when he was visiting us and saw the way we were living, he asked if my husband wouldn't like to go to the U.S. for awhile so that he could earn enough to build a house, maybe just one room, but a place that we could call our own. I didn't want him to go because we were not living in my village then, but in a dangerous city, and I didn't want to be left alone with my four children. There was a lot of violence, and if we were just a little careless, we would find thieves in our house. Criminals were everywhere robbing and hurting people, even throwing rocks. That was in Monterrey, but it was in a neighborhood on the outskirts. You see, there are categories of neighborhoods and where we were renting there were a lot of gangs. But in the end, my husband did decide to leave because of the poverty, and I tried to be as strong as I could because there were times I didn't even have anything to feed my children.

When he got here to the U.S. and started to work again, he sent me some money to buy some land there in Monterrey, and we started to build a room. That was the first thing, and then he came back and tried to find a job in Monterrey so that we wouldn't have to be separated. But it was very hard because he had been gone for two years. I mean he was in the United States during those years, and then he couldn't find a job in Mexico because he couldn't prove where he had been. That's when he decided to go back to the U.S. because he had looked for work for a month without finding anything. In Mexico nobody lends a hand.

So he came here while I found a job so that I could support

Janet

the children. I took work as a servant until he could get to the U.S. and start sending money. But pretty soon he was saying that it was so hard for him to be here alone and that he was going to get together enough money so that all of us could come north. It was so sad because the children had nothing. They had no shoes, no food, and they needed so many things every day. That's what he was thinking, and so he saved money so that we could all be with him.

My husband spoke to someone who told him to just bring one of our daughters first. So she came by plane using someone else's documents. And she got here really fast. It was like a dream. She arrived in Chicago, and when she called me she was already there with my husband. She was fifteen years old when she arrived.

Eight months later I came with my other three children. My husband told me I had to take a bus to Ciudad Juárez on a Friday afternoon so that we could be there by dawn on Saturday morning.

"There will be some people waiting for you to help you cross over with the kids. I don't know if they're going to walk across with you, or if they are planning to go through a check-point, but don't let the kids out of your sight. Stay with them all the time." We got to Juárez, and then a man showed up looking for us.

"Are you *Señora* Janet and are these your children?" One of my brothers was with us, too.

The man said "Are you ready to hike? Because we're going to be walking a lot."

I told him that I was afraid it would be too much since my littlest one was only six years old.

"It's okay," he said, "don't worry. At 7:00 in the evening all the people who are going to cross over will get together. We're going to take a van to Las Palmas to get close to the *Río Bravo* [Rio

Shattered Dreams

Grande]. When the time comes to get out of the van, there's going to be signal."

There were about 30 of us, so there were two vans.

"I'm going to say a special word, and you're all going to get out and run. And don't stop. Get out and run as fast as you can," he told us.

My brother carried my little girl, and I took my other two by the hand, and we ran for about ten minutes, and there was the river. They told us to take off all our clothing except our underwear and to carry all our clothes in our arms because we were going into the water. The same for the children.

That's how we crossed. We waded into the river. But this is where my nightmare begins. Here's the hardest part. We crossed the river, but after we crossed it got much worse. Five hours of walking without stopping—through corn fields, through who knows what—and we just couldn't walk anymore. We crossed a small bridge that only had room for one person at a time, and on both sides there were barbed wire fences and high tension lines, and if you brushed against them, you would fall into the river. Down below there were whirlpools in the water. It was a very narrow road to go along, between two towns. I don't know how, but when I managed to cross with my daughters, somehow at that moment I lost sight of my son. We were in a line. I went ahead, and he was behind us with my brother. So, on the other side, when everyone was getting together again after crossing, I couldn't see him. I hadn't seen him come over the bridge because it was so dark you couldn't see a thing. I didn't know if he had fallen into the water. We couldn't find him, and I started screaming.

The *coyote* said, "Be quiet, *la migra* is going to find us. I've got a lot of people here."

Janet

But I was shouting, "Fernando! Fernando, where are you?"

And I asked my brother where Fernando was. I was hysterical, and the *coyote* separated me from the others because he didn't want me near them.

He said, "He's not lost. See? There he is coming along with those people."

But I said I wasn't going to move until my son was with me. I was going through hell, thinking he had fallen into the water and that we would never find him. In the middle of all of that, suddenly the *coyote* said, "Get down! Get down!" One of those trucks with search lights was coming.

As soon as he told everyone to shut up and get down, there wasn't a sound. I waited until the *migra* agents got close. I waited until they were almost beside me, and then I shouted that I had lost my son. I was going crazy because I couldn't find him. An agent asked me if there were more people with me.

"Yes," I said, "There are more. There are a lot, but my son is missing."

And he asked again, "Are there any more people?"

And I said "Yes, but I don't know who they are."

The agents called for reinforcements because there were so many people. First they made us kneel down, and then they loaded us into the patrol cars, and then they started to look for my son.

"How long has it been since you noticed he went missing," they asked. "Why didn't you say something?"

"I told another person who said my son was right behind us."

Shattered Dreams

I said "Another person" because the *coyote* had said, "If they catch us, don't say that I'm the *coyote*. Just say that we all made the trip together, taking care of each other, because if you tell them, they'll put me in jail."

The agents looked and looked for my son. They took me with them in the patrol car, with my daughter and brother, and we couldn't find him. Then one of the *migra* agents told me the water must have carried him away.

"There's nothing we can do," he said. "Let's go."

They took us and put us under arrest. The only thing they asked me was my name. They gave my daughter some milk, and they took us to Juárez and left us there at the border between Mexico and the U.S. "Now you can go home," they said. "We're sorry about your son. He probably fell into the river. We have your contact information, and we'll let you know if we find him."

Right away I went to talk to my husband; I found a phone. I told him "I lost Fernando. I'm going crazy. I don't know what happened to him."

He told me to talk to the man and woman who had taken us across. "They'll know who he was with."

My husband couldn't understand how I had lost Fernando, and when I told him what had happened when we crossed that bridge, he said, "My God, I don't know what I'm going to do."

Then I went up to the hotel room where they were keeping us and almost right away there was a knock at the door.

It was a man who told me, "Lady, because of you they caught everyone. You have no idea how much money we lost."

I was afraid they were going to do something bad to me.

Janet

"It's your fault nobody made it across," he and others kept repeating.

I told him that what mattered to me was my son's life.

Then a little later someone else phoned the hotel room and threatened me, told me I had better watch out, that this wasn't going to end well for me. I think that even the owners of the hotel have connections. They are all working together because the hotel manager was angry with me too. They talked and talked to me on the phone and said I was in big trouble, that everything was my fault and that they were going to give me a good beating.

At about 12:30 someone knocked on the door. "*Señora*, we've received information that your son is just fine. He's on the other side, safely in the United States."

He had made it across with two young men who had helped him because he was all by himself. Those guys told him they weren't going to continue on with the rest of the group because it was too big and they were going to get caught. So they went another way.

"*Señora*, we're going to try to cross again tonight with you."

I told them I didn't want to. I didn't even want to try. I wanted to go home. I told them that if it was true that my son was okay, I wanted them to bring him back to me. I didn't believe them. I didn't believe he was all right. I thought, "How do they know he's okay?" They urged me to try to cross again, saying that yesterday we had bad luck, but this time it would go well. But I said I wasn't interested in trying again. I wasn't going to risk losing my six-year-old daughter. I already didn't know where my son was. And that's how we passed the day. They called me on the phone a lot, saying I wasn't going to get out of that place. These were the voices of the *coyotes*, men's voices.

Shattered Dreams

At about seven that evening everybody left to try again. It didn't matter to them what had happened. I didn't leave the hotel. I said to myself I'm not leaving here until I know something about my son. When I saw that everyone was gone. I told my brother to watch my daughter, and I went to see the *coyote*'s wife.

When she opened the door she said, "So you didn't try again."

I told her that I believed she knew what had happened to the people who went missing. I wanted to know about my son.

"He's already over on the other side of the border."

"I want him here with me. I'm not leaving. If he's on the other side he's still very far away from where his father is, and he's all alone."

She told me to go back to my room and wait to see what information she could get.

The night passed and, at about 2:00 in the morning, people came back to the hotel shouting and screaming. The hotel was a real dump, and I was so frightened. The men were getting drunk, and I couldn't sleep. I could only watch through the window. They were shouting that because of me they hadn't made it across the border. At about 5:00 in the morning there was a knock on the door. I didn't want to answer.

"Who is it?" I asked.

"Open up, *Señora*," someone shouted.

I asked again who it was and what was happening. It turned out they had my son with them and they were coming to return him to me. Oh my God, when he arrived I quickly ran out of the hotel and called my husband. I told him that I had found Fernando. He told me not to go back home, that he had spoken to someone else and that we should try crossing again.

Janet

"Things went badly for you with those people because Fernando got separated. Try again with this other man because he was the one who helped our daughter Margarita get to the other side."

My brother thought that we should try again, too. I didn't know what to do. Oh my God, I don't know what was going on in my head.

Then my son said, "I was on the other side of the border in a trailer because the men I was with told me that a lot of people get caught trying to cross the way we did." He said, "Mami, I've suffered so much because Dad has been gone. He's not going to come home to Mexico because there's no work. Let's go, Mami, it isn't hard."

He hadn't been through what I had, so for him it hadn't been so hurtful. But I didn't want to try again.

When the van came to the central bus station where we were waiting to go back home, a man approached and said, "I'm the person your husband talked to. Come and get into my car. I'm not going to do you any harm. Trust me."

We got in his car, and he took us to a house and gave us something to eat. "You can trust us," he said. "Your son and your brother are going to go separately, and you and your daughter will go together."

"I'm not leaving my son. I just went through the worst experience of my whole life."

He said, "You can have confidence in me. We're not going to wade across the river or walk across the border."

That's how he convinced me to have a little more courage, and I said, "Okay, let's try it."

Shattered Dreams

About half an hour later a *Señora* arrived and gave us our credentials. She said, "You are these people."

So we drove across the border with fake documents, and they left us in a store in El Paso. From there they took us to the airport and we took a plane. They told us we had to make connections in Dallas and that we were going to Chicago. That's what I did, and two hours later we were in Chicago. I was in communication with the man who was with my brother and son, and he said that they were in a car right behind us when we crossed the border, but for some reason, who knows what, they couldn't put them on the plane. At about 11:00 p.m. they called and said they were about to arrive but that we had to go to the bus station to pick them up. And there they were. It was really them. They did arrive. And that's how we all came to the United States.

I think I have never had a worse moment in my life than when I couldn't find my son. That's what it was like to cross. My husband paid $2,500 for each of us, and $500 to the one we were with when my son disappeared, and that money was lost. I wanted to go crazy. I even ripped my slacks, I was so anxious and angry at myself for wanting to come. I was beside myself. It's the worst thing that can happen to a person—just terrifying, losing a child like that.

When we got here we owed so much money that my husband was scrambling for cash every way possible. So the week I arrived in Postville I got a job at Agriprocessors right away. I started to work on April 22, 2001. At the beginning we worked without papers, but then the managers started to push and say we needed documents. A Good Samaritan showed up and asked who needed papers for work. So that's how I got the documents and was able to continue working when I went back to the plant in 2003.

It took a long time for us to earn the money we owed for crossing the border. After paying what we owed each month there was no money left for anything else. It was hard to understand.

Janet

I said to my husband, "It's just the same here. There we had nothing and here we still don't have any money to pay the bills."

But little by little we began to see things more clearly. My children were going to school, and we began to pay for a car and to look for a place to live. When we arrived we were living with my sister. There were a lot of us. It was the whole family in a two room apartment. The owner realized that there were more people living there than before so she told us all to move out. In the beginning there were no places to rent; everything was full. The only place we found was the apartment above the bar.

I worked at Agri for about two years, but since my shift started at 4:00 in the morning and the work was really hard, in 2003 I left and took a job at the other turkey processing plant for eight months. But there wasn't enough work there and I wasn't earning enough to support us. When the turkey processing plant burned down, I went back to working at Agriprocessors.

Yes, the turkey plant burned down. Well, someone burned it down according to what people said. We went to work there on Friday, December 20th, and then on Saturday only four people went to work, and by ten or eleven in the morning they were saying it had burned down! That was the end of the turkey plant. I don't know exactly what happened, but it was gone. There was no more work for people. That was on a Saturday, and Tuesday was the day people could apply for work at Agri, so there were a lot of people at the plant, but since I had worked there before, I had a better chance.

A supervisor came out and told me, "You can come to work tomorrow for me."

And I worked there until the day of the raid. I never left. I never missed work. I worked holidays. I was always working.

In the section where I worked it was just me—one woman

among sixty men—because the work was very heavy. The manager put me there and said I could do that job which was to separate the fat from the meat or the meat from the fat, and take out the bone. It all came on a conveyor belt, and I also sorted the meat according to quality. I had some barrels to put the meat into, and I put the garbage back onto another belt that was higher up; that's where I put the bones. I did the work of about seven people. I was all alone. That space was for three or four people, but since the supervisor said that I was able to do the work, well, that was that!

The supervisor was an American, a white guy. When you get here to the States, you believe you have to do exactly what they tell you to do, and you do it. You say to yourself, that's what I'm here for, to work. You don't know that people have rights on the job, and then, too, they threaten to fire you. When they told me what I had to do, at first I said I couldn't do it. I didn't know how to sharpen the tools. I didn't know how to cut the meat.

They told me, "You do it, or you can go home."

I asked a Mexican supervisor to tell them the work was too hard for me, but he said he couldn't do anything and that I should go home and never come back.

That went on for fifteen days, and every day I came home with a fever from exhaustion. All I did was work. I never saw my children. I couldn't do anything else. I don't know if it was depression, but I couldn't make sense of that kind of work. I don't know if it was because of the fever or because of the sadness, I didn't want to say anything to my husband because we owed so much money, and we had no choice but to pay. It was all just work and to bed after a bath, and then I was unaware of anything until 3:30 in the morning because my shift started at 4:30.

I spent all my time at that job, and that's when I started to know more about meat. They started giving me more work

Janet

because they said I had learned to do it well. I couldn't have any time off. I had no privileges. I couldn't miss a Sunday. I couldn't have off for birthdays. If we asked for time off they said that we didn't care about our jobs. For instance, for my daughter's first communion I didn't go to work, but I didn't ask for time off, and when I got back they said I shouldn't have done that and they weren't going to pay me for working on a holiday that had been the week before.

"And you're not getting a raise either," they said.

They never gave me raises anyway. It was pure threats, that if we didn't do this or that they would kick us out. And, for fear of losing our jobs, we did everything they said.

I was there all the time, and my worst day at the plant—it was so humiliating—was the day they found a rat inside one of the buildings. That day they took all of us out of the department I was working in because it was the one with the most people. There were like seventy of us, and they took us out to clean the plant. We had to take out all the rubbish. They made us pick it up in our hands. There were dead chickens, all the filth that was in the corners, everything. We couldn't keep from vomiting. The muck was hideous. They found a rat right there wandering inside the plant so they decided we were going to do the cleaning! The 4:30 a.m. shift ended at 4:00 p.m.

But they said, "don't anybody leave. Get in a line, and we're going to go outside."

I didn't know what this was for. Then they talked to the Mexican supervisors and made a list and said, "You take so many, and you take others, and some are going to the chicken processing area, and others are going to clean outside the plant."

My group was sent to where the rotten chickens were, and dead rats, too. It was absolute filth. Just a peek inside would make you shudder.

I told the supervisor, "I want to go home. I'm exhausted, and this is just disgusting."

And he told me that if I left I shouldn't bother coming back. He said they had orders from Sholom, the plant's owner, that we had to clean everything. They sent us to an area near the parking lot and there was a pile of filth you couldn't even imagine.

That day I felt so humiliated, going around cleaning up the crud that was around the plant. I was so disgusted by everything we had to clean up that when I got home I took off my clothes, threw them all in the trash, and took a bath. I was so furious I couldn't say anything to anyone.

I waited to tell my husband until the next day. They had us cleaning on the roofs, that's where they have tubes that carry the chemicals, and all the signs said "Danger." I was afraid I was going to step on something and some dangerous liquid was going to come out. They made us clean under the tanks of ammonia. I didn't want to, and the supervisor said he would help. He gave us a hand as we crossed over and under the tanks, and I was really afraid. Because of that, when there were rumors that *la migra* was going to come, I made plans to go up on the roof to escape, because I knew what it was like up there. But when they did come, I didn't have time.

My supervisor was really mean, not just with me but with everyone. He wouldn't even let us go to the bathroom.

He'd say, "It's not your turn. The line starts here."

He yelled at you for any little thing. You couldn't even turn around. He was really nasty, just there to make threats.

Janet

He'd say, drumming his fingers, "Leave if you want, the door is plenty wide."

If you came in slacks he thought were a little dirty he would fire you, send you home. But in the end, they fired him just like he had fired everyone else who had spent years working there. He was so nasty, so snooty. He wanted everything to be so fast and clean, and he said we were fucking idiots. And if so much as a piece of meat fell on the floor, he would get furious. He wanted us to be there just like slaves. In our place.

Another ugly thing was when the toilets would overflow. The dining room was right next to the bathrooms. We would be enjoying our lunch and there would come the sewer water with floating feces, and we would ask permission to go outside to eat so we wouldn't have to be near the flooding bathrooms, and the supervisor would say no. When you walked into the dining room there was a bench on the right and the doors for the bathrooms were on the left. And then there were some lockers and four more benches. That's where we ate.

They said that the plant used to be a jail. The shower heads were still there, and it does have the shape of a jail—little rooms, hallways and the shower heads. I think the dining room was where the women used to bathe. I believe this is true because there were really old shower heads on the wall. My daughter told me she had heard at school that it used to be the county jail many years ago. I never paid much attention to that. In what was supposed to have been the men's dining room, we had to go to get our checks. They didn't just give them to you. You had to pester them to get your check. That's where I realized there were shower heads, bathrooms, and rooms like small bedrooms. So that's how I imagine the prison.

After some time, I bought a house here. That was four years ago. I was tired of paying such high rents every month. My sister-in-law

Shattered Dreams

sold me one of her houses so that I wouldn't have to pay so much.

She told me, "I'll sell you my house, and we can just do it directly if you give me $4,000 to do the paperwork."

I talked to my husband because I was convinced I would never be able to buy a house through a bank because it was a lot of money, plus I didn't have my papers. What she proposed to me seemed easy. The $4,000 was a lot, but at the same time pretty easy. It took me about eight months to save the money. At first I rented her house, and when I had the money I told her I was ready to buy it. And so we made the deal. She sold me the house for $35,000. The bank had valued it at $8,000. I knew what I paid was very expensive, but that's how I bought it. So we were living in the house, and we were fixing it up. We wanted to do a lot of repairs because it was really run down.

And then on May 12th disaster struck and with *la migra* everything fell apart. I was arrested. *Uyyy*, where do I begin? It was about time to go to lunch when I saw people running.

I asked a woman I was working with, "Why are they going so fast?"

She said, "They're hurrying to change gloves."

And I thought to myself, "That is very weird."

Then another woman yelled, "Run! Run! *La migra* is inside the plant."

Both of us ran. Me and the other woman who were the only ones left in the department. And I thought, "Oh, my God." I was terrified. I didn't know what to do. And I thought about my children. What would become of them? But then an agent came from behind and said, "Stop, I see you."

Janet

And then there was all this running with the agents racing after other people. And then ten more agents showed up in our area.

One of them shouted, "We're going to run you down like dogs!"

The same one told us to go downstairs; all of the different work stations were upstairs. My friend and I started to run again, she one way, and I the other way because we still hoped to hide ourselves. We never thought there could be so many immigration agents as there were. And there I was, running and running and trying to hide and along came more agents who were going upstairs when I was going down. One grabbed my sweater.

"Where are you going?"

I said, "Downstairs," but he replied, "No you aren't. Get in that line."

There was already a long line of all the people they had caught.

They took me down to the men's dining room, and everyone was there, some of them on their knees because they had struggled. It was the worst thing I saw, face after face, all so sad. I was trembling. I was thinking, "Oh no. They're going to take us away." And then they told us to start taking off our work clothes.

One guy told me, "Give me your weapons!"

I said, "I don't have any weapons."

He grabbed my sweater and started shaking me as hard as he could. At the same time other agents were telling us to leave because they were going to take us to another dining room. I didn't have time to take off my sweater. A woman agent told us to march with our hands behind our heads, and we went to a very large room that they were supposed to be making into a new dining room.

And then another agent asked me, "What weapons do you have."

And I said again, "I don't have anything."

I had my hands in my pockets and was wearing three sweaters because the area I worked in was refrigerated. I said I didn't have any weapons, I was just cold. He kept insisting I had weapons and then started pulling off my sweater. Under that I had a thick apron so that I wouldn't get cut on the stomach if I had an accident. First I had a sweatshirt, then the apron, then a sweater, and then another sweater, and the woman started pulling them off me. She wouldn't let me do it myself. She started to throw all my things on the floor. She was really mean when she was taking everything. After she had ripped off all my clothes and dumped everything on the floor, she told me to pick it all up.

Right after that another line of people came to join with ours. I saw my sister, Sofia, there. I saw her, and she didn't have a sweater on. She was shaking, so I gave her my sweater and helped her put it on.

She said she was cold, but I told her, "It's probably because you're so scared."

I never dreamed I would run into her under these circumstances. Then she asked me about Margarita, my daughter, who was working in the plant, too, and all of a sudden I wondered where she was. My God, I hadn't thought about her at all! And now, where was she? Margarita didn't seem to be anywhere. I wanted to tell *la migra* that she was there someplace. Maybe she was hurt. There were about seven women who nobody had seen, and we were worried that something might have happened to them.

Then the agents said they were going to process us. That's when one woman asked me if I had any children in school. And I said yes.

Janet

They asked me if I wasn't at home to take care of them who would be able to do that. I said that if I were gone my children wouldn't have anyone because I was the only adult who cared for them.

Then she said, "So if your children come home after school they normally don't find anyone at home but you? What time do you get off?"

"At 3:30. And my daughter gets out at 3:30. We arrive at the same time. The school bus brings her home."

The agent said that for humanitarian reasons they might let me stay here in Postville, but it wasn't a sure thing. Then they put a purple plastic bracelet on some of us and separated us from the other women. They put us on a bus, and we were there for many hours, until about 7:00 in the evening. Then they transferred us to another bus because the one we were on was going to leave.

On the second bus they searched everything we were carrying again. They didn't want us to have cell phones and they took most of them. They didn't want us to have anything. My daughter didn't show up anywhere. I couldn't see her anyplace. Then I was able to call another one of my daughters and told her we had been caught by *la migra*.

She was crying, and she said, "I know, *Mami*. Are you all right? What's going to happen to us?"

I said, "Take care of yourselves and take care of Patricia. I don't know where Margarita is. From the bus we can see all the people being taken out and pushed into the vans, and she never appeared."

My daughter answered, "don't worry, Margarita is fine." That was all she managed to say before an agent grabbed the phone.

So time passed until 8:00 p.m. when they took us off the bus. That's when they processed us again, in another bus. They took my fingerprints and told me to move along to do some more paper work. I was the last one there; all the other women had left. I really needed to use the bathroom on the bus, but I was afraid they wouldn't see me and would leave with me still on the bus. A man told me they were going to put an electronic monitoring cuff on my ankle, and then I would be able to go home. They put it on and gave me a paper to read and sign, where I promised to take care of the cuff, connect it [for charging], and not leave Iowa.

That was how I left the plant at nine o'clock at night. I started to look for my family because there was nobody at home. I went to my sister-in-law's house and when I went in, my daughter-in-law said, "Let's go."

I explained about the electronic shackle and that I couldn't go away and that for the time being I was safe. I thought she meant we were going to run away to another town or city, but it turned out she was about to give birth. The contractions had already started.

My daughters hugged me close and said, "Why did this have to happen?" I told them that Margarita hadn't been seen anyplace.

"*Mami*, Margarita is hiding inside Agri. She's hiding in a pit."

"My God," I thought. What pit? Where could she be? But there wasn't any more time. My daughter-in-law's water had broken, and I had to go to the hospital with her. Fifteen minutes after we got to the hospital the baby, a little boy, was born. I let my son know. They live in Des Moines, and my daughter-in-law had come to see how we were doing. She wanted to be with us because of the raid. So my son immediately drove to the hospital here.

When he arrived, he said, "Ma, don't worry. Margarita is fine. She sent me a message saying she's hiding with 12 other women."

Oh my God! I was so sad. I couldn't even celebrate the birth

Janet

of the new baby, my grandchild, because of the situation, because my daughter was lost someplace. So then at 2:00 in the morning I went back home.

The next day I got a phone call from my missing daughter, Margarita.

She said, "Ma, I'm fine. I'm still hiding but not in the plant. We're hiding on a farm."

I told her I would go get her right away. We went and picked her up. And then what I did was to send them all away. I sent all my children far from Postville.

I told them, "You go. I can stay because I'm not in any danger."

That day was when the terror began with all the talk that *la migra* was going to be going into the houses, that they were going to take more people away, right from their homes.

With everything that happened I went from having a house to losing it. I didn't know what was going to happen in my case, if they were going to send me to Mexico or what. Even right now, today, I still don't know if they will send me back or if I can stay. I didn't have work so I told my sister-in-law that I didn't know what to do about the house. She told me to give it back to her.

"You don't know what's going to happen to you," she said.

So I said, "Okay, and if you could give me back some of the money, it would be a help because I don't have anything, and if I have to go back to Mexico, I'm going to need it."

She told me what had happened wasn't her fault, and besides, "It was your brother who had spent all the money and not me, and I'm not going to give back anything."

Shattered Dreams

And so I gave her back the house and everything we had paid and put into it was lost forever.

All this time I've been waiting for an answer from Immigration. It's been almost three years. It's been awfully hard to live all this time because I don't think anyone likes to live on charity, to depend on other people, but we continue to live on the donations that come to the church and with the help of people who have found ways to support us. If it hadn't been for this, God only knows what would have happened to us.

There's nothing more to add other than a little bit about my childhood. Well, I was born on September 26, 1967 in San Luis Potosí, Mexico. I was a pretty unhappy child, always believing I was ugly. I felt that my mother never even looked at me, never paid any attention to me. My brothers would always say that they couldn't buy shoes for me because my feet were so big, and it would be better to make me some sandals out of the kitchen door. Maybe it was just a joke, but things like that hurt a lot, and it didn't seem that there was any love for me, and there was no one to teach me about the world.

I didn't feel comfortable with my mother. I would talk to myself in a room alone, pretending she was with me, but I would come out crying. She would ask me what was wrong, and I would just tell her I had a stomach ache. I always hoped to hear her or my father say, "*M'ija*, I love you." I heard those words only once, and that was the first and last time. That was five years ago when I was having a terrible time with my daughter who was going through a very difficult adolescence. But even with all that, I love my parents very much.

I was a very good child, at least I think so, because I was always helping my mother with everything. I liked school in spite of the fact that my father didn't pay much attention to his obligations. He didn't make sure that we weren't absent.

Janet

Can you imagine? I didn't even have a birth certificate, and I was the butt of a lot of jokes at school because of that. Once a teacher sent me home and told me that if I didn't bring my birth certificate I shouldn't come back to school.

And I went home and told my mother, and she said, "What do you want me to do about it? That's why I tell you not to go to school."

And I asked her to talk to my father. "What for? All he does is go around drunk all the time and fool around with other women."

That really hurt me. And I thought, "And now what am I going to do?" I felt like I was in a real pit. And I told my mother that if I didn't bring my birth certificate the teacher said no more school for me.

She told me, "Get out of here. That teacher is crazy."

And so I went and told the teacher I was just waiting for the birth certificate to come, and he said, "That's fine. Sit down." And that lasted the four years it took for me to finish primary school. I don't know exactly how, but by lying I made it through sixth grade and I got my diploma, but my childhood was very poor, and I had a lot of brothers and sisters, and my father was very uncaring. I was always having to beg for money to buy food, and my *mamá* was very, very stupid. She let my father humiliate her and do really awful things, and then she would take it out on us. But I was very sassy, and I took my beatings because I was so angry about the life we were living.

My father would sometimes take my sisters to the fields to work, but I would hide.

I said to myself, "That crazy man doesn't even buy shoes for me and spends all his money on loose women." They didn't make me work. Plus, we were really young to be doing that kind of work.

Shattered Dreams

Once we had nothing to eat, and I mean nothing. I have a very rich uncle and he had no children, and I wondered why we were so poor while he had more than enough. But then I thought to myself, why should he take on responsibilities that weren't his? But finally I looked at my mother who had just given birth to her ninth child and didn't even have gas to light the cooking stove, and I decided to go to my uncle's house. When I got there he wasn't home, and his wife wasn't home either, but the key to the closet was just hanging there.

So I opened the closet and thought, "Let's see what's in here."

I thought I would find a lot of money, and there actually was some there, so I took a little of it.

I said to myself, "It isn't right that he has so much and we have so little."

When I was leaving, I ran into my uncle and he asked me where I was going. I said *mamá* had sent me to buy a tank of gas, and he asked me if I had money. I told him I did, and he sold me a full tank. I had some money left so I bought a whole chicken and some bread for my little sisters and brothers.

I said, "God forgive me for what I'm doing, but I can't ignore our situation." And then I thought, "What am I going to tell *mamá*." I ended up saying to her, "Look what my uncle has sent for you, and he told me to tell you that when Ray, my brother in the United States, sends money, you can pay him back."

That was what I could come up with, and she said, "See how good your uncle is?" I thought, "If she only knew." My hands were burning. And I told her that nobody should go to him for more money except me because I was afraid someone would find out what I had done. And because she didn't know and didn't talk with anybody, she believed me.

Janet

Three days later my mother sent me to pay my uncle back because some money from my brother had arrived.

What was my surprise when my uncle's wife said, "Weren't you here the other day?"

I told her, "No, why?" She said "I lost some money, and that never happens."

I was amazed that with so much money she would miss such a small amount.

I was sweating, and she told me, "don't ever come into the house if I'm not here."

And from that moment on they liked me less, and when I would show up they would close the doors and take out the keys, and I wondered why they liked my other sisters more.

When my mother decided to take us to Monterrey to be with my grandfather, my aunts there also treated us differently from our cousins. The other children were given a lunch with flour tortillas and potatoes and juice, and they would sit down first and eat. When I would try to sit down because I was hungry, the aunts would tell me, "First them, and then you." And my mother would take us out on the patio while our cousins finished eating. Then, we were hoping that we would get the same thing, but they gave us watered-down beans and coffee and corn tortillas instead.

My cousins would say, "Eat it all. Fill yourselves up like hogs." And my aunt wouldn't say anything to them. It was so sad, and you live with those memories and that resentment.

I'll never forget when we went to Monterrey and I could work. I was fourteen years old, and the first thing that occurred to my aunts was that it would be good for us to look for work as servants in a house. Because of our poverty and to avoid always being in my

Shattered Dreams

aunts' house with them, I truthfully did prefer to go to work. They found a job for me as a live-in maid for a woman teacher. It would be just me working in the house.

I went to the house, and three days went by. And then one day everyone who lived in the house went out. I closed the door, and about an hour later the husband showed up. He was an old man. He told me to iron a shirt for him. I did the ironing in the same room I slept in. It was the laundry room, and there was a bed in it. But what the man wanted was to touch me. I got very scared and started screaming, but he said no one could hear me. I don't know how, but I got loose and shut myself up in the bathroom, and he couldn't get me out.

He shouted, "If you say anything to my wife, you're really going to be sorry."

I was crying. When he finally left, I ran to the phone and called my aunt, and I asked her to please come and get me. But she said no, that she didn't want me to make a bad impression with her friends. I asked her "Please, I can't say here," and she hung up on me. I grabbed all my things, and I ran away. I didn't know how to use the buses, and it was 8:00 at night, and I got lost.

I called my aunt again, and I told her I was confused, and she said, "My friend was already here at the house to say you left."

I told her, "If you only knew what happened," but she said, "I don't care. You are a *huevona*."

She didn't want to listen to me. So I was walking along and I went into a park, and three boys came after me. They surrounded me and told me they were going to play with me. Crying, I told them to please leave me alone, and they said no, they wouldn't. They grabbed me and grabbed my legs, and I was struggling.

Then a man showed up and told them, "Leave her alone, you jerks. Don't you see she's not from here? She's scared."

Janet

And the boys took off running. The man told me it was dangerous to be in the park and asked where I was going. I told him I was lost. So he asked where I wanted to go, and I told him to my aunt's house, and he asked me, "But where is that?" I didn't know the address, just the phone number. He took me to a phone booth and dialed my aunt's number. I told her again I was lost.

She said, "How am I supposed to guess where you might be?" And I was crying, so the man took the phone from me.

He said, "*Señora*, your girl is very frightened and I don't know how to help her get back to you, but if you give me your address I can take her there."

She said no, but asked him to put me on a bus by myself and she would be waiting at the bus stop for me. That's what he did, and, thank God, I got safely back to my family. It was midnight. I was really scared when I saw my aunt, but she said, "Go to bed. We'll talk tomorrow." I cried all night. I wanted my *mamá*, but then I wondered why because it would have been even worse. She would have beaten me.

The next day my aunt came, and she said, "Well, you'll have to go to work like your sister because you can't be lazing around here."

And I told her I wanted to go back to be with my mother, so she said, "With what money? You don't have any," and I just hung my head. I said I wanted to tell her why I left the teacher's house. She said, "It's because you don't know how to work and you don't know how to keep a job," and she left. She didn't want to listen to me.

I haven't told any of this to anyone until right now, and it still hurts so much, just to remember what happened makes me shudder. I can still see that man grabbing me and I feel disgusted. He didn't end up doing anything. He was just grabbing me.

Shattered Dreams

He didn't get what he wanted. There are a lot of things in life that you keep silent about, sometimes out of shame and sometimes for the simple fact that no one will listen. You feel like an outcast, and that hurts, but with God's help I have been able to move ahead with my life. I have a husband, four children, two grandchildren and a daughter-in-law, and I want to live for them, for the love I want to give them so that they never feel what I felt.

If there is anything I'm sure of it's that God is great and He is with me when I need Him. I love my parents a lot. I love them for what they gave me, whatever it might have been. Right now when I'm talking, I'm really hurting because my father is very sick, and it hurts even more to see the struggle my mother has with him. But that's life, and it doesn't change what happened, and I ask God for forgiveness for everything, and every day I give thanks for my life.

Amalia

I was born in a Finca Concepción in 1971, or at least I think that's where I was born. Shortly after, they took me to San José Calderas, which is where I grew up. I remember that when I was small there were a lot of poor people in Calderas. There were a lot of houses just made of straw because people didn't even have enough money to buy boards. The houses had dirt floors.

Everyone was indigenous, like my mother and my grandmother who are both indigenous Mayans. Nevertheless, I didn't grow up wearing traditional Mayan clothing but wearing dresses and skirts just like my daughters do here because that's what my uncle wanted.

When I was about seven years old my father left me at my grandmother's house so I could take care of her, and I lived there a long time. I don't remember how many years it was, but I grew up with my grandmother as if she was my mother. She loved me more than my mother or father did. She was the one who taught me how to do the basic things like bathe, wash my clothes, and cook. When she was about to die she told me she was going to die and that I should go back to my parents, but it was so hard for me because I was very attached to her. She was like a mother to me.

When she died it was so sad for me because they took me to my mother's house. I was very unhappy there because I missed my grandmother, and my father had a very strong personality and was really aggressive. But I did have an uncle who loved me a lot. I remember that the soldiers took him away.

My uncle wasn't with the guerrillas, but people said the guerrillas would visit him because he gave them food. Sometimes he went to my grandmother's house and asked her to prepare a basket full of tortillas. My grandmother would do it and then he would take it away. She would say, "Why do you want so many tortillas?" And he would say that he just wanted them, that's all. I think he was feeding the guerrillas, otherwise why would he have wanted so many tortillas? And that's why I think the army took him away. He never came back. Even today we have no idea if they killed him. We don't know what happened to him.

My uncle was better than my *papá* because he would buy me clothes and sandals. On Sundays he would give me 10 or 15 *centavos*. Sometimes he would give us 25 *centavos* and tell us to buy something for ourselves. He would give the money to me and to my brother. I only have one brother. I remember that for one birthday he bought me a doll. I still have that doll he gave me. It's packed away safely. And for my brother he made a little car like a square box. He was a carpenter. My brother was so happy playing with that car because my father could never give us any toys.

The army took my uncle right out of his house. We were outside playing when we saw the soldiers go there. We ran to Grandmother's house to tell her, and she ran out to see what was happening. She tried to talk to one of the men in charge of the army, but they refused to talk with her. They gave us no explanation of why they were taking him away. My grandmother wanted to talk to him, but they wouldn't let any of us get near. My uncle just looked at us and then they took him away.

That time they took my uncle and another man. He was from another town called Chimachoy. That man never came back either, and that's all we know.

People would say that it was bad to get mixed up with the guerrillas, but the guerillas really didn't do anything. One day my father was gathering firewood in the countryside and when he came back home he said a man wearing just ordinary clothes came up to him. He didn't look like a guerrilla.

Amalia

The man said to my father, "How are you, *compañero*."

"Working."

"Look, I'm hungry. Would you happen to have a tortilla to give me?"

"Sure. Pretty soon my wife or my daughter will be bringing me lunch."

When I got there the three of us had lunch together. And after that he just kept coming. My father didn't know how to get rid of him. He would come at night to get something to eat and then he would leave. My father didn't like him coming all the time because he was afraid people would find out and do something to us. One day the man said they were leaving. I don't know how the guerrillas found out that the army was coming, but that's what he said, that the army was on its way so they had to go someplace else.

They would go from place to place. That's how they kept going, by moving all the time and hiding. I never saw that man again. He thanked us for the food we had given him and told us to take care of ourselves.

My father said to us kids, "Whatever you have seen you have seen, but don't tell anyone anything. If someone asks me for a tortilla, I can't say no. I can't deny anyone a tortilla."

I don't understand why the army couldn't get along with the guerrillas. I still don't understand it. The guerrillas weren't doing anything bad.

I also remember that they said a lot of people in the town of Aguacate were with the guerrillas. Who knows how the army found out, but they came and surrounded the village. Airplanes came, and they were dropping bombs all over the place, and though Aguacate is pretty far from Calderas we could hear the bombs going off. Then my aunt, who had a lot of relatives there, said that a lot of people died.

One woman had eight sons, and they killed seven of them, and she just had one son left. I remember that because I went to the burial which was in San Andrés Iztapa. It was so very sad because the woman was crying. There were seven caskets in a row. She told us that her sons would take the animals out to pasture in the hills. Then they would go check on them from time to time, to move them to another pasture and to give them water, and then they would bring them back to town for awhile. She said that one day one of her sons went out and didn't come back, and then another one went and didn't come back either. People said it was because there were being killed outside of town. The army was killing them. So the other sons went out to look for their brothers who hadn't returned, and they didn't come back either. Once the army had left the town, then they found their bodies scattered around. *Ay*, how that woman cried! I remember that even though I was very little at the time. Something like that stays with you forever.

After that the army went up to the town of Chimachoy, and they were there for several months until the guerrillas went completely away. People said that there were women in the town who were weaving with their babies snuggled on their backs, and the soldiers killed them and just left them there with their dead babies. *Ay*, there was so much ugly violence. So since a lot of the people in Chimachoy had family in Calderas, they moved to Calderas. One of my uncle's sons-in-law was taken out of his house by the army, and he never returned.

I remember that for us life was very hard because we were very poor. First my father bought a cow, and then she had calves that he sold. With that extra money he was able to buy a little plot of land. He was renting land at first but then he decided to buy the land in installments. He told us to work very hard. He saved money, but it was only because he made us go hungry.

Amalia

He would say, "Well, today we're not going to have anything to eat, just a few tortillas with salt."

There were times when we didn't even have coffee. My mother would heat water and she gave us hot water to drink instead of coffee and just a few tortillas with salt. When there was an egg, half of it was for my brother and half for me. We worked very hard alongside of my father to earn the money to pay the plot of land that he now owns.

He made me work very hard in the fields. I worked with a hoe and with a machete. Sometimes I was too tired to continue, and he would say, "Hurry up." He would put my brother ahead of me because he was a boy. Sometimes my brother was exhausted and couldn't do anymore, but my father would whack him on the shin with the hoe handle. My brother did the best he could because he was afraid of getting hit. Sometimes *papá* would hit him on the head, and he would have a goose egg. When I helped my father, my mother was unhappy because I wasn't helping her in the kitchen. When I came home late from working the land I still had to do housework. I had to make tortillas, and since we didn't have electricity it was harder because I had to do it in the dark.

When I was little I could only watch my father's abuse of my mother. But, inside I was angry because I wondered why he beat her. He never appreciated me or my mother and he said that we never did anything. It was like that because many men in Guatemala don't value what women do because we do it inside the house. Women's work is harder to see because we clean and cook, but soon everything gets messed up again. My father never appreciated what women did.

My father beat my mother a lot in front of us children. He would kick her and throw her on the ground. I just watched. Unfortunately, in the past we had no idea that women have rights and that we have a right to defend ourselves. My mother just put up with everything my father did to her.

Shattered Dreams

And so that's how I grew up. I worked in the fields with my father and when I began to feel that I could work on my own I went somewhere else where they said a person could earn six *quetzales* a day. I began to go there to work but my father would take away the money I received.

I began to work in the fields cleaning carrots, picking green beans and *frijoles*. I also learned to harvest and thresh the corn when it was ready. Here in the U.S. a machine does that, but in Guatemala we do it by hand. There they hire men and women to strip the husks and put the corn in big piles. We call that *tapiscar*.

There they harvest and clean carrots by hand, too. I worked with a friend, and together we would do two strings of carrots, one for her and one for me. But when they paid us my father would always take my money.

He would say, "You want to keep the money? Well, then you'll have to buy your own food because I'm not going to feed you."

He always, always, took my money and said I was getting spoiled and abusive. Sometimes I needed shoes or clothing and I didn't have any money, but since I was so little I was afraid and always gave him what I earned. I worked with other people in the fields, and when I got to know some of them they started to tell me that if I wanted to leave home and start working in the capital city they would take me. So, little by little, I began to leave my home.

I was learning to fend for myself. A girlfriend looked for a job for me in Guatemala City, and I started to work there because they paid 50 *quetzales* a month. Over time I got smarter and began to think that I knew enough to take care of myself

Once my friend took me to work in the city, and my father had no news of me for awhile. The lady I worked for would not let me out of her house even to do the shopping. She forced me to stay there. She fed me very little and treated me very badly. I was very young, about thirteen or fourteen years old. I was scared and had no courage. I just didn't know anything. So a month passed, and then two, and then three. She wouldn't let me out of the house for any reason. I took care of two children, washed and ironed clothing, swept and mopped the floors. But the woman kept me locked in. Sometimes I wanted to go out with my friend, but she wouldn't let me.

You know, I also didn't know how to read or anything because I never had the opportunity to go to school. I went for a year when I was with my grandmother because she told me to. Some days I would go and others I wouldn't. When I did go, I still had to give my grandmother her medicine, so during recess instead of playing I would run to her house and give her the medicine and water if she was thirsty. Because she couldn't see, I had to take water and food to her in bed. I was about eight when I went to school. I was there for just one year. I couldn't finish the second year because my grandmother got sicker and then she died and they took me back to my father's house. He said that it wasn't important for me to study because I was a girl and someday I would go off with a husband and studying wasn't going to be of any use to me.

So there I was working at that lady's house, doing the cleaning, washing and ironing. She taught me how to do a good job with the washing and ironing, and she taught me how to cook. She would tell me what food she wanted, and I would prepare it.

And I took care of a baby that was about a year old.

My family had no idea where I was. Then my father got very worried and talked with the girl who had taken me to the city. He wanted her to tell him where I was, but she didn't know exactly. At the same time I was very unhappy and wanted to get out of that house because of the abuse and because the woman fought with her husband a lot. To me, he was just like my father, and the same things were happening in that home. I told the wife I wanted to leave, but she wouldn't let me.

It was very hard for me because in addition to being mistreated by my own father, here I was being mistreated by the *Señora*. She would ration the food that I ate, and I often was hungry for more. I've been through a lot. I worked for her all day. I would get up at 4:30 or 5:00 a.m. and couldn't go to sleep until 10:00 p.m. because she and her husband would go out and leave me caring for the children and I couldn't go to bed until they got home.

Another woman, a neighbor, said that I shouldn't put up with her and that no other girls had stayed with her for so long. She asked me why I didn't leave, and she urged me to go. I couldn't get up the courage to leave because I was scared and I didn't know how to take the bus to my village. Finally I insisted that the family let me go and take me to the bus station. I begged and I begged, and finally they took me to the bus and that's how I got home.

When I got back my father behaved the same way he always had, always the same. He still made me work a lot in the fields. Sometimes when we took the mare he told me to be sure the load was equally distributed on both sides and the mare was standing straight up because if the load was unbalanced and fell off it would be my fault. So I was careful to watch how the mare was loaded and to hold her with both hands. He made me carry big loads of produce to the horses, and some were very nice and tame, but others weren't and they frightened me. He teased me because I was afraid, and that's how I learned to put the harness on.

There was a day in which I was trying to defend my mother from my father and he started to beat me, and then she came to my defense. He wanted to hit both of us. And that's when my father threw me out of the house. So I went to my uncle's house to talk to him.

Amalia

My uncle said I should come and live in his house. I had a cousin who was a little younger than I was and my uncle treated us both exactly the same. He didn't play favorites. Whatever he bought for her, he bought for me, too, so I was very happy there. That's when I said to myself that I was going to get a job, and that's how I started to go out, and I met a lot of people who helped me out, and I was able to help my uncle with the food. I was fifteen years old then.

A year later my father threw my mother out of the house, and so I had to start taking care of her. I was working in the capital then and the woman I worked for was very good and kind. She helped me, and in addition to my salary she gave me food to take to my mother who I would go visit every two weeks. She was living near my uncle's house in San José Calderas.

But, a year after he threw my mother out, my father came back and asked my mother to forgive him for what he had done. He said he needed us and asked us to please come back home. My mother didn't want to go back. I thought that in the end he was my father, and I felt a certain affection towards him just for that reason. And we started to live with him again.

Once I started to work on my own I began to accomplish things. I refused to continue giving my money to my father. I bought my own things, and my brother would ruin them. I bought a black and white television, and he broke the cables and my father never said a thing to him. In my opinion, my brother was always the favorite, not simply because I was a girl but because my father always underestimated me.

For a while I worked for a gringo who was from here in the U.S., from San Antonio, Texas. He was with a Guatemalan woman, and she hired me to go to work in their house. I worked for her for several years, and she was very good to me, too, and helped me a lot. She advised me to look out for myself and not let myself suffer just because my father was my father. She said that it wasn't fair for him to abuse me so much.

Shattered Dreams

She asked me, "Do you want to go to the United States? I'm going to help you. We're going to travel, and I want you to come with me."

She got me my passport so that I could come here. I mentioned it to my father, and he didn't say anything. But, once he saw that the *Señora* was getting all my documents ready, he told me he wouldn't give me permission to go. I was twenty years old at the time.

So I stayed in Guatemala. I met a friend who invited me to go see where she worked, and I ended up working there for three and a half years. I worked on a farm called Finca Paulequi. When I started to be away from home more and met a lot of different people from all around I started to wake up. I felt so humiliated. I felt that I couldn't do anything by myself. I had no sisters or brothers to discuss things with. On the farm, I began to work alongside of others, and so I started to have conversations with people who gave me ideas. They said that I was a good worker, that I could improve myself, and even though I didn't know how to read or write, I could get ahead in life. They encouraged me and said that if I did what they told me I would be successful.

And so it was about a year and a half after I started to work at that company when they called me to the office and said they were giving me the position of assistant supervisor. I didn't want the job because I couldn't read or write, and there were a lot of papers to be filled out, and I felt like I couldn't do it. Nevertheless, I knew all the jobs we had to do by heart—all the different kinds of flowers—but I couldn't write. But the boss said there were no buts about it—I was perfectly capable of doing the work of assistant supervisor. So I started going to classes for an hour. Work was over at 4:00 and we started class at 5:00. And that's how they made me study to learn how to read and write and do arithmetic. Sometimes I'd be very tired after work but would go to class anyway.

Amalia

It was at that job that I met my husband. He was working in the warehouse. He loaded the boxes full of plants from the greenhouses. And he came to work very early and left very late. I worked in the greenhouses where the plants were. I would cut the flowers and package them and put them in the cooler. I had to be sure they were the same length and all the flowers were at the same stage of development. I had to be sure the stems were the same thickness because if there was one thin and one thick, one short and one longer, then you lost points for that.

My husband and I first got to know each other when we would go to the bank to cash our checks. Since we traveled everyday on the same bus we got to know each other better. We were *novios* for about two years and eleven months. He wasn't from my village but did have a sister who was living in Calderas. He's from the coast. He doesn't have a mother; he was an orphan. Two hours after he was born his mother died. His father abandoned him and he was raised with his aunt and uncle. Then he went to Calderas to live with his sister, and that's how we met at the bank and on the bus.

My father didn't like him very much and my mother didn't either— because he was an Evangelical Christian and I was a Catholic. I didn't care what his religion was. So my father did give him permission to visit our house. My *novio* spoke with my father because I had told him I wasn't willing to live in his sister's house. I told him that if he really loved me he should move in with me. At the beginning my father said he would give me a place to live. I was earning my pay twice a month and I was helping my father pay for the lights, and I bought the tanks of gas for the little heater. I helped pay for the food, too. But my father never gave us any money. He'll never change.

And since we were going to be together my husband said we should get married. I told him no, because I made him see what my father was like and the kind of life my mother had with him. Because of that I was afraid to get married until after we had lived together for awhile. I was thinking, if I have a child I can get along, but if I have a bad husband there will be no escaping that.

So I waited to see what he was like before we got married. My father disagreed with what we were doing so when we did get married, he, my mother and my brother didn't come to the wedding. We didn't marry in the two churches. We had a civil ceremony. And we went by ourselves. We paid our own expenses and took care of everything. We could only count on his sister, my brother-in-law, and one of my husband's nieces.

We had to live in my father's house, and, though he often promised to help us build an extra room or lean-to, he never did. When I was about three months pregnant with Miriam, my husband wasn't home because he had gone to church, and my father had already been angry at my brother, and so he wanted to beat me. I was doing some sewing on the sewing machine, and I told him to go ahead and beat me if he wanted to, but he stopped, and at the same time he just told me to leave.

When my husband got back, I was crying and he asked me what had happened and I told him. Then he spoke with his sister, who said, "Now that your nephews are in the United States they can help you, so it would be better if you went there, too. With the way you're living here you're not going to achieve anything. Your situation here is just no good."

That's how he decided to come here to the States. He left me at my sister-in-law's house, and I paid rent there. He came in 2003 directly to Postville. My daughter was scarcely three months old when he left. His nephews lent him the money, and he paid the *coyote* 30,000 *quetzales* to bring him.

Amalia

I stayed with my sister-in-law in a little house that was in the patio. But my life was still pretty much the same because I was sad that I couldn't defend my mother anymore. When my father would try to beat her I would defend her, but when I was gone things got worse because there was no one to watch over her. I was always buying her sandals and food because he never bought her anything. All he wanted was for her to make the tortillas, fix his meals, and wash his clothes, but he never saw to it that she had clothes. But she still went on living with my father, and the problems continued.

One day someone told me to go see my mother because my father and my brother had thrown her out of the house. My father wouldn't let me into the house when I arrived. Someone told me I should go to court because what he was doing wasn't right. So I made a legal claim and had to go before a judge. My father had to sign a paper saying that he had to let my mother in the house. But I said to the judge that he never gave food and he beat her so why should she go back.

The judge said to my father, "If you don't want her but your daughter does, then build your wife a little house and support her."

But things were always the same. I was still living in my sister-in-law's patio, and she had a daughter-in-law who treated me badly. We were always having problems with the kids, with the water, and I was getting so desperate. So my husband told me to come here to Postville with my daughter.

I asked my mother if she would leave my father once and for all, but she refused.

"If you want to go, go ahead. I'm already old. You have to go and make your own life and leave me here. I don't know what will happen but just leave me here."

Shattered Dreams

That's how I decided to come with my daughter.

I came in 2005. I made some of the trip on foot and some by bus. The only thing I knew about the trip was that we had to cross the *Río Bravo* [Rio Grande], and I wondered what it would be like. When I came I was very afraid, but I had to cross the river because of the hardships we were facing. Miriam was like Ingrid, my second daughter, is now—about two years and three months old. Many people say that they crossed over in canoes, but they had me cross on foot. I came out of the water soaking wet and shaking from the cold.

The *coyote* who was taking us made up a kind of a family group for us. He told me another young man was going to pretend to be my husband. I don't remember that man's name. They taught my daughter to call him *papá*, and they had him carry her around for awhile so that she would get used to him and not cry. They make people practice before crossing and tell you what to say and do if they catch you. The *coyote* who got us across was from Mexico; they called him *el gringo*.

On the trip over the only people were me and my daughter, the *coyote*, and the man who was coming as my husband. He carried my daughter across. The *coyote* told us where to get out of the river on the other side, but as soon as we got out of the water and started to walk the police showed up and arrested us.

"What are you doing here at this hour of the night? Aren't you ashamed of risking your daughter's life? The river water is freezing cold."

"Yes, but we're here now."

Then the officer put us in the car and drove us to Immigration. They kept me there and they gave us some sandwiches to eat. Miriam was coughing a lot because she had bronchitis and I had her medicine.

Amalia

"Is your little girl okay?"

"Yes."

"If she isn't, I'll take her to the hospital."

"No, I have the medicine here that the doctor gave her." Then we ate something, and they locked us up.

"Don't worry," the officer said. "We're going to get a permission that will let you stay here."

That's how I got in. It was a special permission they gave Guatemalans, some papers that said you could stay in the country. But the people in Immigration never told me I had to return in two months. At any rate, I wasn't planning on returning. I was coming to Postville to be with my husband and to work with him, and that's why I didn't go back.

After they gave me the permission, I went to Dallas because I knew a family there who I had worked with for a long time in Guatemala cleaning carrots. They had a son who lived in my village, and he told me I could stay with his mother in Dallas. I got there and spent a few days while my husband arranged for us to come here to Postville.

In the beginning I felt very sad because I had left my *mamá* in Guatemala. But as time passed I got used to it. I began to work and was able to send her money for her expenses. It was especially hard because years before she had stepped on a nail and was in the hospital for 17 days and she almost died from tetanus fever, but then she finally got well. But since then she hasn't been able to hear anything and she's been deaf for a long time. Because of that since I've been here in the States I've have never had the joy of talking with her on the phone. It's just not possible.

Shattered Dreams

When I got to Postville I was very happy because my daughter could get to know her father. She had been so tiny when he came here. Both of us worked very hard to pay our debts. It was a lot of money because I had to send something to support my mother and we had to pay what we had borrowed to pay the *coyote*. My brother-in-law borrowed more money using a deed for the land he was living on as collateral. He helped me. Sometimes I think that what my father was unwilling to do, my brother-in-law did for me. He told me he trusted me and was confident that I would work and pay him back. I promised him I would.

When my husband first came to Postville he had very bad luck because he worked a very short time in one of the departments before they fired him. He went to Waterloo and the little he managed to earn he sent back to me. My daughter was sick a lot in Guatemala, and what he sent was only enough to pay the doctor. Because of that, when I got here we owed about ninety thousand *quetzales* in Guatemala. It was a lot of money. Since he hadn't been able to pay his debt, now that was added to mine and we had two debts to pay.

When I arrived my husband told me to wait until after the snow to start working, but I said no, because if I waited, then how were we going to pay what we owed? I told him I wanted to work. I worked from 9:30 in the morning until about 1:30 or 2:00 a.m. I did that for about a year. Four times I left work at 4:00 a.m.

I worked in the poultry section, and my job was to cut the wings with scissors. I would come home with my hands swollen from using the scissors so much. And since I wanted us to pay off our debts, I needed to work a lot to send money to my mother, pay the housing expenses here in Postville, and take care of that debt.

My expenses here included, for example, $90 a week for childcare for my daughter. I didn't even see my daughter during the week, just during the weekends, because when I left she would

Amalia

still be sleeping and when I came back she would be asleep again. My babysitter was a woman who came from the same town in Guatemala. My husband, of course, was also working, and we would pick her up after work at about 1:00 or 2:00 a.m. After awhile my husband worked at night and I worked during the day. When he came home at about 7:00 a.m. I would fix lunch, and then I would leave, and then when I got back he would already have gone to work. I would walk home from the plant very late at night, I worked many hours, and I always had to carry my daughter to and from the babysitter.

When I started at Agri I didn't know anything. There in the plant they give you no training on how to do things. The person who starts working there has to figure it out for herself, and if she's lucky she will have some friends who will help her out or otherwise she'll have to just watch the others to see what they do. I watched the others, and I taught myself. First I worked cleaning the chicken breasts and cutting the fat off with scissors. It was pretty hard for me because I had never done it before, and I even cut my gloves repeatedly because I hadn't ever worked with that kind of scissors. After awhile, with practice, it got better.

My second job was to put the chicken breasts on the plastic trays, but really fast because the meat would come along on the belt really fast, and if I didn't hurry the chicken would pile up and the supervisor would run up and yell at me to work faster. He said if any of the meat fell on the floor I would have to pay for it myself and that I had to rush. And I would try but it was awfully hard to package so many chicken breasts in so little time.

They told us we had to package 16 breasts per minute and so while I picked up one breast with one hand I was putting another one down with the other hand. I certainly didn't have time to count how many I did a minute, but after awhile the supervisor saw that I was doing it okay so he didn't scold me anymore. My hands and arms were always tired, and my hands would swell.

Shattered Dreams

Sundays and Thursdays were the hardest because there was a kind of chicken they called "organic." They would bring it in the middle of the day so that before lunch we had to have the tables totally cleaned up for the new batch. We couldn't have a break until we finished with the organic batch. We worked on specific orders at the plant. You would get there in the morning and see how many orders had to be filled that day. Sometimes there were a lot of orders and we had to finish them all. Sometimes the supervisor would say to us that we had to hurry up because we weren't going to get a break until every last piece of chicken on the line was finished. Many times there wasn't enough time to eat or go to the bathroom, and we just had to take it because we had no choice.

When I started, they paid me $6.25 an hour, and I earned that for about a year. Then they gave me a fifty cents an hour raise, and I was getting $6.75, and the next year they paid me $7.25 or $7.35. Sometimes the check wouldn't have the full amount I was owed. I would do my calculations, and the amount on the check was less. That's why I think they were paying us less than we earned.

When I started at Agri the supervisor's name was Gerardo. He was Guatemalan and treated people very badly. Many people were afraid of him because he was always shouting and telling us either to work faster or go home because, he said, there were a lot of people who would like our jobs. He was always swearing at us. After a year, Antonio started, and he was different. He was Mexican, and he wasn't as bad-tempered as Gerardo. Antonio always asked us to do things in a polite way, but the one who really treated us poorly during the hours I was working overtime was Filomena.

She swore and humiliated us constantly. "Hurry up, you fucking Guatemalans. You're just a bunch of *huevonas*."

I don't know if I should tell about this, but sometimes she would touch the women and then say it was just a joke. I didn't believe it because I worked in several plants in Guatemala and they never played that kind of joke. She said it was a joke when we would lean down to get some chicken and she would come from behind and stick in her hand and touch you. We would tell her to stop doing that, that it wasn't right, but she would say she was just kidding and that she did it so we wouldn't fall asleep. We told her to stop because the men were watching and we felt ashamed and angry.

She said, "You think the men are going to watch? They're not looking at anything."

We felt very bad because we knew that she shouldn't be doing that, and she just kept on and on. Sometimes she would bring little toy animals like snakes or frogs, and she would suddenly put them on someone's hand, and then she would swear at the women because they were startled. The women felt very bad and angry because no one had ever done those things anyplace else we had worked. She started with the little animals and then she started the touching. It was very bad. Either the other supervisors didn't know what was going on, or they didn't care because all they wanted was for everyone to work faster and faster.

Filomena threatened us and said that if we went to the office to complain they wouldn't believe us because she was the one in charge. If we didn't like her games then we should find another job or change to another shift. But she knew there were no shift changes and that we had no choice but to be there, and she took advantage.

Another thing that happened in the plant was that they wouldn't pay attention to us when we were sick or if someone had an accident. When I was pregnant with Ingrid, in my last month, I almost fainted once. One Friday we were working and they sent me to seal bags of chicken which was a new product that we were trying out to see if it worked. There was a lot of dry ice, and I started to feel like I couldn't breathe. I told Antonio that I wasn't feeling well and that my mouth was very dry and I couldn't stand it.

Shattered Dreams

He just told me, "We're about done."

When we went out for lunch break—those days we had lunch early, at about 10:00 in the morning—I felt that my heart and my breathing were about to give out. I felt like I was going to faint and my cousin, who was working in the same area, helped me sit down. The supervisor told her to take me down to the office once he realized I was losing consciousness. The same thing was happening to another woman who was pregnant, too. The dry ice was affecting us a lot because we were having very fast heart palpitations, and we told the supervisor but he didn't pay any attention. Even with a face mask on we felt the same, like we couldn't breathe.

In the plant they abused us, they yelled and swore at us, they threatened us, and they took advantage of us because we had no papers. They knew we had to work, that we had no choice but to work there no matter what.

When we were working all those hours I didn't care because my family was happy to be together. Then my other daughter, Ingrid, was born. We came to this apartment, and we lived by ourselves because before that we were sharing an apartment with another family. We had no problems with anyone and got along fine even among ourselves until the raid when everything changed. Everything was different because the family was broken apart. My husband is now in Guatemala. They deported him, and here I am with my two daughters (covering her face and sobbing), and my husband is just waiting to see what is going to happen to me. I don't know what will happen.

I would like it if they allowed me to stay here, to work and give my daughters a better life because I didn't have the opportunity to study, and with my father I didn't even know what toys were. I was seven years old and walked around barefoot because my father wouldn't even buy me sandals. I want what's best for my daughters, I don't want them to live in poverty. My husband says that we must

Amalia

wait and that maybe there is a chance, but at the same time there he is alone in Guatemala. He feels lonely with him there and me here. It's hard, but what can we do?

Right now he's trying to find work there, but all the people they deported are also looking and there are no jobs. Sometimes some of the men go to the countryside to gather bundles of firewood. They are paid just 25 *quetzales* a day. You can't buy anything with that amount of money so he's living on the coast with my sister-in-law.

I would like my daughters to be something some day, to have a good job not like the ones I have had because I can't read or write. I can scarcely sign my own name. I want my daughters to graduate, as they say, and to have better jobs than we have. I'd like to leave them an inheritance, not a lot of money but a career like secretary or teacher.

I want to have my family back together again. I want my husband to be living with us because Miriam is always asking for her father. Sometimes it's hard for me to explain to her why he isn't with us and what happened, but she doesn't understand.

"My *papá* didn't smoke and didn't drink. Why did they take him away?"

"That's not why they took him away. It wasn't for smoking or drinking. It's simply because we don't have the papers to be in this country."

"I want him here with me! I want to go out and do things, and nobody takes us out anymore. When he was here he would take me to McDonald's and he'd take me to eat at the Chinese restaurant, and now, nothing!"

He would also brush her hair and fix it up and she'd look so pretty. She has missed all of that so much, and we all need him

Shattered Dreams

here. I feel so desperate and anxious, and I can't have a car, I can't drive. I feel trapped. (Short pause in the interview as Amalia tries to control her crying).

On May 12th, the day of the raid, I started work at 9:30 and about ten or fifteen minutes later I saw people running all over but I didn't think it was anything. I mean I didn't think it could be Immigration because people had run out twice before because of short circuits that had caused small fires.

I thought it was the same thing, but then a woman who was next to me said, "Amalia! Amalia, let's go!"

I just stood there in the same spot, and I asked a Russian woman, Monica, what was happening. She said she didn't know why people were running, but when I left my work area the supervisor, Antonio, said to me, "*Ay*, Amalia, it would have been better if you hadn't come to work.

"Why?"

"Because *la migra* is right here right now."

He just scratched his head, and then I saw my husband and I said "And now what can we do?"

Another *compañera* said, "Immigration has arrived." She was very afraid, too.

What I thought of first in those moments was my daughters because Ingrid was with the babysitter and Miriam was at school. We kept running from one place to another, and we didn't have anywhere to go because they had us completely surrounded.

Finally my husband said, "Let's stop running because one way or another they have us."

All of a sudden, one of the men from Immigration who spoke

Amalia

Spanish very well yelled at us to sit down and get rid of all the clothing and tools that we worked with. We threw down everything, and I just kept thinking about my girls. I started to cry because I couldn't imagine what would happen to them because all of my nieces and nephews and everyone else in the family were also detained because they all worked at the plant. Then they took us to the butchering section, and they separated us; they took all the men someplace else and the women stayed. I wanted to go over to my husband to get the key to our apartment because both of us worked in the area called "cut up."

An agent shouted at me, "don't go near him!"

So I went over to where the women were, all so frightened. One of the women I worked with said she felt pain in her heart, and then she fainted. I think it was because of the fear and because they had us trapped. Then one of the female agents came over and told us to move away from her. She began to fan the woman who had fainted, and she came to. They had us there for a little bit of time and then they took us down to the basement.

I headed over to join the women I worked with, especially the ones I got along with the best, but the Immigration people wouldn't let me.

I asked why and an agent told me, "You're not going there."

Another agent asked me, "Why are you crying?"

"I'm crying for my daughters. Ingrid is only a year and a month old and I'm still breast-feeding her."

"Just tell the truth and nothing will happen to you."

"But they've already taken away my husband. What's going to happen to my daughters? Who's going to stay with them? I don't know anyone here. Everyone I know has already been taken away."

"Just tell the truth and wait."

I was very worried because we had spent a long time in the basement. I didn't see my husband again that day, and I've only seen him once, in prison, since then.

They put some different colored bands on our wrists and divided the women into groups. I didn't know why some were taken one way and others went someplace else. Then they took my statement, and I told them the truth about how I had entered the country. When there were five or ten women who had finished with the interrogation they took us as a group and put us on a bus. They kept us there pretty much the rest of the day. I was still crying because I was so worried. About 2:00 in the afternoon they gave us a sandwich, but I couldn't eat because I was so overwhelmed with worry about my daughters. I couldn't imagine what would happen to them if they took me away.

Then they started taking some of the women off the bus, but I couldn't tell if they were letting them go home or what. I saw them leaving, but I didn't know if they were going to a different bus or home. After a while there were only two Guatemalans left, me and a woman who worked with me, and there were some women from Mexico. I was the last one off the bus at about 8:30 in the evening. They interrogated me again. They told me they were going to let me go because of my girls, but they were going to put a shackle on my ankle and that I shouldn't worry because they would deport me in four to six weeks.

When they put on the electronic shackle they told me I had to charge it and I was responsible for plugging it in every day and if I didn't they would call me and I'd be in trouble if I didn't do what they said. But I didn't know how because I'd never seen an ankle bracelet like that. In the beginning I only charged it for a little

Amalia

while. My daughter was so small, she was just learning to walk and when I plugged in the shackle she would unplug it and it wouldn't get fully charged. They put the GPS on me on Monday and the following Wednesday they called me and said it wasn't charging properly, so I started to plug it in at night so that it would be fully charged and they wouldn't call me.

When I left the plant after they put on the GPS shackle I walked towards the train tracks and an Immigration officer wished me luck and I said thank you. When I got to the tracks, I ran into Mr. Boss [a local Evangelical preacher], and the owner of the Guatemalan store, Toñita. Mr. Boss said he would take me to the church and that it was getting dark and that I was one of the last ones out. When I arrived at the church I was amazed to see so many people who were already there walking around and asking about their families.

I asked about my husband, and they told me he had already had his first court appearance at 4:00 that same afternoon and that he was in Waterloo. It was so very sad for us because my husband and I lived in an apartment with our two daughters and now I was alone with them. When I went to get my daughters at the baby-sitter's place, she wasn't home. She'd left and gone into hiding because she was afraid Immigration would come get her, and I didn't find my daughters until the next day about noon when a North American lady brought them to me at the church. That night of the raid was terribly sad because I was alone and without my husband and daughters and wondering where they all were. I didn't sleep at all worrying about the girls. Ingrid was still breast feeding. After that day nothing was ever the same.

About ten days after the raid and my husband's arrest, he called me to say he was in Waverly because they had transferred him to that jail. During those days I had met Priscilla, an American friend, and thanks to her I was able to visit him. She took me to the jail where they were holding him. I took the girls, too, and was able to talk to him in prison. That was the last time because he was just in that jail for two months and then they transferred him to Louisiana. It was very far away, and all we could do was talk on the phone for about three minutes each time. It was very expensive. He was the one who would call, and I had to send him money orders so that he had the money to do it. I couldn't have called him if I had wanted to.

He told me he was very sad, that he wouldn't wish what he was going through on anyone because the food was very bad. They treated him very badly, and they said he and the others were criminals. The truth is—he and his friends—they weren't criminals. They were caught working. They weren't stealing or doing anything bad. He said that if someone did something wrong, even if it was another cellmate who did it, everyone was punished. They would shut them up in a dark and cold cellar. I got so sad when he told me these things because it wasn't fair to treat them like criminals when they weren't.

The raid changed my life a lot. Everything was different. Before the raid we were working, and, though we were working very hard and they treated us badly, we knew we'd get a check that would allow us to survive, to buy food for the children, and to send a little something to our family. Now, after the raid, it's been hard because now I can't work. They are holding us here without allowing us to work and they're making us depend on charity. Before the raid none of us knew that there were people who gave food or who helped people who had no jobs.

In the beginning I was very ashamed to receive charity because in my country they teach us to depend only on our own efforts and not to rely on charity. It's very painful for me to talk about the fact that we live off charity, but that's the truth. We survive on hand-outs from other people.

Amalia

My husband has been deported now, and he's back in Guatemala, and he says when I talk to him that he gets sad when he sees other little girls the ages of Miriam and Ingrid. He says it makes him sad because he imagines that his daughters must be like those other children, and he is struggling because he's so alone.

Although after the raid nothing will ever be the same, it has served to teach me the idea of having rights. Before that I didn't have a clue, and I couldn't get up the courage to do anything for myself. I would just ask my husband to do everything. I never said, "I'm going to do this" or "I'm going to do that." He was always the one who did everything because he knew a little English. Now that I'm alone, I've had to do things. I've had to force myself to learn. I was always afraid to talk, but now, after the raid, little by little I've been learning to do my own things. But this has been hard for me. I've met a lot of people who have encouraged me. Before, for example, I was too afraid to order something at McDonald's, but now I believe I can. I do a lot of things because there is nobody who can do them for me.

I feel stronger and less fearful. Before I was really scared of Immigration, but now that they caught me I have nothing more to be afraid of. Before, the mere sight of a police officer scared me because I thought he would catch me, and then I had heard that if you were caught they took your children away from you. And I thought to myself, no way am I going to leave my daughters here if they deport me, but now that doesn't worry me. I go out of the house, and I know that if they arrest me again and deport me then my daughters go with me. I know my rights.

Shattered Dreams

Lupita

I was born in a village called San Antonio Aguas Calientes, and my mother and father are artisans, and they also farm the land. That's where I grew up, with my brothers and sisters. I was the third child born to my parents. We all started school when we were seven years old. Since my mother had to be away from home every day to sell our weavings and other crafts in the market, I would stay with my father. My *Papá* took care of us. He would take us to the fields, and we would work with him there.

I was about nine years old when someone stole all of the weavings and materials my mother had taken to the market to sell and that put us practically in the street. We were left without a cent. And that's when my mother began to get sick every day. She had terrible stomach problems, and I think it was because she was so sad. We didn't even have sugar for our coffee and had to drink it bitter.

My father spent his days working the land, but the harvests were poor and what he earned wasn't enough to feed us. We fell into years of poverty. We grew corn, beans, and other vegetables like carrots. Since we had no money he couldn't buy fertilizer so the fields were unproductive and the little they did produce often didn't sell. I and my brother Miguel would go to market with my father to try to sell the crops. We were just kids, but we worked in the market anyway. When we could, we would buy sugar and other things we needed just as if we were grown-ups.

That's the way we lived.

I made it to the fifth grade, but my mother didn't have any money to continue sending us to school. One day I asked her for a notebook and twenty-five *centavos* to give the teacher for supplies,

Lupita

but she didn't have any money for those expenses. I didn't want to go to school anymore because the teacher punished us for not bringing the twenty-five *centavos*. I cried and said to my mother, "I'm not going to school."

By that time I had learned traditional weaving from my aunt.

Once she had asked me, "So, do you want to learn how to weave?"

And I said, "Yes, I do."

My grandmother said, "Why didn't you tell us?"

It was because I was just seven years old and didn't know enough to ask.

I would sit with my grandmother and put on the backstrap loom and spend time weaving with her. My grandmother couldn't do any of the complicated weaving. She could just do the *tzutes*. That's what we call the men's kilts, which don't have designs, just the woven thread. A lot of people placed orders with her and she would finish long rolls of the material, using every bit of thread.

My uncles were the ones who taught me how to make blouses, *huipiles*, and tapestries. By the age of eight I knew how to weave. When I was nine and my mother had lost everything that day in the market, I told her that I was going to help her and I would do the weaving so that she could go to the market and sell again. But it was never the same. We never really recovered. I started to weave early every morning because I didn't want to study.

They called me from school, but I said, "I have to weave to help my mother."

I tried to keep on studying little by little, but it's hard to keep up.

Shattered Dreams

My Mom asked me why I didn't want to study anymore. I just said I didn't want to. About that time I wove a blouse for my mother. I have a picture of her wearing it. My mother told me she loved me very much and was so sorry she couldn't even get out of bed. She was very sick. All the doctors said she needed to have an operation that cost about $7,000. With my mother so sick, I had to take care of my younger brothers and sisters. Antonio was still tiny and I had to carry him around and care for him, and then my mother had two more babies.

After a while my mother started to sell in the market again, but we didn't have a lot of goods, and sometimes she couldn't sell much. When we had village *fiestas* I would never leave the house to enjoy them. We had no money, and with all my brothers and sisters to care for I wasn't free to go out and have a good time. I didn't have a lot of girl friends, just the neighbor girls, and I was always at home so I didn't meet people. When my mother would come back from market she would ask me, "don't you want to go out?" And I would say, "No, I don't feel like it. I'm sleepy and I want to go to bed."

I only said that because we didn't have money and if I went to the *fiesta* with my little brothers and sisters, they would ask me for things that were for sale, and then when I said we had no money I was afraid they would start crying and getting upset.

My neighbors would say, "don't you want to go to the bullfight?" June thirteenth is the festival of Saint Anthony, but we don't celebrate it directly on the thirteenth but on a weekend like the twenty-first or twenty-second. The bullfights are held out in the outskirts, not right in town.

And I would say, "No, I'd rather stay here."

And I would take my little brothers to play in the street in front of the house. Since they were boys I would get out a ball for them to play with. There were never many people in the street since they were all at the *fiesta*.

I would sit and watch and sometimes the boy from next door would come out and say the same thing, "Lupita, aren't you going to the *corrida de toros*?"

"No, I'm staying here with my brothers."

"Don't you want to go out and have some fun?"

Of course, I liked going to *fiestas*, but I would always say no.

And they would say to me, "Come on. We'll go with you to keep you company."

"Not while my mother is away in Antigua."

But my father did go to the *ferias*. Especially to the chapels because the custom in my town is to decorate the four village chapels. He had to be at one of the chapels because the men took turns taking care of them. People go to visit the altars, and priests go there, too, and so my father had to go. I would stay home and when he returned I would have the food ready. On those days I would prepare the special holiday meal, *pepián*.

Because I was so small and had to care for my brothers, my father would often say, "Just make some soup, and that's what we'll have for dinner."

That was really what I mostly did, take care of my father and brothers. My mother would often come home late at night.

Sometimes she had money; sometimes she didn't.

She would say, "I didn't sell a thing."

And my father would say, "That's okay. We'll get by.

Shattered Dreams

Sometimes they would send us to the store to ask for something on credit, like a pound of sugar. We felt so ashamed and didn't want to do it.

"No, *mamá*, please don't make us go."

And she would say, "But I don't have any money."

"Okay. It's all right. I'll go."

Around that time they invited me to weave in a museum that was in Antigua. It was on the grounds of the University of San Carlos, but it wasn't part of the university any more.

When I started working there I remember I was weaving a white tapestry and all the teachers would pass by and there I was, weaving. I was so excited. And that was where Sebastián would walk by, because all the kids had to get to school that way. He was in the second level. I was twelve years old then, and every time he walked past he would look at me. That's how we met. Then he started asking around who I was, and it turned out that some cousins of mine were Sebastian's neighbors.

They knew each other, so Sebastián asked, "Who is that girl?"

And they said, "That's our cousin."

"Your cousin! Why haven't you introduced us?"

And that's how it started. That's where everything began.

One day my cousin said, "Why don't you come and have lunch at our house tomorrow?"

And I said, "Sure, I'll be there," but I had no idea what was really going on.

Lupita

I was completely naïve, and when I showed up the next day one of the cousins said to me, "Come in. We're making some soup."

So we were in the kitchen, and all of a sudden, Sebastián showed up and very politely asked if he could come in, "*Con permiso.*"

"Come on in. We'd like to introduce you to our cousin. Her name is Lupita. Lupita, this is Sebastián. He lives next door and is a friend of ours."

"Oh, hello, *mucho gusto*," I said, but I was kind of annoyed.

And he said to me, "I'd like to get to know you better."

"I don't think so. I really don't want to talk to you." I was afraid my mother would find out.

"Don't worry. If we just talk in here nobody will see us. Your family won't know."

I said, "Well, that may be, but I don't like to lie to my mother."

My cousins said to us, "We're going to leave you two here fixing the potatoes, and we're going to the store. We'll be back soon."

And they left us all alone. There were just the two of us. I was just shaking. Sebastián was thirteen years old, and I was twelve.

I wondered to myself, "What if my aunt and uncle come home?"

Well, but there we were, just he and I.

After awhile my cousins came back. They brought soda and some other things. They owned a little store. I was always close friends with my cousins, and they still love me a lot.

And they said, "Help yourselves. Let's sit down and eat."

And Sebastián said, "Let's eat and talk some more." His hair

Shattered Dreams

was all combed, and he smelled good, like men's aftershave.

I didn't want to eat. Still, there was something that I felt, some attraction. I think it was love at first sight. And from then on we have been together. But I was trembling, my little bones were shaking like mad.

I said to my cousins, "I need to go to the bathroom."

"Well, go on then. You aren't stuck here, are you?"

The house had two doors, one in the front and one in the back that opened onto the outside latrine and another street.

I left and went out the back door. But I didn't go to the bathroom. I went directly to the street and started running home. My house was pretty far away, in a whole different village. But I ran and ran and ran. Later my cousins told me they had waited fifteen minutes, and when I didn't come back from the bathroom they went and looked for me, but I was gone.

I was just about a block away from home when Sebastián caught up with me.

"Hey! Why did you run away?" I was all sweaty from running.

"I can't do this. I don't want my father to hit me."

But at any rate, that's when we started to get to know each other.

A year passed and my mother would just send me to the store every once in a while. Sebastián and I would see each other then, five minutes, ten minutes, and we had no real chance of talking.

During that time, my mother would say to me, "don't you want to go to Antigua to sell *típico*?" [traditional clothing and crafts]

Lupita

And I would tell her I didn't want to, that I preferred to stay at home weaving and taking care of my little brothers.

But then she would say to me, "But I feel so sick and can't go myself." So I always ended up going.

My older sister Virginia started to sell *típico*, too. She had already started to work for my cousins for a monthly salary, selling clothes. The two of us worked, and my sister said, "You can do your weaving, and I can sell it to one of the cousins, and then we'll give the money to *mamá*.

We had no money for ourselves. Everything was for the family. That's what we did for awhile, but then one day my sister said, "Lupita, I met some Americans at the Artisans' Fair." Every December in Guatemala we have big fairs where we can sell our products to international buyers. My sister always went to those fairs to sell with an American lady.

But then my sister said, "I'm going to leave and go north, to the United States, but I'm not going to say anything to *mamá*."

"*Ay*, no," I said. "What if *mamá* dies? I don't think she can take it if you leave."

But she said to me, "Lupita, you have to take care of *mamá* and our brothers and sisters for me." But I started to cry, and I cried all night.

She had brought us a farewell cake and said, "Come on, let's eat this nice cake."

This was in December.

"But it's not even Christmas yet," my mother said, but my sister wanted us to eat the cake anyway.

But I knew that it was a goodbye cake. My sister told me not to be sad. She had a boyfriend at that time and told me to go tell him

Shattered Dreams

to wait outside a little bit and she would be out to see him soon.

When she came back she said to me, "I said goodbye to him. I'm leaving tomorrow."

But I could tell she was really upset. She was only sixteen years old at the time, four years older than me. So she left, and after about eight days my mother asked, "And your sister? Isn't she coming home?"

"No, she isn't coming home."

"Well, do you know where she is?"

"She's working."

And then, when we got a letter from her saying that she had arrived in the U.S., everything was fine and she had found work, my mother said "didn't you tell me that she was just someplace nearby working?"

I told her, "I didn't know. She just told me to wait for a surprise."

And so, as soon as my sister came north she began to work. They paid her $200 a month. And she sent money to us all the time, but since my mother was so sick, the money all went for medicine.

Mamá had a terrible ulcer, and she was in such pain all the time. She would double over from the pain, and we didn't know what to do. And it was even harder for us to try to make do without my sister.

Christmas was normally such a happy time. *Mamá* would make tamales and we'd all eat together. But after my sister left, there were no more tamales.

"No, *M'ija*, there aren't any tamales, but I can make some for you if you want."

Lupita

"No, thank you."

And I remember that I wrapped myself up in my blanket. I said, "*mamá*, I'm asleep and I don't want to get up." I knew my mother would be crying at midnight.

I said, "I don't want to get out of bed, I don't want to light firecrackers, I don't want to do anything."

But my sister always did write to us. Back then there were no telephones in our village so she would write and tell me, "I'm going to send you some sweaters."

And I was so happy when she sent me a sweater.

So a year passed, and I was thirteen years old. Sebastián said, "Now that I'm fifteen we can become *novios*. I'm going to talk to your father and ask his permission for us to see each other and have conversations in public."

"No, my father will beat me."

But he went to talk to my father anyway.

"You're both so young," my father said. "If you want to meet at the door of our house to chat just as friends that would be all right. But nowhere else. Just here at our house."

And another year went by. And Sebastián knew that I had to take care of my brothers and sisters. So when I was fourteen years old I went to the town fair for the first time.

Sebastián said to me, "I'll help you. I can carry the baby, and you can hold the hands of the other little ones.

There was Antonio, Leonarda, Esperanza, and Miguel and the one year old baby that had to be carried. I was taking care of all of them.

Shattered Dreams

And Sebastián said, "Let's go to church first." So he carried the baby, and I pulled the others along, all holding hands.

Everyone was looking at us. "Oh, now they're *novios*," they all said.

So Sebastián would help me when we went to church for Sunday mass. And other times he helped me and played with the children, too. I don't know where he got the money to treat us but he did. I think his father paid him to help make wooden coffins.

Sebastián would say, "I finished making a coffin today and my father gave me the money we earned. Let's go share it with your brothers and sisters."

I said, "I don't have any money."

And he'd always say, "don't worry. I do."

At that time, I had a teacher who liked me a lot and wanted me to continue studying. She thought it was very important for me to go on with my studies even if there were some days when I couldn't make it to class.

She said, "You're a very hard worker, and your grades are good."

So I tried to keep up with my studies. At fourteen I would go to class sometimes and others times I wouldn't because of my brothers and sisters. One day the teacher said she had a relative who was looking for a woman or girl to take care of two children. She asked if any of us knew of a girl who wanted a job like that. They were going to pay 300 *quetzales* a month and that was a lot of money.

And I said to her, "I would like that job."

"You?"

"Yes, me."

Lupita

"But she's looking for someone older, responsible, and who knows how to cook."

And I said to her, "I know how to cook. I can make tortillas, and I make food for my father when he goes to work in the fields. My mother is sick, and she can't do it." I told her the whole story.

"I take care of seven brothers and sisters."

"By yourself?"

"Yes, all by myself."

"Okay. Let's talk to your mother about this and let's also see if you can continue your studies."

And my mother said, "No, not this daughter, too. One has already gone away. I don't want to lose another."

But I said to her, "I really want to go because my sisters and brothers don't even have clothes to wear. We hardly have enough money to buy one set of clothes a year. Please, I want to go; I want to go."

For this job I had to go live in Costa Rica. My teacher set up everything and arranged for me to meet with the *Señora*, who was her sister-in-law. Her name was Marigel.

"So, you would like to come to Costa Rica to work for me? Do you know how to cook?"

I said, "Yes, I know how to cook, but I don't know what your children eat."

She said, "You're not going to have to take care of all the cooking."

She was very happy when I said that I would accept the job.

Shattered Dreams

"You're still young but my girls will be very happy. I think you are just the right age for this job."

"I hope so."

"You will only need to make meals for the children and to wash their clothes in the washing machine."

I didn't know what a washing machine was.

"You will help them brush their teeth and give them baths and play with them. And you will take them to the park."

And I said I would do all that, but what I was really thinking about was helping my mother and father.

"Okay. We'll be leaving on Monday, but I would like you to come with me tomorrow," the *Señora* said.

My mother was beside herself. "Do you really want to go with those people? You don't know anything about them. What if something goes wrong?"

I said to her, "*mamá*, I have to take the risk. My sister has left, and I can leave, too. I can do it, too."

So finally she gave me permission.

I got all my clothes together. It wasn't very much, just two skirts and two blouses.

Sebastián showed up later that evening, and I told him I was leaving.

"Where to?"

"I'm going to Costa Rica. I have a contract for two years."

"Two years!" What are you going to be doing there?"

Lupita

"I'm going to care for two little girls."

"No, don't go" he said. "I think we should get married."

I said to him, "We're way too young to get married. I don't want to get married now."

"You don't want to get married?"

"No, I don't. Not yet."

"But you're fourteen years old, and you'll be fifteen before long."

"Yes, I know, but I'm leaving."

And I left. The *Señora* was a student, and she was graduating on Friday. I left my house in the village on Wednesday. On Thursday we went shopping and she bought clothes for me, too.

On Friday she said to me, "I'd like you to dress in your traditional clothing, and you can serve sandwiches to the guests. And you can give some treats to the children and serve a meal to the young people. Before that I'd like you to clean the table with furniture polish. I don't want you to be stuck in the kitchen."

She loved me very much since the first day we met. She told me, "On Saturday we're going shopping again, and on Sunday we'll visit some people. And then on Monday we'll be going to Costa Rica."

And that's what we did.

When we went to Costa Rica she was able to get a passport and visa for me very quickly. As we landed, I expected to see very tall buildings. I asked myself, "What will Costa Rica be like?" And when we arrived, it looked exactly like Guatemala!

I spent over a year and a half in Costa Rica. The *Señora* was almost like a sister to me. She told me that I didn't need to cook for her or anyone else, just for myself and the children.

She said to me, "My clothes are your clothes, everything in the closet belongs to both of us. There is no difference. You're going to be like a sister to me, and I will love you very much. I'm going to send you to school with the nuns so you can get your diploma."

I ended up not going to school because I wanted to take care of the little girls. I taught them how to cook and to make tortillas by hand.

Then the *Señora* was given a scholarship to study in England, and she asked me, "Do you want to go to England with me, or do you want to go back to Guatemala?"

At that time my mother was going to have an operation, so I decided to go home to Guatemala.

That's the worst decision I've made in my life. I think it was a mistake because if I had gone somewhere else maybe I would have been able to travel and see other places, and I might have graduated from high school.

Sebastián told me he was waiting for me. He wrote to me every day. I had a lot of his letters that I carried around in a backpack.

He was always asking me, "Are you coming back to Guatemala?"

The 300 *quetzales* they were paying me to care for the girls didn't come directly to me. The money was sent to my mother in Guatemala. The also gave me about 100 *quetzales* to spend, but I said it was a lot of money because I didn't have any expenses. They gave me everything. I told the *Señora* that I wanted to send that money to my parents, too, because they were so needy. My sister in California also sent them money every month so they were able to save for my mother's operation.

I was fifteen years old and about to turn sixteen when I went

Lupita

back home. I didn't tell anyone I was coming because I wanted it to be a surprise. My mother was not at home when I arrived so I sat in the doorway. There were a lot of people and a lot of food.

It was a holiday!

After mass everyone showed up at the house. I was already inside and had begun setting the table and serving the food. When *mamá* came in and saw me she just burst into tears.

"When did you arrive? Why didn't you tell me? What if you had been robbed? Who knows what could have happened to you in Guatemala City?

"Well, nothing happened, and here I am."

"You are so brave!"

So my *mamá* was very happy, and she asked me if I would go to mass that evening. I told her I would.

There was a neighbor who had been a little boy when I left but was all grown up. He said, "Let's go to mass. I'll go with you."

'And what if Sebastián sees us?"

And he said, "Sebastián? No problem. He has a lot of girlfriends."

And I got angry and said, "Okay, let's go to mass together."

Then when Sebastián showed up, he said, "*Hola.*" And I said, "*Hola.*"

He said, "don't you want to talk to me?"

So I said," Yes and no."

"Why not?"

Shattered Dreams

"They told me you had a lot of girlfriends. I heard all about it."

"No, those are all lies."

"Okay," I said. And we started to talk, and we were soon back to being *novios*. We were never really apart from the age of twelve. Soon I wasn't spending a lot of time at home. About a year later Sebastián and I were engaged and wanted to be together. I was only sixteen then.

My father-in-law said they were going to approach my parents to ask for my hand. They came to our house. In San Antonio the parents of the boy take sweet bread to the women of the house. They brought two *canastas* for my mother, one with loaves of bread and another with bread, fruit and vegetables. They also brought articles of clothing as gifts.

I said to myself, "So much food! And if I don't want to get married? Will I have to give all this stuff back?"

"If you marry another boy, you'll have to pay it all back."

And I was scared. There was so much involved in getting married. The bride had to weave a *huipil* and *tsute* for her mother-in-law and you have to give a *toalla* to your father-in-law, handwoven and with his name. I started to weave and my mother helped me, too.

My mother said, "I'm going to have another woman do one of these."

But I didn't get married. I started to think about my parents-in-law and wondered where in heaven's name they found the money to pay for all the things they gave when they came to ask for my hand. There's no money in my town! My parents don't have money, and you have to spend a fortune for a wedding— five or six thousand *quetzales*, including hiring a marimba band.

My poor parents are going to spend so much money, I thought

to myself.

I talked with Sebastián and asked him if he really wanted a church wedding.

He told me, "I do."

And I said, "I don't."

"Don't you want to get married?"

"Let's just get together and wait for later to marry."

"Okay, if that's what you want."

And I told my mother, "I'm going to live with Sebastián."

"Are you sure that's what you want to do?"

"Yes, I'm sure."

"Okay. I can't tell you what to do, but it's going to make me very sad and angry because you really should wait for the wedding."

I told her I didn't want to wait, but I didn't tell her why.

And again Sebastián asked me, "Are you sure you don't want to get married?"

And I said, "Look, your parents are going to spend so much money for something that is over in a few hours, and then they're going to end up in debt. It's better for us to wait and earn some of our own money so that we can get married. Yes, one day we will get married but only when we have earned the money ourselves and we know it was our own hard work that made it possible."

And so we started to live together. I moved into my

parents-in-law's house. When I first arrived they asked me "Aren't you going to wait for the wedding?"

My mother-in-law put on her *tsute* and the two of them went to my parent's house to see what had happened. My mother explained to them that it had been my decision to move out and to not have the wedding. And it was okay with Sebastián, too.

So that's how we started our life together, and I lived in Sebastián's parents' house for almost a year. When my daughter was born I was living with them. After she was born, my father-in-law said, "You can go and live on our plot of land with Sebastián's grandmother. Another daughter-in-law might be moving in."

There were seven boys in Sebastián's family!

"If another daughter-in-law moves in, you might not get along, and then you'd start fighting. It would be better for you to have your own house and begin your life together."

And that's what we did. My mother-in-law gave us a dish, a cup, a *batidor* to make our coffee, and a pot in which to cook our meals. And we went to live by ourselves in our room made of cane stalks, our kitchen made of cane. Everything was made of cane. And we did well. We were working and getting along. Sebastián began working for the police. He would come home every weekend. I was weaving every day from morning until night because the money he earned wasn't enough to support us. We did have enough to eat, but sometimes Sebastián didn't have money for the bus so he couldn't afford to come home. Then, when we had two children—Andrés was born after Patricia—Sebastián decided we should sell fruit to earn more money.

We went to the capital city to buy baskets of mandarin oranges. Since we bought them wholesale, they cost us less. A large basket cost 15 or 20 *quetzales* and had hundreds of oranges. We sold them

Lupita

for 10 *quetzales* apiece and made a profit. We started with the oranges, but the second time we also bought *pateras*. Do you know what those are? They are like a stick or a long pod shaped like a machete, and when you split them open, they have something like cotton inside that you can suck on. We sold that and also *caimitos*, which are kind of like a plum. We sold all kinds of fruit.

My mother-in-law suggested that we also sell onions and chili peppers because they were in big demand. We started to make more money.

My mother had a refrigerator and offered to give it to us so that we could sell frozen things as well. I told her we would pay her for it once we earned enough. So then we were also selling ice cream bars and *chocobananos*.

My son was four years old, and we were still selling produce. When I was pregnant with Daniel we were able to make a house of adobe bricks and live there instead of the cane hut.

Sebastián said, "Instead of just using the house to sleep in, why don't we open a little store."

He began to make the sales counter with wood that he bought, and he made shelves, too. He was still working with the police, and when he was at home he was also helping his father. He made all the furniture, so we didn't have to spend much money. I think that helped us a lot. And we started to buy ribbons—not many, maybe a dozen or two—and cartons of fruit juice by the dozen.

Then one of our neighbors who had a workshop and a lot of men working for him asked, "Why don't you sell *refacciones*." That's what we call a snack during break with sodas and something to eat. Here in the U.S. Spanish-speakers call it *merienda* but there we always said *refacción*.

The neighbor said, "You can make food for the men and earn

more money. On the weekend we'll order from you because I pay them only on weekends." I told him I would ask Sebastián.

I never did anything by myself. I always had to consult with my husband about everything. He's very jealous.

I said to him, "Your cousin, *Don* Lino, talked to me about selling food to the men who work in his workshop."

"Who's going to be doing the selling?"

"Well, it'll be me because I'm the one who's at home. But *Don* Lino will be coming with the men."

"And how are you going to do it? What are you going to give them?"

"I can make *chiles rellenos*. If I give each of them two *chiles rellenos* for 2 ½ quetzales, that's a lot of money."

"Okay, if you really want to do it, then do it. But be very careful."

So I started that business. On Mondays I would sell *chiles rellenos* to everybody. On Tuesday the young men from the workshop would come at 10:00 in the morning, and I had to have everything ready for them. I also had rolls, and they drank a lot of soft drinks. They paid me every weekend, and I could earn as much as 500 *quetzales* each week.

I said to Sebastián, "Now we have enough money to buy more and have a better variety of goods in the store."

And we began to buy corn by the *quintal* and sell it by the pound. Then I began to have bigger plans. I was still weaving at the time.

I said to Sebastián, "Let's buy some little chicks. We can buy 50 and keep them in the corral. We can heat them with a light." I had such a big imagination.

Lupita

"When they're grown I can butcher them and we can sell them by the pound."

And that's what we did. We sold chickens and sometimes there was so much demand we ran out, and I had to buy more chicken to sell. There was a man named *Don* Pedro who sold the chickens to me by the pound, but still alive. I had to butcher them and take off the feathers myself.

Despite all this, my husband said, "We're all right, but we really are still hurting for money."

The children were growing up, and we had other responsibilities, too. My grandmother helped us a lot, but it wasn't enough. I had a little cousin who was very, very poor. She didn't have a father and her mother couldn't take care of her. I went to talk to my aunt and asked her to let my cousin live with me. I told her I would help her go to school. I said I would buy her clothes and everything. So my aunt agreed. My cousin was such a tiny little thing. It was like adopting another daughter but she helped a lot around the house.

Sebastián started to talk about going north. "There's no way we can earn enough money here."

He had left the police and started working as a bodyguard for an ambassador. Then the ambassador said he was going back to El Salvador which is where he was from. The ambassador said he wanted to leave Sebastián with a job with a wealthy family, and he found him a job as a chauffeur for a rich lady. She treated him so badly, and he would come home exhausted and angry. It was hell, and we still weren't earning enough to pay all our expenses. The store was doing only so-so, and there was no way we could get ahead.

Sebastián kept saying, "Everything we earn goes to food, electricity, water, so many things. I want to go to the United States."

Shattered Dreams

I called my sister and told her that Sebastián wanted to go north like she had done.

"It would be better if you could come. It's easier for a woman to find a job. Get your papers together. The reason I'm working is so I can help you with things like that."

I got all my documentation and my children's papers, too, and I went to the U.S. Embassy. We thought it was easy. We went to Immigration and told them we wanted to come here, to the U.S., and they said no. They turned us down.

So I told Sebastián, "I'm going to get a visa as a weaver, as an artisan."

But I kept thinking more and more. I wanted to help my parents, and I couldn't. I was able to give them a little money from the store but just such a small amount.

Sebastián said, "This poverty is terrible. I'm going to the United States. Yes, I'm going as a *mojado*."

And Sebastián headed north. He suffered a lot along the way. When I didn't have news of him I got very sad. He hasn't called, he hasn't come home, I would think to myself. Every time he did call, he was still in Mexico.

"When are you going to get to the U.S.?" I always asked.

When he left, he took all the money. I stayed at the store with nothing. I had no sugar in the store to sell, no corn, nothing. It was empty. I thought to myself, where am I going to get money for my children? They have to go to school. I need money for electricity, for the water. I tried to get ahead again. I continued to make food for the men from the workshop. That's the one thing that kept me going.

Lupita

I had to get up really early, at 4:00 a.m., to go buy fresh vegetables for the store, and I finished working at 8:00 p.m. Then I would close the store and start cleaning, sweeping, and mopping. I finished with everything at about 10:00.

For awhile a nephew came to stay with us. He was studying and was about to graduate. He helped me a lot.

He said to me, "You need to take better care of yourself. You're going to get sick."

My *Papá* said, "Go on, get to bed. You never get enough sleep."

I was really skinny, but I said, "If I don't push myself, we won't have any money."

And every time Sebastián called he was still on his way north. I got to the point where I was owing 800 *quetzales*. Two months went by, and he had found no work. When he finally got across the border he couldn't find work there either.

When he called he said, "I have no money."

"Don't worry," I would say. I always said I had money. I never said, "I don't have any money." I always told him that between the store and his parents we were doing okay. I said, "Your father takes us to Antigua to go shopping. Don't worry." And it's true that his parents helped us a lot.

"But the children, do they have clothes?" he said.

"They have plenty to wear," I would answer.

And all that time with no money!

But Sebastián was always saying, "When I find work you will have everything you need."

Shattered Dreams

And I would answer, "Okay, everything's fine."

But there I was alone in Guatemala thinking "My husband has gone away. What will become of us here?"

Finally he managed to get into the United States. Then he called and said, "Guess what? I ran into a guy from our village, San Antonio. His name is Santiago. Yes, he's from back home, and he's going to take me to a place named Postville. He says there is a plant there where he has been working."

"All right, if there is work there, God willing, you need to go."

And he went to Postville. He told me all about the plant where he was working. At first he was working in the turkey processing plant. Then he was working in Agri, and he sent me photos of where he was working as a janitor. I was still working in the store. And then he sent me a little money, but I knew it was only to pay off the debts we had because of what we had to pay the *coyote* for his trip north.

I kept on thinking of getting a visa for the U.S. I said to myself next year I'm going north. I started to get my paperwork together again so that I could apply for a visa as an artisan.

"There's a young man who goes to the U.S. a lot. Why don't you go and talk to him?" my mother said.

So I did. I told him I wanted to visit the U.S. and see my husband. "He's been there for almost two years. Yes, he sends me money, but I need to know how he's doing."

He told me we could try for June because there was going to be an event in California where people went to view merchandise. He thought I could find something to weave there. First we went to the consulate and asked for the visa like I did the first time.

Lupita

We talked to a man. Well actually, first we talked with a lawyer, and she said to me, "You want to go to the consulate?" When I said yes, she asked me why.

"I want to travel to the United States, but I don't want to go alone. I'm going to go with some other weavers." I was planning on coming with Griselda and with two young men from a village just beyond ours. I don't know what we thought we were going to do in the U.S., but I was so excited about traveling.

Then she said, "You have an appointment at the consulate next Thursday at 10:00 a.m."

When I left I said to the man who was helping me, without giving it too much importance, that I had the appointment. He was very excited and said to me, "I'm sure you're going to be able to travel to the U.S. They wouldn't have you go to the consulate unless they plan to give you a visa." He was very happy. I wondered if it could be true.

He told all of us to dress up a lot, to be as elegant as we could so that the people in the consulate would think we had money and would give us the visas. He also insisted I take the document showing I owned a house. They ask for so much paperwork at the embassy. I took my children's birth certificates, and Sebastián's, too. I took the deed to the house and the tax papers from the store to show that it was all very legal. They asked if I had money in the bank and I told them I had 50 *quetzales*.

My Dad worried about the bank account. "You're going to show them those 50 *quetzales*?

They've turned people down who have thousands, *m'hija*, and there you go with your 50 *quetzal* bank account!"

"Well, that's all I have. And I made my own house, too."

Shattered Dreams

"I guess if you're lucky they'll take you," my father said, and we set out for the embassy. When we got there the man who talked to us was black. I had never seen a black person in my life!

"Hello, are you Lupita?"

"Yes, I am."

"And you father's name is Miguel, right?"

"Yes, it is."

"Well, you are going to get a visa."

"Really? Me? What do you mean?"

"Go to the window over there, and they'll give it to you."

I will never forget that young man. He was the first black man I ever saw, and I will always remember him.

I went to the window, and they asked me if I wanted to travel. And I said "Yes, I would like an American visa."

"I congratulate you because you are a woman and you're very brave. You're going to have to travel by yourself because we're not going to give visas to the others."

When I looked at the visa it was for ten years and I was almost overcome with joy. I had such a strong pain here on my side that I could hardly walk. My father and my in-laws were waiting for me outside.

My Dad asked, "How did it go?"

"*Papá*, they gave me the visa!"

He couldn't believe it. "They really gave you a visa? Let's go celebrate." And we went out to a restaurant called *El Pollo Campero*.

Lupita

After looking at all my papers my father said, "After such a long struggle you are finally going to be able to travel to the U.S. You spent three years coming and going with all the documents. Now you're going to see your husband at last."

When I called my sister in Los Angeles, I said, "Virginia, I have a surprise for you."

"What do you mean? What surprise?" She had never expected it.

"Imagine! I have a visa! I'm going to travel to the U.S. I'm going to be with Sebastián"

"No," she said. I think she was a little jealous. "You're not going to stay with him. You're coming here to stay with me. I'm going to send you the money for the ticket. It costs nearly a thousand dollars."

And, of course, although I wanted to make the trip, I had no money, so my sister paid, and I arrived in Los Angeles. She told me she wanted me to stay with her for a while.

Sebastián called me from Postville and said, "Why didn't you come here with me?"

I just said, "It's okay. I'm with my sister."

My sister had a friend named Maricela who worked on the cleaning crew of a store. The very day I arrived, she called my sister and asked, "Where's your sister? Has she arrived yet?" I was sleeping because I was so tired from the trip.

"I have a job for her, but it starts right now. If she doesn't come now there might not be another chance."

My sister felt so bad about waking me up, but I told her, "don't worry, Virginia, in Guatemala I'm used to working long hours. I hardly sleep, maybe four or five hours a night."

Shattered Dreams

I took the job, and they picked me up at 8:00 that night. I started to work that very day cleaning in stores with those huge machines that wash and polish the floors. One of the other ladies taught me how to do it. During the day I would go to work with my sister cleaning private homes. At night I was working with that company cleaning stores. When Sebastián called I was never home, at night or during the day. Then Sebastián decided to go to Los Angeles, and my sister was really happy.

"Guess what?" she said. "Sebastián loves you a lot because he's coming to be with you. I asked you to stay with me and not go with him because I wanted to test him. You had been apart for three years. Here in the States you never know if your husband has found a new girlfriend, and then the wife shows up and there's fighting. I was worried about that happening to you, and then there you would be far from your country and I would be here in Los Angeles, far away, too."

I think she was acting out of sisterly love. We were very close.

"I didn't want you to go with him right away. The money didn't matter to me. I just earn it, and I would have been glad to give it to you, but I wanted to be sure that Sebastián truly loved you."

When Sebastián came to Los Angeles it was just three days after the attack on the Twin Towers in New York. I remember that day. I was sound asleep after working all night, and my sister woke me up. "Something is happening here in the United States."

I'm not sure exactly what she said to me because my sister speaks very little Spanish, but she said that the Twin Towers had been destroyed.

We heard the news, but Sebastián had already bought his ticket to fly to California. He told us that all the airports were completely closed. I don't remember the exact date he arrived.

Lupita

My sister asked him, "Are you still planning to come?"

"Yes, of course. That's where Lupita is, and I want to be there, too."

We went to the airport to pick him up. Because of the attack in New York, passengers weren't arriving in the regular areas of the terminal. They had people get off the planes behind the airport. We got lost trying to find Sebastián. When we saw him, he was already in the street with his suitcase. Everything was pretty chaotic in those days.

My sister said, "Do you recognize him?"

I saw him and shouted, "Sebastián, here we are!"

We hugged, and to celebrate my sister took us to a restaurant.

My sister was so happy that we were all together. We lived with her, and she made a small studio apartment attached to hers—made a kitchen in it and everything—and she gave it to us to live in. We settled in and spent maybe a year there. Sebastián was working for a landscaping company.

It was about that time that I started to have headaches. We lived on Cathedral Street which is just past Park Place in California. Since I was working with the janitorial service at night and cleaning houses with my sister during the day, I was earning a lot.

Sebastián's job as a gardener was only for eight hours. He wasn't happy with the situation.

He kept saying, "I come home and you're not here, and then when you do come home you have headaches. I think we should go to Postville. I know that they'll give me a job in the plant, and they'll give you a job, too. Then we'll both be working the same."

Shattered Dreams

And we came to Postville. When we got here, he went to get his job at the plant, and they wouldn't give it to him. I think that after what happened with the Twin Towers there was a lot more control in this country. It took him two weeks to get his job again. At that time, Joe was still the manager, and he knew my husband well, so when he did start at the plant again they gave him his old job as a "yellow hardhat" [supervisor].

I went time and time again to apply for a job, but they kept saying there was no work for me to do. Then I noticed that new people were coming and as soon as they showed up they were given a job. Sebastian began to ask around about why they wouldn't hire me when they were giving jobs to others, and one of the men told him, "If you give Casam $500 he'll make sure your wife is hired."

"But then we'll have to wait," I said. "We have to pay the rent, and we've gone a month with no income. We have no money, and we have to send some to our children in Guatemala."

I had to wait seven months before I could get a job at the plant. My first job was in the area called *cadap* ["cut up"]. We did the final cutting of the chickens and put the pieces on Styrofoam trays. The supervisor said to me in English, "Too much money." [This was to indicate that area job paid well with lots of hours.] "Okay, thank you," I said and went to work.

At that time, I started work each day at 9:00 a.m. and finished at about 1:00 or 2:00 a.m. Since Sebastián was working as a janitor on the night shift, we hardly ever saw each other. He would come home from work at 10:00 a.m. and I had already left before 9:00. And then when I came home at 1:00 a.m. or so, he wasn't there because he started at 6:00 p.m. The only times we saw each other were from a distance at the plant and then we would say hello or wave to each other. If we ran into each other during lunch break, we would talk and talk because that was the only chance we had.

Lupita

We went along like that for about three years. They paid me $6.25 per hour. The supervisor knew I was a fast worker. As a weaver I had learned to weave very quickly, and it was the same for me working cutting up chicken. I thought to myself that I had wanted to work and this was what I had wanted. Thank God they never yelled at me like they did at some of the others, but it was as if the more work I did, the more work they gave me. They piled on the work, and when I said I was tired and the Styrofoam trays were coming too fast, they told me that was the job and I had to do it or leave.

I would reply, "Well, I want the job, so it's okay."

What did really bother me was everything that I witnessed there. There were children who had to do the same hard work. They had to pick up heavy pieces of meat, and they had to do everything so fast. I thought about the fact that my son would one day do the same kind of work. That was before I saw the kid who cut his hand. He cut off his finger. And we had to just go on working!

We were busy cutting and putting chicken on the Styrofoam trays when one of the young men yelled, "Lupita, there goes my finger!"

"What happened?

We stopped the conveyor belt, and everyone gathered round. "What happened? What happened?"

"My finger, my finger, my finger!"

We thought it must have gotten in with the pieces of chicken. I never saw it. I thought it was a better idea to start looking for it on the belt. But it wasn't there. We looked in the boxes of chicken that were already packed. It wasn't there either. "Where is the finger?" we wondered. It finally turned up stuck behind the meat saw where he had been cutting. *Ay*, even though we were frightened and almost frigid with shock we just had to get back to work.

The supervisor said, "Go on working. Get to work," as if nothing had happened.

They didn't wash the saw. They didn't wash anything. We just had to keep on working. And even though I would have liked to go to the office with the boy to be sure he was taken care of, we weren't allowed to. We had to pretend everything was normal. It was his problem, not ours, even though we had seen the accident.

That's the kind of work we did. I worked like that for three years. Often I could scarcely breathe. Sometimes they dumped dry ice where we were working. All of the women would get sick, and they wouldn't let us take a break.

Or, one of us would say, "I need to pee. I want to go to the bathroom, and I'll be really quick."

It was a problem because when we did have a break we couldn't use the bathroom. There was one bathroom, and there were about 75 people who needed to use it at the same time. We had to decide whether to eat lunch or go to the bathroom. What I got used to doing was to take a yogurt and a soft drink in my bag, and then when I went to the bathroom I would be in the stall peeing, eating and drinking. Break was already over when I was done. Three years of that!

Finally our children came from Guatemala. My daughter was almost grown up, and she said she wanted to get to know us because she had forgotten what we were like. My in-laws also said she was growing up so quickly. She was nearly sixteen years old. Sebastián told them not to come because there was no work and no money, but my daughter told us she was going to go to her aunt in Los Angeles. The kids managed to get their visas to pass through Mexico, but all their money went in crossing the border. When my

Lupita

daughter finally called, they were already at the border.

My daughter said, *"Mamá*, we're here!" But she was crying. *"mamá*, what should we do? Please come get us."

"And where are you?"

"We're here in the U.S. We crossed the border."

"You need to get on a bus and come here. There isn't anything I can do."

It was so hard on us. But she brought her two brothers. My daughter brought her two little brothers! My sister-in-law had travelled with them and came all the way to Postville. She stayed here working about a month, too, but her children were back in Guatemala, and so she decided to go back to be with them.

Once my children were here I wanted to stop working at the plant, or at least stop working all those hours because I couldn't spend any time at all with them. They went to school in the morning, and we didn't see each other. I got home at about 1:00 in the morning, and they were asleep. I would leave food prepared for them, but sometimes they would eat and other times they wouldn't. When I woke up in the morning my kids were already leaving for school, and by the time I was wide awake they were gone.

I started asking the supervisor Casam for a schedule change.

"No, you can't change shifts because no one knows how to prepare the Styrofoam trays like you do."

"Please, please, let me change from the night shift."

"No way, there is no changing shifts for you."

"My children have arrived, and I want to spend time with them. It's almost Christmas, and I want to be with my kids."

Shattered Dreams

So he said, "I'm going to give you vacation time, but I'm not going to make any changes in your schedule."

And I responded, "Well then, pay me more. I want a raise."

And he said, "No, no, a lot of money. Sebastián earns a lot of money, and you earn a lot of money."

I responded, "We have to pay rent, and buy food. If I can't have a raise then change my working hours."

"Find someone to help you with the trays of chicken and I'll think about it."

He never agreed to change my shift. I had a sister-in-law, Elena, and I told her, this is where I work and what I do. I'll teach you everything, and then when I leave you can stay here in this section. But even after I trained her they wouldn't change me to the day shift.

During the time I was asking for a change, Casam went to Sebastián and said, "I have a good car for you, a Blazer. Buy it from me."

"If I buy it, will you change my wife to the day shift?

"Yes," Casam, said, "that's the only way."

The following day Sebastián told him we would buy the car. We had to pay him in installments. We didn't have money to pay cash. That's how we bought the Blazer that we have now.

The day after Sebastián agreed to buy the car, Casam came to me at work and said, "You can go home now."

It was 7:00 p.m. He was shouting at me which was strange because I always worked hard so they almost never yelled at me.

"You can go home."

Lupita

"Really? But it's only 7:00."

"Yes, you can go home and see your kids. Tomorrow you need to be at work at 6:00 a. m.

"So you've put me on the day shift?"

"Yes." And I was so happy. And then one of the other women I was working with started to cry.

She said, "*Chaparra*, you're leaving? You aren't going to be working with us anymore?"

And Adela, who worked right next to me, said, "*Vieja*, why are you leaving?" and everyone else started to cry. I think they felt bad because I always helped the other women, especially when I finished my own job I would help them finish theirs.

"I have to make a change to be with my children. My girl is almost grown-up now, and I don't want anything bad to happen to her."

"Well, okay. Leave. Go on."

And I left at 7:00 in the evening. The following day I went to work at 6:00 in the morning. Little did I know that this was going to turn out to be my worst nightmare.

I was so happy to begin the day shift but they changed me from the packing area to butchering and Casam told the supervisor, Mark, "Mark, I've brought you this *Señora*, and she's a very fast worker. You can put her with the knives. She can handle them perfectly."

"Yes, *Señora*, is what Casam says true? Are you a fast worker?"

"I don't know, but I needed to change shifts because of my children."

Shattered Dreams

They put me in the butchering area, and my job was to cut the wings off the chickens. The problem was the chickens went past on the belt at a rate of sixty per minute. Yes, sixty per minute! Sometimes the chickens came with both wings broken and I had to cut those off. I got so tired and my hand would fall asleep, and I would say to the supervisor, "I'm tired. My arm hurts."

"You wanted a change, and this is your change. Don't complain because this is what you asked for."

"Maybe another person could help me. We could each do half."

"No way."

When I wanted to go to the bathroom he wouldn't let me go. And there was a lot of bleach. Behind the belt was where they washed the chicken in the bleach. The bleach ran through a drain. Here was the counter and right below was the draining bleach. The chicken was also covered in bleach. I was sneezing all the time, and my eyes were always watering, and I could hardly see. Sometimes I said, "I can't see. My eyes hurt. Let someone help me, please."

And no one helped me. When I asked to go to the bathroom the supervisor told me I couldn't because there was nobody to take my place on the line. Sometimes I asked as many as ten times.

"Wait 15 minutes. Then you'll have your break."

But I had already been asking for two hours. They just kept saying no and no and no. Finally, after six months of that work they finally moved me to another position where my job was hanging the chickens on hooks. This was also hard work because many of the chickens were dirty, and I had to wash them before hanging them up. The knife I had to use was also very heavy. My arms and my shoulders hurt. I asked Mark why he put the other women, the Mexicans, to work putting plastic rings on the chickens, a red one if the chicken was dirty, and a green one if the gall had burst. They

Lupita

didn't have to stand to do it, all they had to do was sit and fasten those little rings.

"Why don't you let me work for awhile putting on the rings?

"No, I'm the boss here, and what I say goes, and this is where you need to work." He always said the same thing.

I was getting angry because I saw that when new women from Guatemala started he would always give them the hardest and heaviest work.

I asked, "Why do you give us, the Guatemalans, all the hardest work?" I was always protesting, and Casam said I was being racist, always talking only about the Guatemalan workers.

"I'm not racist. You are the racist. Because you give your people"—the Mexicans, because he was Mexican—"the easier jobs and you give those of us from Guatemala the hardest jobs. I've been watching you."

"*Ay, Señora*, you are always complaining."

When a new girl came to work they put her with me and asked me to show her the job.

"Teach this young lady how to work."

I said, "That's not my job. It's yours."

"No, you have to show her."

"But you are the supervisor."

She was so very young, maybe sixteen, and she introduced herself and asked my name.

I told her, "don't worry, I'm going to teach you. I just had to talk

Shattered Dreams

to him that way. The supervisors aren't good people. They want all the easy work and make us do all the hard stuff. But they don't pay me more. They pay very little, and then they want us to do their work."

"Don't worry," she said, "I'm going to learn."

The two of us started to take the chickens off the hooks, clean them, and throw them into the barrel. There were chickens that weighed as much as eight or ten pounds.

One evening I told my son that when I got home from work I was exhausted from picking up the heavy chickens. My son was weight lifting and he had weights at home.

"Mom, I'm going to help you. I'll teach you how to use my weights and that way you'll get used to lifting heavy things."

Once I started doing the exercises, the work with the chickens wasn't as hard. But when they saw how I picked up the heavy chickens and threw them, they saw I was strong enough to do it and they made me work alone.

"Why do I have to do everything all by myself. I'm a woman. I get tired."

"You're just a complainer, full of sour grapes."

"I complain, but I do the job. You're a man, but you wouldn't be able to take what I'm doing."

"And who says I can't?"

"Come up here and pick up this knife and work for a full day. I know you wouldn't be able to do it."

Not even a man could handle the kind of work I had to do.

I remember once when they decided to put Esmeralda—she's

Lupita

the one with the GPS on her ankle—in my job, but Esmeralda's husband is Mexican so he was able to help her. Again, I said I didn't think that was fair.

"You're always looking around, watching everything, spying."

"Yes, I am. I see everything. When someone from Mexico starts to work here you give them the easiest jobs, but when it's a Guatemalan you make us load the chickens and do all the heavy work. Even the Mexican men get easier jobs then the Guatemalan women. Why do you do that?"

Then he asked me, "How can you tell?"

"I watch you when you're talking to someone else, and I can read your lips. I know when you are saying bad things about Guatemala."

"Maybe, but this is what you asked for—a shift change."

Whenever I saw Casam I asked for a raise. When I told him I wasn't earning very much he would always say, "Sebastián earns a lot!"

"My husband doesn't do my job; I do my own work."

"If you want to work, fine, but if you don't, go home," was always the response.

That's what they told everybody. They threatened us. If you wanted to keep your job you just shut up and took whatever they doled out.

There were rumors about an Immigration raid a short time before it happened. I asked Casam about it because I always went and talked directly to him with questions.

"Casam, is Immigration coming like people say?"

Shattered Dreams

"No, not true. Immigration can't enter the plant."

We were all hearing these same rumors so one day they told all of us to come to a meeting before going home after work that evening. We all had to attend.

Many workers were saying, "We're exhausted. We're covered with chicken poop. We're wet. We want to get out of these clothes. We want to go home."

"Nope, you have to wait."

At the meeting some of the Mexican supervisors told us in Spanish that we shouldn't skip work for fear of a raid because Immigration couldn't come into the plant. They said it was because Sholom was paying Immigration and for that reason they couldn't raid the plant. And the following days we just went back to work as usual.

I remember a really humiliating day for me. It was a Friday, and I asked Mark if I could go to the bathroom. I asked him over and over again and he paid no attention to me. He pretended not to hear me. Finally I said, "Mark, I've peed in my pants."

I was totally wet. He came running and said, "Go to the bathroom. Go clean yourself up."

I went to the bathroom, but it was too late.

The following Sunday, when I was back working, I said to Mark, "Can I please go to the bathroom?"

And he started to tease me, "Yes, you'd better go to the bathroom before you wet your pants."

"Well," I said, "maybe wetting my pants was worth it."

After a while they switched me from job to job—butchering,

hanging the chickens, putting on the red tags. My arms always ached. I was usually at the end of the line, so when the others finished and started their breaks I still had to finish.

The supervisor always said, "You have to hurry and work faster. There can't be any chickens left in the barrels when you take a break." By the time I made it through the remaining chickens, the others were coming back from break. That only left me with time to go to the bathroom but not to have anything to eat. I got angry and went to the main office. I asked the woman there why they couldn't give me a full break like everyone else. I was always left there hanging more chickens while the others were resting and eating. But the people in the office just said that was the way it was and that was my job.

When it was time for the afternoon break I said, "I can't work any longer. I haven't the strength." The work was really so hard.

The supervisor just said, "You're such a good worker. Go on back to your job."

I don't think he understood me. I don't think he could do anything other than give orders. It was when I was working with the very heavy chickens that I had the accident with my hand. The job was so, so, very hard. The knife went into my hand here on my palm and came out here on the other side. He wouldn't pay any attention to me at all. The next woman on the line said to me, "Go to the office for help. Just let him stay there chatting with his friends."

I didn't say anything to him but went directly to the office. I thought it was just a little cut, but when I went to the bathroom to wash it there was blood all over the place. The whole bathroom was full of blood!

One of the "green hardhat" supervisors, Filomena, was there and she said, "Son of a bitch, you really fucked up that hand! Get to the office right now."

When I got to the office all they did was wash my hand with hydrogen peroxide and wrap it, but it wouldn't stop bleeding. I remember that my brother Miguel came to see me.

"What happened?"

"I cut my hand, but it's no big deal."

"It looks pretty serious to me. Your work station was all bloody. I went to see."

"But they told me it wasn't anything serious."

They covered the cut with a lot of gauze. You can't see where the knife went in anymore, but here you can see where it came out. This line right here is the scar. The wound used to look pretty big, but it has shrunk a lot. I didn't even get a break after that. They didn't let me have even one day off. Nothing, nothing, nothing. I just went on working. I had to learn to work my fingers in a different way. When I picked up the containers of chicken my cut would open up and started bleeding again. I had to work only with the knives again because I couldn't lift the heavy loads. When my hand was better I told them that I could hang up the chickens part of the time, and they got mad at me for wanting to change.

I told them, "I don't want to keep doing the same thing all day. You change jobs for others all the time, but the Guatemalan women are always stuck here."

We were also paid less. Esmeralda, for example, earned $7.75 an hour and I only earned $7.25.

My God, I thought, it's only because we're poor that they do this to us. If we had money we wouldn't work in these conditions.

After a lot of asking and asking and a lot of exhaustion, they

Lupita

finally allowed me to work depluming the chickens. By that time they had started to fire a lot of people. I had been working taking the feathers off the chickens for only a week when they fired me. They told me that there wasn't any more work and that they had to lay off people. I cried, and so did a lot of other people. Eighty people left that day. They fired eighty people! When we left they told us that if they needed more people to work they would call us. I was sure they would never call me because I always demanded my rights and they never paid any attention to me.

At home, Sebastián asked me what had happened. I told him how all of us had been fired. He went to talk to the people in the office to get my job back, but they said no. I went back on Sunday to see if I could get in. Esmeralda was back at work. She was fired the same day I was. And Tracy, Mark's niece, was working, too, and a lot of others, but they didn't call me. It was like the fourth day, and I stopped coming to the plant every morning, when an "orange hardhat" [manager] went to Sebastián and asked him why I hadn't come back to work. Sebastián told him that nobody had called me. The supervisor told him that I needed a new ID to get back inside the plant, but that they needed me and wanted me back. But where could I get the documentation? We didn't know who had the IDs. How could we bring a new ID if we didn't have one? In the end, thank God, I wasn't able to go back because if I had I would have been taken in the raid.

While I was working at the plant they caused so many problems—abuse of children, and abuse of expecting mothers, too. My cousin's wife was pregnant and she began to have contractions right there in the plant, and they took her to the hospital from there, so her baby was born on her last day of work. They didn't give you any breaks for any reason.

They didn't let us do anything. When I was working in "*cadap*" I ended up losing a lot of weight and went down to 105 pounds.

Shattered Dreams

I was very skinny.

Union people came to the plant to see if we could organize. That's how we met *Don* Felipe. He asked us to sign for the Union but we said that if we signed we would be fired. We said we wanted to work and needed the jobs.

After the people from the Union showed up, Casam asked me, "Did you sign for the Union?"

"No, I didn't."

"Yes, you did. They told me you did."

"Who told you that? Show me that person!"

"No, but I know you signed."

"No, I didn't."

Then there was another large meeting for the workers. They gave us fliers with drawings of little devils. They said to us that the Union people were devils, that the Union was Immigration and couldn't come into the plant. They told us the organizers were bad people who didn't want us to work for the plant. That's what happened when the Union came, and that's why nobody signed up. The company also said that some lawyers were going to come to help us and that we were going to get really good insurance.

One of the rabbis rented a room in the church where Mr. Boss preaches. They asked us to meet there. I went to the meeting and asked if I could get a work permit. I took my passport and all my documents. They asked me if I had some witness, someone who was a citizen of the U.S. and could say how long I had been in the country, and that I had paid taxes and other things. There were so many requirements, and we didn't understand or have what they asked for. We said we didn't have the documents they were asking for so they said they couldn't get our papers. I still have all of the documents I could gather. I thought that at least one day they would be worth having. I gave them to the lawyer after the raid so that she could see all the promises they made at the plant, all the broken promises.

They told us that there would always be work for our whole families, for all the parents and grandparents. We would never be without work. And we believed all that until what happened [the raid] happened. But I'm angrier at Immigration because we were working, and even though the work was terribly hard, we had jobs. We were able to help our families in Guatemala. I helped my parents and my brothers back home. Now we have no money because of what Immigration did. We suffered a lot of trauma because of what happened and what continues to happen, and worrying about what will happen. After the raid, my oldest son didn't want to go to school anymore. He said to us,

"Why should I study? In this country we're nobody."

Shattered Dreams

Sebastián

Part I: Sebastián tells of his trip north in an interview

I was living in my village of San Antonio Aguas Calientes, in Guatemala, and working, but unfortunately I faced a lot of discrimination. I worked as a chauffeur, driving a car for a wealthy woman who had tons of everything but treated me very bad.

I can tell you about one thing that happened, as an example. I had to brake suddenly like happens to any of us if someone just appears in front of the car. You're not going to just drive over them! So I hit the brakes and the *Señora* started to scold me and asked me, "Why did you do that?" I told her a guy on a bike had just gone in front of the car without paying any attention, but she didn't like that explanation because she was sitting in the back seat reading the newspaper. She said, "Watch out!" and then hit me on the head with the paper. She told me to be more careful if I wanted to keep my job. At that time I was supporting my wife and my children so I didn't have a choice and I just had to put up with it. After awhile I got tired of her abuse and that's when I decided to come here to the United States.

Before working as a chauffeur I was in the National Police force during the governments of Vinicio Cerezo, Jorge Serrano Elias and Ríos Montt. Now it's called the Civil Police. During that time I wasn't earning much either, but I was lucky to be assigned to serve the ambassador of El Salvador, and that's really when my adventures began. He was very kind to me, a real ambassador. Yes, he was a politician, but he was very good to me. He knew that I could be trusted, and I did security for him, and he gave me really

Sebastián

beautiful weapons to use—Uzis, nine millimeters, thirty eights—guns I had never seen before.

We got along well, and I was happy with that position, but after awhile he told me that he didn't want to see me suffering in the police force and earning so little. He wanted me to leave and said he would talk to the government to let me resign because in those days you couldn't quit the police immediately but had to give at least one month's notice. But he helped me, and he filled out some document that I took to the Head of Police who let me leave right away. Then he got me the job with the *Señora*, and you know how that went!

And so that's how I decided to come to the U.S. I remember that my parents were crying.

When I left my wife, Lupita, at home, she was crying, too, and said "Please don't go." It was a Sunday morning at dawn when I left. Through a friend, I had found someone to help me get to the U.S., and I put the 7,000 *quetzales* I would need to pay for the trip in my underwear. I tied the money firmly in my pants, and my father said to me, "But you aren't very safe. Take this machete," and he gave me an enormous knife. "If anything happens to you, you can use it." That was because I had so much money in my underwear.

I remember my parents took me to a place they call "*el trébol*" in Guatemala City. That's where you can get all the buses to the coast. As I got on the bus, they were crying, and I told them, "First of all, I'm going in the name of God, so pray to God that I make it," and I got onto the bus. I said to the driver, "I want to go to Quatepeque" because I had the name of the *coyote*. I remember his name was Charlie, and he was from that town. At that moment, I felt—well, I find it hard to explain. I felt very sad because I had left my wife and children crying, and my parents said that was the last time I would ever see them, and that's basically true. It's been 15 years, and I haven't seen my mother and father since I left them on the road as the bus drove away. Fortunately, my wife is here with me now.

I left Guatemala City at 3:00 a.m. and arrived in Quatepeque at 8:00 in the morning. When I arrived I felt a little confused, but the *coyote* had told me to find a taxi, so I went up to one and said "Do you know, Mr. such-and-such?" And the driver said, "Yes," so I asked him how much it would cost for him to take me to the *coyote*'s house. It was 15 *quetzales*, so I took the taxi, and we had to drive up into some mountains, and then I could see like a little hill where the *coyote* lived. The taxi driver asked me if the man I was looking for lived there, and I said he did. But the driver went to the door to be sure it was the right place, and it was. When I got out of the taxi, I asked the driver if he would like the machete, and he said, "Yes", so I gave the machete I had been traveling with to him. It was a big machete with a very sharp blade. And I went into the *coyote*'s house.

"Are you the one who phoned me? Is your name such-and-such? Okay, come on in."

He called to his wife and told her to get me something to eat.

We went into a room, and the *coyote* asked me how much money I had.

"7,000 *quetzales*," I told him.

"Where is it?"

"I have it with me."

"Don't be worried," he said.

And I could see that there were other men from my village there, so I thought that he wasn't lying and I could trust him. I rolled down my pants and reached inside my underwear, and I

Sebastián

gave him the money. There were about five more men there and when I got a good look it made me laugh because they were all from Calderas, sitting around and talking and waiting to leave. They were all people I knew from home. So the *coyote* called his wife and told her to bring the food and said to me that the next day we were going to talk. She gave me all sorts of food—beans, eggs. A good meal.

He told me to sleep well because, "Tomorrow you're going to get up early. The first thing you have to do is study the Mexican national anthem."

These are the tricks you have to learn to make it all the way through Mexico. The *coyote* told us that when the police asked us if we were from Mexico, if we said yes, they would say, "Okay, let's hear you sing the national anthem." And then you would sing it for them. "And who is the president? And who is the mayor of your town?" For example, the *coyote* told me "You are from this town, and your mayor is Mr. X." And he told me that I was from San Luis Potosí, and he told others they were supposedly from Arriaga, and so on with everyone. He had a tape of the national anthem and we would sing along with it and practice. And in the end we could remember a little of it.

There were some twelve people who were going to cross the border. The day before we left, the *coyote* got really drunk. He said we were ready, that we had studied well, but that we weren't going to leave until the following day. He said he was going to get drunk to ask the road for good luck. We were getting ready for the next day, and I remember that I still had 300 *quetzales* from the trip. It wasn't going to be of any use to me, because we were going to be leaving the country. I gave the money to the *coyote*'s wife for her to give back to my wife, and my passport, too, but in the end I found out she had just kept them.

And that's how our adventure began. It's really strange to watch a *coyote* who knows all the tricks. For example, I was wearing a new pair of shoes from Guatemala because he had told us what kind he wanted us to have—black shoes, really, really black. So the *coyote* had his own cobbler who would cut the shoes like this, and take this part out, and then we all were carrying Mexican pesos in both shoes. Every single one of us had money in our shoes. So for example, the *coyote* had a lot of money with him, but if the money ran out, he took some from each of us to pay the expenses. He had that special cobbler who put thousands of pesos in our shoes, and we would walk around as if nothing was up. We would be shooting the breeze and strolling around just like normal because the money was wrapped in plastic. In Mexico they don't seem to detect the fact that people might carry money that way.

So we started on the trip, and I remember that one day we arrived in Tapachula. I think it was December 14, 1989—or 1987— and the following day was going to be Guatemalan Independence Day. The *coyote* put us in a hotel for two days. I must have been about 23 years old then. It was a great *fiesta* in Tapachula. On the 15th it was pouring rain, I remember, but the *coyote* was awful. He wanted to leave then, but we couldn't because he said the border patrols were watching more than usual and there were more police than most of the time because they thought many Guatemalans would feel more confident during the *fiesta* and try to cross the border into Mexico to make it to the United States. There were also a lot of roadblocks set up.

In the end we had to wait until the 17th to cross into Mexico. We slipped past a border patrol post and that was really hard for me because they chased us shooting all the way. We were carrying jugs of water, and—*híjole*!—one of the guys who was carrying the most water dropped it all because he couldn't handle it. We were running and running.

There, near Tapachulas, was a place they call Chahuites. At

Sebastián

8:00 in the evening the *coyote* told us we were going to take a bus to Chahuites, but we weren't going to go all the way into town. He went to the bus driver to arrange for us to get off at a certain place, and then we were supposed to run really fast into the brush because there were a lot of thieves in that area. So the bus got to a place in the road near a border crossing, and it had to make like a U-turn to head towards Chahuites. And we did what we were told and ran into the brush, but we were chased and shot at by those Mexican bandits. But we didn't stop. It was raining hard that day, and we hid in the woods, and thank God the Mexican immigration guys were inside their sentry post to stay out of the rain and keep dry. Since it was raining so hard, they couldn't see. There were some soldiers as well, but they were in the hut out of the rain, too, and that's how we were able to get past. We all got together there in the rain, and I was thinking there was not going to be any bed for me that night. We were all kind of helping each other to not fall down in the mud.

The twelve of us hadn't gone far from the immigration booth and we had to go very slowly because, as you know, when you walk in water, the water makes noises. And since it was water and mud, our shoes kept getting stuck, and the *coyote* didn't want us to make noise, and we were just like frogs—*plaff, plaff*. So we went really slowly and managed to get past the shack, and I remember we walked about four hours more to get as far as possible from there. We came to a bridge alongside a road, where buses and cars and everything were driving past. We were inside Mexico now, and the *coyote* told us we had passed the first immigration post, but there were four more to go. And, the last one, that one is in Laredo, Texas.

"Son of a bitch" I said. All the time I was asking myself, "Are we about there yet?"

"Don't even think about it," my friends said. "It's still really *faaaaaar* away." So that's what happened, and we slept beside the bridge.

As we were traveling, I never lost sight of the *coyote*. I stuck to him, wherever he went. I remember he told us to huddle together back to back to sleep. No one could sleep lying down, just resting against something. He told us we would take turns; each one of us would be a look-out for an hour. He said, "First it's your turn, then it's your turn," and he gave us a watch to know when to wake up the next person. We were watching to see if there were any cars, or any animal, or any other thing coming too close. There we were sleeping right next to the bridge, and it was pretty hard because we were all wet.

We all got up at about 4:00 a.m., and the *coyote* said "I'm going to the road now and I'm going to signal one of the buses, but I'm only going to go with four of you because if the driver sees 12 of us all together he won't stop. And as soon as you see the bus is stopped, the rest of you come running as fast as you can to get on."

And that's what we did. I was wet all over—my shoes, my shirt, everything—but the bus did stop, and the *coyote* talked to the driver who said "Okay," and he paid for all of us, but everyone on the bus was looking at us because they knew we were *mojados* [wetbacks] that we were from Guatemala or El Salvador. They only had to look at our faces. It was about 3:00 or 4:00 in the morning. They were all going to work, and we were going to cross the border.

We were headed to a place called Esquintla. This was precisely right after Hurricane Mitch, and that's another reason I came here to the U.S., because we had some terrible storms, and my house was destroyed, and everything was in ruins in Guatemala. So, when we got to Esquintla, everything was destroyed there, too—the bridges, the river beds. We stayed there all morning. We didn't eat anything because we had gotten separated for a while, and the town wasn't very big. But the people were very hard-working. They

Sebastián

were farmers and farmhands and every morning they would start work at 6:00 or 7:00 a.m.

During the time of Mitch, for people to cross over the river to the other town, everyone had to use a zip line. Since the bridge had been destroyed, nobody could get across—not buses, not anyone—because the bridge had fallen and the river was full of rocks, and trees and more. Soldiers and firefighters were helping people get across with the zip lines and then helping them back to the other side after the day's work.

I don't think they were paying any attention to if we were legal or illegal. They just asked, "Where are you going." "To the other side." "Okay." And that's how we crossed, but the bridge was almost a half a mile long, the river was so wide. So we were suspended up high, and I could look down into the river and see the trees and the rocks it was carrying, and I mean rocks. Big boulders. Everyone else was crossing, too, and on the other side more buses were waiting. There were also people selling food— *atole, tostadas* and everything—for people to take to work with them. In the end, they didn't ask us if we were Guatemalans or immigrants or anything. They just wanted to get people to the other side of the river.

From there we went to another town, and I don't even remember its name. This town had also been destroyed by the hurricane and there was only one hotel left, but people could still stay there. It made me think of Old West movies, where there is one hotel in town all by itself and everyone comes to stay there. The *coyote* was familiar with that hotel, and we ended up staying there for almost a week. We would go to the river to bathe. It was a dirty river, the water wasn't clear, and it had all sorts of things floating in it. We looked for places where the river slowed down and pooled a little, and that's where we would wash in the dirty water. We had to watch out and if anything looked suspicious we would get back into the hotel.

Shattered Dreams

The hotel was almost deserted, but we were afraid to leave it for long. The *coyote* said we should go to bathe in the river only three at a time. One of those days one of my friends was at the river bathing when a helicopter landed nearby, and since he was curious he went to look at it. It was a military helicopter.

They asked him, "What are you up to?" "Nothing." "Okay, come over here and lend us a hand." And they had him unloading sacks of corn from the helicopter. We were all laughing like crazy, and the *coyote* was furious.

"Son of this and son of that! They're going to take you away. I can't be responsible for you."

And later on the guy was laughing so hard, "I was working with the army." And that's the kind of thing that happened.

Finally, we were able to get out of that town, and we walked to a place called Arriaga. Much of the time we were walking, all night every night through the fields and the hills. In all, we walked about two months. Yes, two months on foot. A little ways by bus, then walking, a little more by bus, then more walking. I remember the day we arrived in Arriaga. It was a very pretty place. We went to the outskirts to stay for awhile. There was nothing there but rocks, except there was a tremendous water tank, but other than that it was horrible. And I remember that we spent a week or two there. I don't remember exactly why we couldn't leave, but I think it was because there were so many check-points set up by immigration and the army. The place where we were was pure wilderness. We could see from there—see the soldiers—but no one could see us.

While we were there the *coyote* brought us everything we needed, food and everything else. I was getting really bored and anxious, but I was always as close as possible to the *coyote*. We were still all together, the same guys who had started out. On the first day there we couldn't sleep, and on the second day it was the same.

The *coyote* said that every night the water tank would empty out so, "We can all sleep inside the water tank, but at 5:00 a.m. we'll have to get up because at 5:00 they fill the tank again."

And it was true. At 11:00 p.m. the *coyote* had a flashlight to show us the way, and all the water was gone from the tank because the people had used it all up during the day. The tank was totally dry and very big. There was a little entry on top, and a ladder, and we took off the lid and set it beside the tank.

We went into the tank and it wasn't cold in there. I didn't get very far from the *coyote*, I didn't go deep into the tank but slept right next to the ladder, in case anything happened, so that I could run. And everything was exactly like he said because at 4:50 in the morning you could hear the water whistling—*whooooooo*—and we were all racing to get out. A lot of the guys wanted to sleep deep inside the tank because they slept better there, but not me. The water tube was pretty wide, and the tank filled up fast, and we all had to be outside because if anyone stayed in they would have died there.

Finally the *coyote* came and told us we were leaving the next day. From the place where we were hiding we could see pretty far, but there was a curvy stretch that we couldn't see beyond. We were taking buses. The *coyote* kept checking for us, and a first group went on the bus and passed the area we were worried about. Then we were on a bus and were going to pass through the same area and all of a sudden we saw soldiers. The *coyote* told the driver to stop because we couldn't go any further. Thank God, he stopped. "I'll stop, but you better be quick." We were heading right towards the Immigration police, and the driver stopped only a minute, and we were climbing one on top of the other trying to get out when we saw that patrol getting close to us.

Shattered Dreams

I was right behind the *coyote*, and we were all running like a herd of sheep—jumping and jumping and jumping through the weeds and bushes. There was barbed wire, but I ran right over the *coyote*. We kept on going until we were in heavy brush. The Mexican police won't follow people into those areas, but we thought they were following us and kept going. Finally a long ways away we hid in a gully at the foot of a tree when we realized we were right on top of a beehive. We were running away from Immigration, and we were running away from the bees. That trip was really awful—terrible—but we finally made it past that town, too.

Along the way we were eating all sorts of foul things. We only ate canned food. We ate sardines, bread, stale tortillas, and everything until we got to the border. The *coyote* had us carry Mexican pesos in our belts, too. If the police searched us they would take the money. They took money from me. One day we were on a bus and some police made us get off. They're very clever at this. I don't know how they do it, but they just look at your face quickly and can tell you're from Guatemala. All of the people on that bus were Mexican except us. I was sitting next to a man who was very elegant, with a nice business suit. I don't know if he was maybe a doctor or lawyer or what, but I sat down right next to him. There were some newspapers, so I started to read.

When a police van stopped and the officers got out, they came onto the bus and went straight to the back. I was at the front, near the driver. I saw that the police were bringing my friends up to the front of the bus.

"You, you, and you, off," they said.

I didn't know how they managed to do that. I told myself to just play dumb, when an officer came up to me and said, "You, too."

"Me?"

Sebastián

"Yeah, you. Come on." "Oh, shit," I said.

I got off and went over to the others. There were five of us. The police asked me where I was from.

"San Luis Potosí."

"Okay, what part of San Luis Potosí?"

"From such-and-such place."

"And who is your mayor?"

"Mr. So-and-so."

"Who is the President?"

"García."

"Well, come on now," they said to me, "You aren't Mexican. Tell us the truth. No way are you Mexican. Mexicans don't talk like that, you jerk. People from San Luis Potosí don't talk that way."

"And how do you want me to talk to you?" I asked.

"No, you're Guatemalan, not Mexican. Come on, tell me the truth or I'll deport you. How much money do you have with you?"

"But, I'm Mexican."

"And you're still giving me that line? Look, do you want to be deported? How much money do you have?"

"*Ay*, I'm sorry, officer. I am from Guatemala."

Oh, I had forgotten. The *coyote* had given us a kind of ID, and I showed it to the police.

Shattered Dreams

"That ID isn't from Mexico," he said. "So, how much cash do you have?"

I said I had 500 pesos, but I told him I couldn't give it all to him. "I'm asking you to leave me with 100 pesos for the journey.

I'm heading north."

"That's what we like. Now you're telling us the truth."

"But please leave me with at least 100 pesos for the road. I have to pay my way."

The bus was waiting for us.

"Give us the money."

"No, please leave me with 100."

"No, 100 pesos, no, but I'll let you keep 50."

"Okay, just go to hell."

So I turned all my money over to the police and they gave me 50 pesos back. I got back on the bus a lot poorer. They also let the others go, but they took money from them, too. They took all the money some had, and they left.

At that time we were on our way to Mexico City. It was funny to us that the buses didn't let people off at stops on the highway but all go directly to the main bus station. When we got to the central bus station in the capital, they made us all get off, like they do in airports. I grabbed a newspaper, like I was a reporter or something, and there I was reading my newspaper. There were police all over the station, on every floor, watching over everything. What I wanted to do was get out of there, find an exit. There was one of my friends right behind me, walking next to some lady, and I could see

Sebastián

that they were going after him. There was nothing I could do. They caught him, and they took away everything he had. They searched him all over, made him strip down to his underwear, and even took his shoes because they knew about the money people hide there. He had money all over the place and they took it all and even left him shoeless. And the *coyote* was furious.

"Why did you let them do that? Why couldn't you find a way to explain yourself to them?" and on and on. "I don't have any more money to keep supporting you." The police had taken money from almost all of us, most of the money that we had left. The *coyote* still had more money with him because he was aware of all the dangers and how to get by.

And that was what it was like until we got to the border, near Laredo, Texas. And it was even worse there, it was incredible. We went to a park, I don't remember the name, but it was a beautiful park. We didn't have any more money for food. I only ate nuts from the trees in the park. I don't know what kind they were. They would fall from the trees, and I would eat them like peanuts. Soon I had to do something I had never done in my own country—beg. I would watch the people in the parks with their barbecues; grilled steak and all the family having fun together. My heart would break watching them with their children, all eating meat, drinking their sodas and beers—happy—everybody looking clean and healthy. And I was dirty. I stunk, and my hair was long, just like a thief.

One day I saw a couple that had a lot of meat left over. I went over to ask them if they had a little bit of meat they could give me.

"Yes," they said. "Take all of this. And take some tortillas that we didn't eat."

I was so happy to get all that food and the bottles of soda that were only half empty. I took it all back to the *coyote* to share it with the other guys. We would all eat together. Each of us had to go out and find food, like little ants searching everywhere. The *coyote* just waited where he was for us to bring him food and everything. At that time there weren't other people in Laredo doing what we were doing there on the border.

In the end we had spent about 20 days there when the *coyote* said to us, "Tomorrow we're going to cross the river. The river is just a short walk from here. Let's go have a look at it so you know what to expect."

So, we went to see the river. You call it the Rio Grande, but we call it the *Río Bravo*. There was the river, and on the other side was the United States. This is Mexico; if we're over there, that's the U.S. And I was amazed because I thought I could just go over there and then I'd be in the United States just like that.

But the *coyote* said, "It's not so easy. What we have to do is get across without Immigration catching us."

"And what is that," I said, "Immigration? What is this Immigration?"

Well, in the end I crossed the *Río Bravo* ten times before I was successful. The road to the other side was long and difficult. I crossed once, they sent me back. I crossed again, and they sent me back, and so on. Immigration got to know me well. I was back and forth.

One day one of the Immigration guys said, "If you're planning on crossing again, please do it someplace else." I think he was really bored with me. "Whatever you do, don't let me catch you again. If you want to get into the U.S., please cross at some other spot. I catch you every day." He was kind of laughing, and I thought it was pretty funny.

Another funny thing happened when we were crossing one day. Normally we crossed in our underwear because we would carry

Sebastián

everything else—pants, shirt, shoes—over our heads to keep them dry. We had only one hand free to do whatever we needed. The *coyote* was the first to cross. That day it was nearly dawn. We were all in single file, holding hands as we went through the water, but this time we had only removed our pants. All of a sudden it felt like one of my friends was going to fall. No, wait a minute, I'm lying. One of my feet went into a deeper spot in the river. You know, sometimes there are uneven places in the river, and when my foot went down, I dropped my pants and let go of my friend's hand. Everyone began to yell at me.

"Son of a bitch, son of this, son of that."

"What the fuck was that all about?"

"What are you doing?"

"Go to hell."

What could I do? My pants and my belt were being carried away by the river, so I let go of his hand to grab for them, but they were gone anyway. We were near the shore, but when we got out of the water I didn't know what I was going to do without pants. But God is so great that I saw a tree and caught in its branches was a pair of pants. I grabbed them. "What a mess" I said to myself, because they were much too big for me but at least they covered me up. But when we had finally crossed the border that time, Immigration was already waiting for us.

Whenever they sent us back across the border, they deported the *coyote* along with us. This is why I say that the one person I stuck to all the time was him. When he wasn't nearby I was full of doubt. I had to be with him as much as possible so he wouldn't abandon me because I had paid him a lot of money. If I went with someone else I would have lost him and lost my money. And finally he began to mistreat me and complain.

"Why did you do this, or this, or that," he would grumble.

And I would say, "Go screw yourself."

Each time they caught us they took us in to get our names and fingerprints. And then we would say we were Mexican so they always took us back to the bridge between Mexico and Laredo, Texas. But we had to be really careful there because there were plenty of thieves, and the *coyote* was real insistent that we get away from that spot on the border as soon as we were turned loose at the bridge. Once you are on the U.S. side of the bridge it's safe, but on the other side it's bad. And this is what happened, ten times.

Finally the *coyote* was fed up with us. He said this was the worst trip he had ever made because all the things that had happened to us never happened during his other crossings. He said most of his trips were direct, and if there were any problems they lasted two or three days. But we had been trying to get across for two months, and we were never successful. He told us he was tired of us. By then most of our group had actually been able to get to the other side without getting caught. On the last trip I had been caught again but most [of the others] made it. I stayed in the park by myself because the *coyote* didn't want to try with me again. It was raining hard, and I spent the night sleeping in a tree, just like a monkey. It was freezing up there, and we didn't have sweaters or anything, just a shirt and slacks. I couldn't sleep on the ground because there were so many thieves, and they could kill you. I was up in that tree crying bitterly because they had left me there, but the next morning I saw the *coyote* walking through the park because he had been caught and deported again.

The group had left me behind that time because some money I was waiting for hadn't arrived. The *coyote* was treating me so bad

Sebastián

because I had asked a relative in the U.S. to send me some money and he wouldn't. So the *coyote* said that as far as he was concerned he couldn't count on my money anymore. If they wouldn't send any more from the U.S. then I wasn't important to him and he could leave me wherever he wanted. But I continued to struggle. I cried a lot, the road was long and hard. The *coyote* told the others that the following day would be the last time he would try.

"You know what?" he said. "I'm sick of all of you. If they catch me it's all over. I'm coming back to Mexico and then going home to Guatemala, and you all can figure out what the hell you're going to do here. I've lost a lot of money because of you."

The next day at 5:00 a.m. they tried one more crossing. The *coyote* left me behind, as I said, because I didn't have any more money. The park was about an hour's walk from the border, so they had all left at about 4:30. I was crying and crying, and I just couldn't think of what to do. I didn't have any money to call relatives to tell them I was there all by myself, that the *coyote* had abandoned me, that I was so lonely. I thought about going back to Guatemala, but how? I had no more money left.

I was there in the park eating the nuts that fell from the trees, and I was so sad, but then I saw a friend from the same group of Guatemalans I had come with. His name is Alfredo. I hugged him, and he hugged me.

"You're still here?" he said.

"Yes, I'm here all by myself." And I was crying.

When they say that men don't cry it's not true; men do cry and I cried a lot that day.

"I didn't make it" he said. "Immigration sent me back. The others got across, but they caught me. That's why I'm here now."

Shattered Dreams

"And what are we going to do now that all the others made it to the other side?" I asked.

"Should we go back to Guatemala? Should we stay in Mexico?"

"Maybe we should turn ourselves in to Immigration," I said. "But it's all over. We have no money. The only thing is I still owe a lot of money in Guatemala that I borrowed to pay for the trip, and if we don't find jobs in the U.S. they'll kill us."

But then I said, "Let's try to cross tomorrow one more time, early in the morning, just the two of us with the help of God." And he agreed. I remember we used to call this friend *"conejo"* [rabbit]. We waited all that day eating those nuts from the trees because we had no money. We slept in a garbage bin next to the park, one of those big green ones, because there were so many thieves around. It was raining hard that day. There were a lot of things in that trash bin that stunk badly, but there we were inside it sleeping. We didn't have a watch or anything, so we just guessed the time and got up. We walked all the way through the city. There was a lot of water everywhere, but I felt pretty good because we had already gone this way before, and we knew exactly where the bridge was between Mexico and the U.S. We hid under the bridge. The *coyote* had shown us a place where the water in the *Río Bravo* was shallower. And there we were just the two of us. It made me sad when at that very moment the crickets and the frogs began to sing. It was near dawn, and the birds were starting to sing, too. I would really like to have a recording of those sounds.

Just on the other side of the bridge there was an Immigration truck with four big spotlights illuminating the bridge. We had been told before that sometimes they're watching the bridge with those lights but really they're sleeping. We listened very closely for a while. There was also one light shining on the river.

"Okay, let's cross, in the name of God" I said. "I think those

Sebastián

S.O.B.s are asleep. Let's get down really low, and let's not take our clothes off this time."

We went across the river very slowly, and I don't think they ever saw us because they were sleeping. But on the other side of the river it was all swampy and full of reeds and you could hear all the crickets and other things. So we made it across the river, and it was about 5:00 a.m. We walked up a little hill towards a road for the Immigration vans. Right then one of the Immigration cars was coming along the road, and I said to my friend, "Immigration!" So we raced back down into a gully, and they shined their light but couldn't see anyone. When we saw that they had left, and looked down all the streets and couldn't see anyone, we came out. We were all wet. That's why they call us wetbacks, because when we get out of the river we are really wet. It's a terrible word, *mojado*, and it's very offensive to some people to be called that.

We started into the city. Beyond about the first five blocks it was safe. Crossing one, two, three blocks you could run into Immigration. So after crossing the river we made it five blocks and then the dogs started to bark. You know, dogs can condemn you, too, because when they start barking and making noise the agents suspect there is someone walking around and they'll come right away to see.

But that day was so great that while we were heading back to the river to hide, there was a person who lived right next to it, a Hispanic, who called to us to ask what was wrong. He had a little door that opened on to a small room and from there he could see outside, and he told us to come into his house. There was another man with him. We were pretty scared because we didn't know if they were going to turn us in or if they were going to kill us. But they told us to hide inside their house and that soon Immigration would come by looking for us, and it was true. In a few minutes they showed up and drove by the house very slowly. There was like a porch and the agents got out of the van and were poking around there to see if they could find us. Finally they left.

The man who was in the house asked us, "Where are you going? Are you headed north? How much money do you have?"

We hardly had any money left after crossing the border. I said I didn't have any money, and my friend had seven dollars.

"Only seven dollars," the guy said. "You think you're going north with seven dollars? No way."

"But we know a friend who's waiting for us in a house near here."

"Who is this friend of yours?"

"Well, I don't know exactly the name of the place but it's just up that way."

"Okay," he said. "I know that house, and I can take you there. Give me the seven bucks."

He had a big car like a Pontiac parked out in front of the house, and he had a daughter about ten years old. "*M'ija*," he said, "go out and start up the car for me."

And then he said to us, "When I tell you to, go out and get into the car. I'm going to take you where you need to go so Immigration won't catch you. When I tell you to get into the car, do it fast. I'm going to help you, but for seven dollars I can just get you to a safer place. If you can get a few more blocks from the border you'll be okay.

The car was running and his daughter, just a little thing, maybe five or six years old, came into the house and said, "*Papá*, there's nobody around." And he said to us, "Okay. Run, *cabrones*." And we raced into the car. They seemed to have a system all worked out. Right near the house there was a stop sign. The man told his daughter to walk in that direction, and he followed her in the car with us crouched down in the back seat. When the daughter got to the stop sign she signaled him, and the car went ahead and crossed the street. Then he stopped to pick up his little girl and drove us two more blocks where we got out. He was using his daughter as a look-out to see if Immigration was around, and, for seven dollars, drove us just like a taxi. We knew the way to the safe house and made it there by dawn.

Everyone was lying around asleep. It was about 6:00 a.m. The house was under construction, and I guess they just abandoned it. It had two floors. I saw that the house was filthy—trash here, there, everywhere. But that was where we slept. When the *coyote* saw us, he was surprised.

"You're here?"

"Yes, well we got across."

"That's what I like! Good Texas *coyotes*! You've got guts. So what happened?" And on and on he went.

But we still had to go from Laredo, Texas, to a place called Cotulla. We were already inside the United States but had to walk all night because it was very, very dangerous to be so close to the border. There were still tons of Immigration agents. We had already entered a lot of times that way but this was to be the last time. We walked and walked, and walked, and crossed streams and finally got to the railroad tracks at a spot where the *coyotes* said the trains stopped. He told us we would get on a train, and if it stopped at Cotulla we were supposed to get off there, but if it kept on going it would take us to directly to San Antonio. "But this is the last time I do this with you guys," the *coyote* said. "Whoever gets left behind is just left behind forever. This is it. I've already lost a lot of money because of you."

Shattered Dreams

All this time I was praying to God. I stuck to the *coyote* every step of the way. I decided that wherever he went, I would go, and if they caught him they would catch me, too. We were walking all night, in and out of *barrancos* that were full of snakes and skunks and all sorts of animals that run around in the desert. We got to a place full of cactus and had to try to hide because at six or seven every morning an Immigration helicopter would fly overhead checking on everything. We were close to the trains and one of them started to whistle—*tuuuuuuu*. The *coyote* told us that meant it was about to leave. And when it blows out air, that's when it's starting on its way. We were just a short ways away from the train, and the *coyote* told us to run and hide in the boxcars but to go really fast because the Immigration officers might see us. And while we were looking for a good car to jump into we saw that a helicopter had started to circle round, and we stopped running and hid in a ditch.

It was just like the movies, like a Vietnam War film. All of us huddled in that ditch and the helicopter circling overhead. And then the train started to move. "*Vámonos*. Let's go. Let's go." And we raced towards the railway cars, and the police saw us and started to chase us, and we jumped into one of the cars, and we saw that there were more people inside. They were Salvadoran and had been waiting to get on the train, too. But we got in with them. There was a pregnant women in the group and all this was very hard on her. Someone told us that the Immigration agents had called for reinforcements because there were so many people. So, the *coyote* told us to get off the train again, and it stopped so we jumped off. Three of us were off running again, feeling hopeless and bitter. There was no place to hide, not even a big rock or anything.

And then we saw that one of the box cars was open wide, but it had like iron bars for sliding doors. One friend got on first, and I followed. We were going to try to hide ourselves on top of the box car. When my friend tried to climb up higher, the iron door fell on top of him. When I saw what was happening I jumped head

Sebastián

first off the boxcar but my friend wasn't quick enough. He began to shout, "*Ay, Ay.* Oh, dear God, what have you done to me? *Ay, Ay.*" My head had almost been crushed, but I could see that his leg was all twisted. His foot was totally turned the opposite direction. And he started to yell, "*Ay, mamá, mamita.* Where are you, mommy?" over and over again.

I began to shout to the *coyote*, "Charlie! Charlie!" And the other train was starting up again—*sssssssss*. Everyone in the group had gathered around.

"*Mamá, mamá,*" he said, "my foot, my poor little foot, *mamita*, please." I could see that his foot was totally turned around as if he was just a rag doll. The *coyote* came running, "*Mi amor*, my love, what has happened to you? What's happened to your foot? No, it's all right, you'll be fine. Don't worry my dear one."

But then the *coyote* said to us, "We all just have to ignore what has happened. What are we going to do? Turn ourselves over to Immigration because of him? This is your last chance. The train is already leaving. What do you say?" And since we were all there for the same reason we decided to leave our friend. We said, "What can we do? He can't continue north now, and we won't have any other opportunities." And so we watched him there all by himself. He stayed and we left.

The *coyote* told him, "I'm going to leave you, *hijo mío*, my son."

But he did go and yell for the police to come and take care of our injured friend. And the train started to move and move, faster and faster, and we got into a boxcar and yelled to the *coyote*, "Charlie! Charlie, the train is leaving!" And the *coyote* didn't want to leave our friend's side, and he was crying and crying. "We don't want to leave you, but…"

You might not believe this but all of us in the boxcar were crying, too. The *coyote* came with us because this was the last chance to

Shattered Dreams

help us reach where we needed to go. He had an obligation to fulfill with all of us. And he did. We could see that there were helicopters flying all over the area, and the *coyote* told us not to lean out of the boxcar for any reason. He said he was going to get us safely to our destination. And it was true.

Later we heard that the guy we had left behind was taken to Houston. They amputated his leg and he was given a prosthesis. People were helping him to buy food and pay rent, and now he's back in Guatemala with his wife. It was very hard for his family and nobody wanted to tell them exactly what had happened. No one wanted to point the finger at a member of anyone's family. They were going to blame the *coyote*. Then I told people exactly what had happened because I witnessed everything.

Everyone calmed down. The most important thing was that he survived and is alive.

The evening after that accident we arrived in Cotulla and from there the *coyote* took us to San Antonio. Cotulla was up in the mountains, and we were picked up there and left in San Antonio. This was where the *coyote* left us. Even once in the U.S. it was still really hard. The first day I had nowhere to go and didn't know what to do, but the next day a friend from home who had been in Texas a long time showed up to help me. He was living like a Texan. He had come to pick up some other friends, and I asked him if he could help me, too. I said, "I don't know what to do."

"Okay, let's go," he said. He took me and showed me around and then I started to work for him.

I was working in construction. The job was very difficult because the ground was hard as a rock. I was only making enough money to eat. The *coyote* had told as that once a person gets here they only have to lean down to pick up gold from the streets— *chsssssss*—as if it were so easy! He said this and that, dollars here and dollars

Sebastián

there. It was pretty funny because while we were on the journey the *coyote* kept talking about car washes and how by just washing cars we could earn all sorts of money every week. And he said we could find other jobs, too. But once you're here it isn't the same. I hadn't understood before because they really do a good job of brainwashing you, but what they say is a lie. It never stopped being risky in Texas because even when we were doing construction work a helicopter came and we had to hide.

My family was very worried. I started to work and earned enough money to buy a phone card and so I was able to call and tell them that I was well. Then they were very happy. My father gave thanks to God that I was alive, and my wife and children cried, and my grandmother did, too. The whole family did. I complained bitterly to my wife that I didn't have a job, that I had no money, and that I was suffering a lot. And she told me not to be so sad, that at least I was in the United States and not just dumped somewhere along the border, thank God. I had decided myself to come to the U.S. so it was my job, my role, to continue working and that's what I've been doing.

I worked in Dallas for about a month. A friend from my village put me up or, better said, he lent me a hand. I remember well that when I got there my hair was very long from the two months of travel so my friend cut it for me. Then after three days he took me to work with him in construction. Manolo is my friend's name, and he's a very good person. The days passed, and we shared everything among ourselves and with other friends. One day my friend Manolo told me that there was a city called Postville with a company there and another man from my village was working there, and he said he would get his phone number.

On December 30, 1995, I talked to the guy in Postville, and he asked me my name and my father's name. And I told him who my mother and father were and that I was from San Antonio Aguas

Shattered Dreams

Calientes. I asked him his name, and he said, "Antonio" and that he knew me. I told him about all the hardship I had experienced on the way to the U.S. He said that in the Agriprocessors plant there was work, and good work with good money. He said it was a company that butchered chickens, cattle and lambs. He also said that the work was—excuse the expression—"pure shit," but I told him I knew what hard work was and it would be okay. I didn't have any money so he sent me some by Western Union to pay for my trip. The bus fare was $175 and I remember he sent me $250. He's a good friend, and knowing me from San Antonio Aguas Calientes he said he wanted to see me working here.

We left on a Saturday and arrived on Sunday. I was so happy that there was someone I knew waiting for me. When we got to the bus station and I saw my friend, we gave each other a big hug and he welcomed me and told me not to worry because he had a job and I wouldn't lack for anything. I thanked him and thanked him. He brought me to the city of Postville, gave me clothes and shoes, and told me to eat. He introduced me to his other friends, and they also welcomed me to their house, and I felt so happy. I gave thanks to God for all He was doing for me.

After a few days he told me that he would talk to the people at the plant about hiring me. After a week, they called me and asked me to go and apply for the job. I ran out of the house and to the plant. Before I left, my friend Antonio told me that the work was very hard and terribly filthy, but I answered that I didn't care. What I wanted was to work.

Part II: Written by Sebastián himself and describing work at the plant.

I started work on a Sunday. They gave me knives, an apron, and gloves and told me to begin at 5:00 that afternoon. When I started that afternoon they took me to a place they call *carap* ["cut up"]. It's a very cold place, and I started cutting off the chicken wings. It

Sebastián

wasn't easy at all because the belt the chickens were hanging from went by very fast and if I missed one they yelled at me. I had to do it, but I couldn't. They took me off that line and put me somewhere else. After awhile they put me in the area where they slaughter the chickens. There were four rabbis there who did the killing. My friend Antonio was working there, and I was glad because he showed me what to do. I saw how my friends from Guatemala had their faces all covered in chicken blood. I ended up staying in that area. My normal work there was in butchering, but after 2:30 a.m. we would sometimes go to cut-up.

They didn't give us much time to eat. We had to change clothes quickly because they yelled at us. There was a supervisor named Casam. I didn't think he was a very good person because he mistreated my Guatemalan companions and I couldn't do anything to help them. Our breaks were very short—we were supposed to have fifteen minutes but they let us have only ten. We ate in a very dirty place. I think pigs live better than we did. Our microwaves were old and dirty. I think they were from the '70s because they didn't heat the food well. There were only three of them anyway. People were eating their food cold. I remember that I only brought a sandwich. We didn't even take off the work aprons we were wearing, and we ate with our faces covered in blood and with chicken feathers on our faces and hands. They didn't give us any time to wash. The bathrooms were also filthy, and there was dirty paper all over the place.

Sometimes I just kept working and skipped lunch. My other friends suffered, too, because Casam was very nasty when he was shouting. Some went back to work with tortilla still in their mouths and others just ate standing up. He would say in English, "Let's go, *mojados*." And we got up and left the dining room because if we didn't get back immediately they would fire us.

During that time I was working eight hours a day and they were paying me $6.25 an hour, but I needed more hours because I had a lot of debts back home in Guatemala. It was the money I owed for the trip here. I talked to a friend of mine, Pedro. He's from Guatemala, too. Anyway, he's a very good person, and I explained to him I needed more hours and asked him what I should do. He spoke to the supervisor, and they gave me more hours but I didn't mind the hard work because I wanted to pay off my debt. I still owe money, but they haven't asked for it. I put up with all the abuse, and when I left work every day it felt as if I didn't have arms and hands.

On Sunday I would start work at one in the afternoon and would get out at six in the morning. Casam was always yelling at us and calling us *mojados* and making us work faster. If we wanted to have a drink of water he wouldn't let us and if anyone insisted he would fire them. I think he was a very crazy man because he abused people. He wanted us to work like machines, and sometimes he would even hit people.

Several months passed and I asked to change shifts. I wanted to work in cleaning, though that was pretty hard, too, because we had to work with strong chemicals without any protection. I remember when my friend Antonio had an accident. He hit his head on an iron bar and fell about four meters. I was crying a lot because I thought I was going to lose the friend who had given me a hand. Ambulances arrived, and they took him to a hospital in La Crosse. I didn't know what to do because we worked together, and I was beside myself. All my friends were crying, too, but we couldn't stop working or we would have been fired.

I remember when I got back to my room I was still crying, and the others asked me what was wrong and I told them that Antonio had an accident. They said I was his friend and should go see him, but I didn't have a car. One of my friends said he had the keys to Antonio's car, and he gave them to me.

I left for La Crosse on a Monday morning without knowing the city at all. I brought underwear and juice for Antonio and drove

Sebastián

there by myself. I found the hospital and asked for my friend, and they took me to see him. It was a very difficult moment for me because I never thought I would see my friend like that. I began to cry again, and I asked Antonio how he was, but he just looked through me. He was unconscious. I watched him with tears in my eyes, and I felt very sad. He didn't speak at all and I kept saying, "Antonio, it's me, Sebastián." I spent about three hours with him. I asked the nurse if he was going to be all right, and she told me not to worry, that he would be fine.

I left the hospital and when I got home everyone asked how he was, and I told them how he had seemed to me. Days passed and he finally came home. All of us had to take care of him. After a while he was feeling better. He had fractured his skull, and he had something like 32 stitches. After two months he went back to work. We kept on working together, and I was always watching out for him to be sure everything was okay.

I remember that it was like hell working for Casam. Tired of so much abuse, I talked to my supervisor and told him everything that Casam did to us, but he didn't care because Casam was a very important person in the company and he could do whatever he wanted to anyone. All of my fellow Guatemalans were suffering, but because of our poverty we had to put up with whatever came our way. That man fought with everyone who spoke up. We weren't allowed to talk about the bad things that happened. I remember that when we were working in the chicken slaughtering area, it was pure filth. Sometimes there weren't chickens coming on the line but it wasn't our fault, it was the rabbis who were slow, but Casam didn't care. He yelled at us anyway. Working with him was our Calvary.

I just prayed to God for all of us, asking that He give us strength to continue and to keep us calm. All we wanted was to work even though they treated us like animals. I watched how underage workers were mistreated. The United States wasn't what I thought it was like when I was living in my country.

Days went by like this, and because of the abuse I talked again to the supervisor and I told him I didn't want to work with Casam any longer because he treated everyone so badly. Then I worked only in clean-up, but it was the same because Casam was in charge all over the plant. He went on shouting and swearing at everyone and pushed us to do the cleaning as fast as we could. They wanted everything right away. All of my friends worked very, very hard. We worked with water that was boiling. Imagine, it was 160 degrees. We didn't have the proper equipment, there was no ventilation, and we had to work with very strong chemicals. We used two different types of bleach—number 5 and number 12. We mixed the bleach with something they called "Master" and other chemicals because if we didn't, the machines would be dirty and cause problems.

Every day the butchering would finish up at one or two o'clock in the morning, or maybe two thirty. I watched how my fellow workers were mistreated and pushed to the limit, and we just waited for the killing to be over so we could start working like crazy cleaning because the supervisors were all over us, pushing us to work faster and faster. We had to finish the cleaning in three or four hours, and we complained that we couldn't wash everything in that time, but they didn't care.

I remember I had a supervisor who was American. When he started he was very nasty, always pushing us to work harder, and we did what he said. One day I was working in the area called cut-up where it's very cold. I was cleaning three of the belts that go round and round at the same time. They had to be cleaned while they were still moving. As I was wiping them with the chemical-soaked cloth, all of a sudden my right hand slipped and got caught in the belts. I screamed because it felt like I had broken my fingers. The glove I was wearing tore, and my hand started to bleed. The

Sebastián

American supervisor took me to the office for them to fix me up. They put some kind of water on my hand, who knows what it was, and another one of the bosses named Joe iced it. He told me to move my fingers, and I couldn't do it at all at first but after a while I could wiggle them, and he said that it had just been a bump.

They took me to another office and told me to sign a paper. I asked what it was, and he said it was a "warning," since I had been careless at my job. I was really upset, and it seemed so absurd to me. That supervisor said that I would be allowed only one other "warning" and with the third, I would be fired. So I said, "Okay" and went back to my job. I told my friends what had happened, and I was laughing and mad at the same time. I said to the guys, "Let's be careful because here instead of healing your injuries they give you a warning." Everybody laughed, but they didn't really believe me. But a lot of horrible things happened, and I just took it and so did all the others.

Once the new supervisor had seen some of the very serious problems he began to treat us well, and we all loved him during that time. He realized that we earned very little, and so he went to talk to the boss, Joe, and told him not to charge us for the clothing and equipment we had to use. For about a month they stopped charging us for everything, but Joe didn't like it at all and got very mad so they started to take it out of our salary again. More time went by and the American saw how unjustly we were treated, and finally he got totally discouraged, and he quit.

Then we had another manager who was a lot older, about 68. I think his name was Mr. Green, or something like that. He was just nasty. He treated everyone terribly. Everyone was afraid of him because when he got angry he would start shaking and then pass out. He had some kind of nervous condition. Then the ambulance would come and take him. It was a problem for us. Days would go by, and then he would show up again. When he was gone from work we were all happy, but when he came back everyone hated him because he was so demanding. Even when everyone was working hard he would jump on us. My friends couldn't understand why he was like that. Working with him was hell.

I remember one Thursday a kid named Brian who was just 17 was working at about 11:00 p.m., and just because he was talking with another worker Mr. Green came over, grabbed him by the shirt and took him to another area where there were large machines and told him that from then on he was going to have to clean them every day. He was yelling, and Brian got really scared and started crying. I told him to calm down, that Mr. Green was old and that was the problem. That kid was living in my house.

Tired of so much yelling and problems, the workers decided as a group to find someone to translate for us at the main office and tell them our grievances. We had to find someone from outside because if it was someone who worked at the plant they wouldn't listen to us. We found someone and told him all of the problems we were having. He went to the office and spoke with Sholom, the owner of the plant. The following day, a Friday, they told us that when we finished working they wanted to see us in the office. The work ended at 10:00 a.m., and I said, "The soup is hot," and everyone laughed.

We went to the office, and there was our boss, Joe Fleming, and a secretary named Katrina. She interpreted for us, and they asked us what we wanted, and we began to present our concerns.

We said that Mr. Green was mistreating us, that we wanted a raise, and we wanted more safety measures. We also asked for fans because we suffered in the heat. We wanted them to replace Mr. Green because he just made trouble for us. The bosses told us not to pay any attention to him because he was just old. But we kept insisting that we wanted him removed. We also asked for a raise because the workers in all the other areas of the plant had been

Sebastián

given raises. Then Mr. Fleming got furious, but we insisted that we wanted better workplace protection and safer equipment. He was so tough and hardheaded that he managed to shut us up in the end. I was so amazed and angry.

After awhile they hired another supervisor who was American, and when I saw him I started laughing because he looked so strict. He even strutted like he was angry, maybe to scare us. I said to the others, "There's our new supervisor." He started to work, and the first thing he said to us was that he was very demanding and wanted things done well. Everyone started to laugh, and he said, "I'm not kidding!" He turned to me and said he wanted everything done on time, and they put me in charge, but the truth is he didn't know a thing about machinery. I had to teach him how to use all the machines, and there were several different kinds. He got mad a lot because we didn't do exactly what he told us to do, but we all knew how to do our own jobs the best way.

Time passed and the new supervisor became aware of the abuse we suffered and the lack of safety measures for the machinery. Sometimes the mechanics would turn on a machine without paying any attention to who was there. Sometimes someone would start some machinery when we were working right there, and we had to shout to warn people. It was terrible. Very dangerous for all of us. The new boss, whose name was Bob, worked with us for four months. He told us he was going to quit because the plant was disgusting. He had worked at other companies, but they never treated the workers as badly as we were treated. He had a lot of fights with the infamous Casam because Bob was American and not afraid to answer back. Finally he quit, and we began to work again under Brian, another American who was very nasty. One day a Guatemalan named Sergio was working in an area we called Evis [Evisceration] where there's a lot of dangerous equipment, and Brian just went crazy and grabbed Sergio by the neck and dragged him outside and almost hit him. There were a lot of people around, and Sergio felt completely humiliated and went off crying. He couldn't stand the shame.

Time passed and things got worse because there were rumors about an Immigration raid at the plant. I remember an incident one day with a new manager named Rolando, a Chicano "yellow hardhat" [supervisor] who spoke Spanish very well but looked really fierce. There was a kind of barrel that was filled with water, and that day the idiot hadn't closed it properly and the water poured out and he got his shoes wet. Do you know what that fool did? He took off his wet socks and put them in the microwave to dry! Imagine how filthy that is! Everyone was so disgusted. Without knowing what had happened, I heated my tortillas in the oven because we were having a break, and one of the *Señoras* told me not to eat them because the "yellow hardhat" named Rolando had stuck his socks in it. Then I didn't feel at all like eating. I spoke to the supervisor, but he just made us clean the microwave and that was it. Everyone hated Rolando because he was very hard on the workers.

In 2008 the bosses at the plant ordered us to get new Social Security numbers and different names, otherwise we would be fired. It was terrible. A lot of people had to pay $400 to make the change, and then we had to reapply for our jobs. It was a mess. I was about to do it when that terrible moment arrived that I'm going to describe.

We started working the evening of May 11th at 11:00 p.m. Everything went along as normal that night. We were finished cleaning at about 8:45 on the morning of May 12th. Some of my friends and I were going to reapply with our new numbers and names so we went to the office, but there were a lot of people applying for jobs. They told us to come back at noon. We insisted that they take care of us right away because we were exhausted. Imagine, we had been working all night and were very sleepy! So a

Sebastián

friend said, "Let's just go and get some sleep." So we left the plant, and when we got to the gas station called *Keys*, we saw helicopters and a small plane flying and a friend told me to hide because Immigration had just invaded Agri, and I was terrified because my sons were at school.

It was the first day my wife had begun to work in an egg plant so she wasn't in Agriprocessors. I was so scared and I didn't know what to do. The helicopters and the airplane were terrifying. My daughter was crying, everyone was crying. It was like they were hunting rats. I watched what they were doing at the plant on TV and how a lot of people just seemed broken. They were even hitting the women. At that moment I sat down at the table and began writing about what had happened. There is so much more to tell. There is so much I would like to tell you all, and I hope you understand what I have written because it was all very real and true.

Shattered Dreams

Susana

My work at Agriprocessors was that of Quality Assurance Auditor for an outside contractor. It was my responsibility to ensure the high quality of the product according to the contractor's expectations. I oversaw the fabrication of sausages from beginning to end, from the time the spices and meat arrived until the finished product left the plant. I had to train the employees on good manufacturing practices since they had no idea and no training in how to handle the product properly.

I began working for the sausage company on May 15, 2006. I was trained in Chicago before starting to work at Agriprocessors. My first day working at Agri in Postville was Sunday, May 28, 2006, and I worked there until May 12, 2008, when Immigration carried out the raid.

The day of the raid I went to work just like every day. I got there a little early, just before 7:00 a.m. I was surprised to see that the machine wasn't printing the expiration date on the packages, and the department supervisor, a guy from the U.S., told me I could hand write the date myself. I told him that I wouldn't do it. Usually, when I refused to do something like that, they would take whatever time was needed to make repairs—four, five, eight hours—until we could get back to work correctly, but that day the supervisor kept insisting every ten minutes. Finally he asked me to speak to my boss in Chicago, and I said that my boss would say no, and he said it didn't matter, that I should call my boss anyway. So I did, and the boss said it was okay because there was a big demand for the product and the warehouses were almost empty and it was urgent for us to fill the orders.

So the supervisor got people working right away. He told

Susana

everyone to hurry up. Before they started, one woman asked if he knew whether Immigration was going to come or not, and if so, was he going to tell the workers when it was about to happen. There had been rumors about a raid. He said he would notify everyone in plenty of time, but that they should get to work right away. They asked him several times, and he always said that he would warn them so that they could leave. The workers really believed in him. They thought Immigration would never enter the plant because the manager, Sholom, paid the agents not to come. They had always understood that their wages were so low because some of the money they earned had to go to prevent a raid.

One of the things that surprised me was that the supervisor had the machinery working at top speed but only half of the people were working that day because of the rumors. So I lowered the speed, and the supervisor sped it up again. He said we needed to get the product out by 10:00 a.m. I was about to leave because I had to go check the kitchen when the supervisor commented that people were really upset due to the rumors. I told him that, just the night before, my husband and I had been talking about the fact that a supervisor we knew, who no longer worked at Agri, had told me I needed to have a copy of my passport with me at all times. At that moment, the supervisor asked me if I did have a copy handy, and I said I didn't. I asked him if I would need it. He stared at me and with a sneer he told me, "I don't know."

He stayed there, and I didn't think much of it. People were still working very fast. It was only 38 degrees Fahrenheit but people were sweating. I went back in and lowered the speed again. The "green hardhat" [department leader] named Sophia, who was the head of the department, went and turned it back up. She got very angry with me. I asked her if she didn't realize that people were working too fast because there weren't enough workers. She got mad and left, so I went and slowed the machine down a little, and then I began to help make boxes.

Shattered Dreams

One of the ladies asked me if it was true that there had been an I.C.E. raid in Waterloo. I said no because there hadn't been anything about it on the news. They went on insisting that it was true, that there had been a raid, so I said I would go check on the internet when we had a break and tell them if there was any news.

We went on working, and then at 9:00 a.m. it was time for break. I would usually go to my car to rest, but that day, since they had asked me to find out, I went to the office to check the news on the computer. I didn't find anything about any raid, but there was an article that said some I.C.E. agents were in Waterloo. Well, I got scared, but since I hadn't eaten anything or used the restroom, I decided to go to the bathroom and then go back to where everyone was working.

When I was going upstairs, I ran into the boys who worked in the kitchen, the ones who mixed sausage meats and made sausages. I told them that if the kitchen wasn't all cleaned up they had better go back and do it right away because I was going to check. One of them named Nelson said to me, "Susana Coral, when you see how clean the kitchen is you're going to want to give us a raise," and went off laughing with the other workers.

So instead of going back to the packaging department I went to the kitchen. When I got there everything was in order except one oven that wasn't working. I went to the room with the oven controls and there I ran into Norberto D—, one of the mechanics. I asked him why the oven wasn't working and he showed me the design and started to tell me what was wrong. Then he told me the company had laid him off and that the managers said that he needed to change his papers before coming back to work.

"Why are you working then?" I asked him. "You should have stayed home."

Norberto said they had called him and told him to come back

Susana

because no one else knew how to do his job. I told him that was even more of a reason for him to refuse to come in, so that they would value what he was able to do.

"No, he said, "I need the money, and I have to work."

Just at that moment someone called him on the radio and said something that I couldn't understand and he couldn't either. The person who was calling sounded frightened because more than talking he was yelling. So Norberto thought there was a problem in the chicken department, and he ran off towards that area.

Before he went he told me, "Wait for me here so I can explain what's wrong with the oven." That was the last time I saw Norberto free.

About five minutes later, Mercedes G—, a woman who cooked the kidneys, came in and told me that she had overheard two Russian women, Ana G— and Stephani, the "red hardhat" [Quality Control], saying something about police. Mercedes was very frightened, thinking it might be Immigration. I tried to calm her down.

"No, Mercedes, how can you believe that?" I told her.

But she was beside herself so I went out, and it was true that those women were talking with Stephani's brother-in-law. They appeared to be very upset, but when I asked them what was happening, they told me there was a problem with quality control and that it wasn't in my section so I shouldn't worry. They told me to leave—they would take care of it.

I went back to get my notebook and Mercedes came back in and said to me, "Susana, Immigration is really here."

I went out again and found Andri. I said to him, "We're friends, right? Please tell me what's happening."

Shattered Dreams

He told me, "It's Immigration. Go to the packaging room and tell the people working there."

When I went to packaging all I saw was an apron that someone had just tossed on the floor. People were running out. I went back to my room and there was Mercedes, crying.

The only thing I said to her was, "Go, and may God help you. Do what you have to do."

That was the last time I saw Mercedes free.

I called Ricardo, my husband, at home to tell him that I didn't have my certified passport, that I only had my driver's license and that he should come and bring me my papers. I was crying like crazy. He didn't answer the phone, and I left a message. I went up to the office to get my purse and went downstairs to try to call again, but he still didn't answer. I went back out and ran into Luisa M—. They had already detained her. I asked her about the others, and she said they had all run out. She asked me to call her husband and tell him to take care of the children because she had been arrested. At that moment a lot of women began asking me to call their husbands, but when I tried to go back to the phone an Immigration agent told me not to move from where I was because the plant was under investigation. I told him I had to make a phone call, and he said that there would be time to do that later.

At that moment, the general plant manager was walking by and I spoke with him. I asked him to call my husband. He was able to walk around freely wherever he wanted and could have made a phone call to my husband to ask him to bring my papers. He told me not to worry that he would call Ricardo and tell him what was happening. I knew inside that he would never call my husband because he didn't have his phone number. He was just saying that to patronize me. He made me very angry and indignant, that son of a bitch piece of shit. He said the same thing to all the women just to placate them. He had always promised the workers that he would help them, that Immigration would never come to the plant.

So I had to stay there. I saw Luisa M—, Irma L— and Marco T—. Of all the people I saw, I only remember those names.

The women were crying, and I was telling them that they had their children and no matter what the agents said they had to tell Immigration that their kids were at home waiting for them. At that point Irma L— asked me to please pick up her daughter at school and to keep her with me and take care of her. Marco T— gave me the keys to his car and his cell phone. A lot of people gave me their keys and the things they had on them. I wrote down in my notebook what each one gave me and who I had to give everything to.

They took us to the cafeteria and told us to sit down. About five minutes later they said that everyone who was a citizen should go to one side, all of the legal residents should go to another side, and all those who were undocumented or who couldn't prove their status should stay seated. I stayed because I didn't have my papers as proof. I was with Luisa the whole time, and I told all the women I was going to stay with them. They told me to try to leave so that I could go and take care of their children. They were in tears, and they begged me to leave. That's why I finally went to the area where the citizens were being held.

When it was my turn to be interviewed, the agent asked if I was a citizen. I told him I was. He said I didn't look like a citizen. I told him I was born in Guanajuato, Mexico. He asked me how I had become a citizen. I told him that I did it the same way all those who weren't born in this country do it. And how was that, he wanted to know. I had become a citizen on December 11, 2003 after filling out applications, waiting, taking exams, and paying fines. He asked me how it was possible for me to remember the exact date, and I said maybe it was because you don't become a citizen every day. At that point I was crying and I was furious. They asked me if I had any identification, and I said I had my driver's license. I told them that if it was enough they should take it and if it wasn't enough they could take me away because I didn't have any other proof with me.

Then they started asking about my husband and if he was working at the plant. I told them he wasn't, but they kept pushing.

"Is he illegal?" they asked.

"No, he isn't. He just returned from Mexico where he went through the process to become legal."

But they kept insisting, and asking me to tell them which one of the men working in the plant was my husband, and they said they could start the process right then and there to legalize his status. And I kept insisting over and over again that my husband didn't work in the plant, that he wasn't undocumented, but they kept on pushing.

After a while those who had already been questioned were released and were walking past me. I remember Alice S—, they hadn't asked her for identification. And Peter S—, the manager of the sausage department, and Danny B—. There were a lot of other people there, and they were laughing and joking as if nothing was happening. It made me so angry to see that even though they were perfectly aware of the situation, they were just kidding around. All of them were from the United States.

They took us out of the building, and we were outside for about half an hour. They were bringing people out from different parts of the plant because there were a lot of workers. While we were outside I managed to make eye contact with one of the managers. I don't know how I was looking at him, but he lowered his eyes and never made eye contact with me the rest of the day. They brought the men out with their hands tied behind their backs with white plastic handcuffs. They brought some out just with their hands on their heads, men and women. Then they told the people with me that they were going to let us leave. I said that I needed to go inside to get my things, the computer and all my work papers. Two agents accompanied me, together with two supervisors who had to turn the machinery off because it was still running.

When we were coming back out there were people lined up on two sides of the hallway. As I walked past I was crying the whole time. Many women I didn't even know talked to me and told me to take care of their children. When I tried to get closer to the women, the agents told me to keep walking. When they saw that so many people wanted to talk to me and that I wanted to stop to see what they were all saying, each one of the agents put his hand on one of my shoulders and took me outside. The other two supervisors went on ahead, but no one talked to them.

When I got outside the men were there, also in two lines. One of my workers looked up, his eyes full of tears, and asked me to help him, but there was nothing I could do. I was stumbling and feeling faint, and the agents wanted to grab hold of me again, but I told them not to touch me, that I preferred to fall down rather than let them touch me. So they waited five minutes until I was feeling better and at that moment they started to bring out other people who they had been holding in the offices at the entry to the plant. There were a lot of people I knew in that group, but the ones I remember the best were two of my workers, Carlos M— and Ramiro A—.

When Carlos got closer he called me to him, and I was able to sneak a little closer without the agents realizing. I asked him how I could help him. He begged me to ask the supervisor to be sure to pay the vacation time he was owed, to be sure the plant didn't keep his check because his daughters in Guatemala needed the money.

After that he just looked at me and said, "It's been a real pleasure to know you. I'm really grateful to you."

Shattered Dreams

It all seemed to me so sad and ironic. I said to Carlos, "How can you thank me? Look what we're doing to you. Whether or not I agree with all this, I am part of this country which is doing so much harm to you."

He replied, "You're not from here. You are one of us," and at that they shoved him, and he had to keep on walking.

Later, while I was recovering, Ramiro walked past. He worked in quality control. He asked me to put my hand in his pants pocket and get out his cell phone and keys. Alice, one of the managers, heard us and said she would do it.

Ramiro said, "No, I want Susana to do it."

Alice insisted and when she tried to put her hand in his pocket, he pulled away and said, "Please, Susana, take my things."

So I walked in front of Alice and took Ramiro's phone and keys and she grabbed them from me and said she was going to turn them in. Ramiro tried to tell her to give the keys and phone to me, but she refused, and I reached out my hand and tried to take them away, but I only got the phone and she kept the keys.

Two agents escorted me to my car and searched it to see if there were any undocumented workers inside. I got into the car but, before I even got out of the parking lot, other agents stopped me and searched again. Then I called my brother and told him to please tell his wife to be careful because they were saying that Immigration was going to go through the whole state of Iowa. And I told him that Immigration had come to the plant and they were taking everyone away. He told me to calm down, that there wasn't anything I could do. I yelled at my brother that I was sick and tired of everyone saying there was nothing I could do.

Susana

"There must be something we can do to help these people," I said.

Then I hung up because two officers from the sheriff's department stopped the car and searched it again and made me open the trunk to see if there was anyone hiding there. When I left the plant I was in shock.

Before I drove completely out of the plant grounds, I saw another Mexican women who was leaving. Immigration had let her go, too. She saw how upset I was, and she invited me to her house for coffee. I felt like getting out of the car and tearing out every hair on her head. I thought to myself, "How is it possible to think about having coffee while a raid is going on in the plant." To me it was incomprehensible. I can understand that Americans might not feel anything because these were not their people. But how was it possible for a Mexican woman to be so calm. That was something I just couldn't understand.

When I was driving out of the plant there were a lot of North Americans that had even brought folding lawn chairs so they could sit and watch the spectacle.

I heard someone say, "There goes one of them. If they let her out it's because she's legal."

I shouted at them, "You have no idea what's going on in there. All you care about is consuming what those so called 'illegals' have made."

The woman said, "I'm sure she's legal."

And again I shouted back, "No one is illegal in this country."

From there I went to the church [St. Bridget Parish] to see if I could help. When I arrived only Pablo, the Hispanic lay pastor, and

Sister Mary [McCauley] were there. First I looked at Pablo, and he just looked back at me. I asked him what I could do to help, and he said there wasn't anything I could do. I left Pablo's office and saw Sister Mary.

She asked me, "Were you there?"

"Yes." She didn't say a thing; she just gave me a big hug.

We immediately started to make a list of everyone they were taking away. We began with the people who worked with me. I also went to the school to pick up the children whose mothers had asked me to take care of them. The school wouldn't let me take them; they would only release the children to their parents. I went back to the church to continue making the list. I called Luisa M—'s husband because she had asked me to. I told him that she had been detained and that he should stay inside the house and take care of the children. Then I called the wife of one of the "red hardhats" named Ramiro G— to tell her that he had been detained but that I had his cell phone. I told her that the manager of quality control had kept his keys.

And I made all the phone calls that people has asked me to do and tried to get in touch with everyone. I did all of that at the church. I had left my husband Ricardo without a car because our other car needed to be fixed. We live in Decorah, about half an hour from Postville. He had been looking for a ride and had borrowed a car from the bakery. I went to pick him up in Frankville, a town half-way between Decorah and Postville, because they said there were road blocks on the roads in and out of Postville. That's what the owner of the bakery in Decorah had told him. He was the one who loaned Ricardo the car so that he could bring me my papers. I didn't realize there were road blocks because I hadn't left town.

I picked him up and then went back to the church to continue making the list of the people I knew who had been arrested. Then

Susana

I went back to the plant, to the parking area, to see if I could help and to wait for the women and see if they would be let go. I hoped I.C.E. would release them to take care of their children because if they didn't the children would be all alone, and I thought that the government of this country would never be so cruel as to leave children without a mother.

I had worked at other meat processing plants before and had never seen so much abuse of the workers. Many people ask me why, if there was so much mistreatment, I didn't denounce the plant. Well, it doesn't do any good to complain about something if the victims aren't willing to talk. You can help and give advice, but the victim is the one who has to decide what to do. When I told people they had to put an end to the abuse, many of them said that even with all the mistreatment and low pay, it was still better here than in their own countries.

The bosses knew that and took advantage of them. The workers put in more than 12 hours a day, the starting pay was $6.25 an hour, breaks were shorter than they should have been, and many times at the end of the week the company didn't pay all the hours worked. Many women complained that they were denied permission to take their sick children to see a doctor or that they wouldn't allow the women to use the bathroom when they needed to.

During the time I was at Agriprocessors there were two rumors about a possible I.C.E. raid. The first one was in 2007, and there were quite a few days when people didn't come to work. There were many times in which different departments were working with less than half their personnel because people didn't show up. Some of the workers were afraid Immigration was coming. It was kind of funny because I don't know where they came up with the dates and times I.C.E. was supposed to be arriving. For example, many times people said they were going to come on Monday at noon, and, of course, there was no raid. Then people would say that for sure they were going to come on Tuesday and that way the rumor would go on for the whole week until Friday when nobody showed up for work because if Immigration hadn't shown up on the other days then for sure they would come on Friday.

The other big rumor was in 2008. On Sunday, May 11, the day before the raid, a lot of people didn't show up for work because of the rumors. A lot of people skipped work on the 12th, too. Many people believed the rumors, but there were a lot who no longer did. There were many people who had complete confidence in the plant, and if you had told them Immigration was coming they wouldn't have believed you. People had blind trust in Sholom Rubashkin because many times he had said that he paid Immigration not to come, and that was how he justified the low wages. A lot of workers told me that. They thought the plant was very safe for them because they believed I.C.E. was being paid to stay away.

A few weeks before the raid I heard many rumors that the plant was firing people, telling them to get new work documents and reapply for their jobs with the new papers. To me they were just rumors because people just mentioned them to me, but I had no proof since I didn't work in other departments and I had no contact with Human Resources. I did find out that the rumors were true when I realized that many people had done just that; they had changed their papers and returned to ask for the same jobs. The plant rehired some but didn't rehire everyone. This had a negative impact because the years that people had been working didn't count, and when a worker was rehired he had to begin again as a new employee. That was another way in which the plant exploited people and took advantage of their poverty.

What I remember the most about the raid is all the chaos. Everyone was so scared—you could feel fear in the air. But the one thing that is always in my mind and that I think I will never forget is when I had to walk between the two lines of people who had

Susana

been detained and how they looked at me and begged me for help. That is something I will never forget. I have that image in my mind, and also I remember vividly how I looked at Cruz L— and how he looked up at me. And also when I saw another young man named Nelson who worked with me and who looked up—his eyes full of tears—and then lowered them again as if he were ashamed. And I will also never forget Carlos M— and how he was marched passed with his hands on top of his head and begged me to remember to ask the supervisor for the two weeks of vacation pay he was owed. And then he thanked me. I'll never forget how he thanked me, because with everything that was happening at that moment he still thanked me. Those are the images I will never forget.

All of this has had a strong impact on my personal life and my plans for the future because we think that this situation only affects immigrants without documentation, but that isn't true. It affects all of us—as legal residents, as citizens, as Americans. It affects all of us in some way whether we recognize it or not. And it has made a big difference in my life because—how can I say this—because for me the day of the raid was like the day my brother died. That feeling of impotence when you know you have to do something but you don't know what to do. It was the same feeling that I had many years ago when I was only seven and I couldn't do anything and my brother died. And that day during the I.C.E. raid at the plant it felt exactly the same. And I said to myself, I'm not a little girl anymore—no, I'm not. I'm a big girl, and I can do something. I don't have to stand here with my arms crossed. And that's why I'm still here helping. I'm working for the Church to help the people affected by the raid. I'm not going to fix the world but, my God, I am going to stay here until everything gets settled more or less.

And I also discovered that I had some qualities that I hadn't been aware of—specifically leadership skills. I never ever considered myself a leader, someone who could make things happen. I mean never. Now I've done work that I never believed I was capable of and that has really given me much more self-esteem. When my father was living at home he made sure to make me believe that a cockroach was worth more than I was and that I would never amount to anything. And so I have always carried that baggage, that belief that even though I've always been working I just couldn't achieve anything, not a thing. I didn't believe I could accomplish anything because my father said so, and I was told that time and time again. But now I realize that this simply isn't the case and, thanks to that, I'm considering going to law school which is something that I have always wanted to do but never did because I didn't think I was good enough to study law. Now I'm really considering it.

Sometimes I say that I am just a big little girl because I still consider myself a child. They say that you always have a little child inside you, and I think this is true. I and the rest of my sisters never had normal childhoods. We were always working to help our mother, and we were so poor we couldn't even afford toys. A lot of times we didn't have money for food, much less playthings. I would make little skirts for the corn cobs and those were my dolls, and the boys used stones and pretended they were little cars and that's how they played. I helped my mother as far back as I remember. I carried water from the well, ground the cornmeal, milked and fed the goats, cleaned the beans, swept the floors, planted crops, plowed between the corn rows, and a lot more. So I never really enjoyed a complete childhood. I say complete because while I did play, I didn't play as much as a normal little girl, and I had no toys. Maybe that's why when I was 15 years old my greatest desire was still to have a doll, and why I now have more dolls than I had in my whole childhood.

If you want to know much more about my childhood I have to say I hardly have any memories from when I was a little girl. I do remember that my mother sent me to school when I wasn't even four years old. There was no kindergarten so they put me in first grade. I remember that we had class under a tree. After a while they made a little room of stones and that's where we had classes. Since I was so little I didn't learn to read very much but I would draw the smoke from the trains and little pine trees. That's all I did.

I remember *maestro* [teacher] Pedro very well. He was very kind and for the *Day of the Child* [April 20] he would give each of his students a notebook, a pencil, an eraser, and to the boys he gave a slingshot and to the girls a plastic box shaped like a rooster. So the *Day of the Child* was a big party because *maestro* Pedro was the only one who ever gave us gifts. There was another teacher there at the same time whose name was Angel. He was very strict and would pull our pigtails, and since we would cry and our noses would run he would call us "filthy pigs," and hit us more. By the time I was in third grade I still didn't know how to read or write so my grandfather taught me. He wrote on the ground, and he would say, "What does it say here?" If I didn't know he helped me. I learned to multiply, to add and subtract.

He taught me in the dirt because we had no paper.

Then another teacher came named Librado. He was from Durango. He hit us a lot. When we got a math problem wrong he would hit us on the palms of our hands three times. He had a gigantic ring that he would put on his knuckle and then would knock us on the head with it. He was very interesting because when he was writing on the blackboard he would throw the eraser at any student who was talking. It was like he had eyes in the back of his neck.

After that teacher, another one named Lorenzo came, and he's still in the village. The only thing that mattered to him was seeing the mothers. He was always saying, "Poor *Doña* Andrea. Poor *Doña* Tere." He didn't teach us anything. When I finished sixth grade I didn't know how to divide, though I did know how to read and write because my grandfather had taught me. When I read I could

Shattered Dreams

do it well because he had taught me to respect the commas and the periods. I dare say I was his favorite granddaughter at that time because when he would go to the city he always brought me a gift. Before he left he would take me aside and ask me what I wanted. I loved balloons, and I'd ask him to bring me a bag of balloons.

He would say, "I'm going to bring you an orange, too, a navel orange with a big belly button, an orange that has a little bitty baby orange on top."

Those oranges seemed so very big to me, and I remember I shared the little one on top with my cousins. That was something he brought just for me. He brought the others presents and oranges, too, but just the plain kind. I shared the balloons with everyone. Maybe that's why he brought them for me, because he knew I would share with the others.

When my grandmother on my father's side would go into town, my grandfather was left home alone. He always wanted me to make his lunch then. He wanted me to make his food because we both like salty things. I would heat the tortillas and leave them for him, and then I would go take care of the goats. He taught me to shoot a stone with a slingshot so that I didn't have to run after the goats so much. I would aim the stone at them from far away, and they would come back. We also milked the goats together. He milked his, and I milked mine. If he finished first he would help me, and I did the same thing for him.

Grandfather told me I had to drink milk because it was good for me, but I didn't like milk. So when he would go to the city once a month he would bring back a kilo of bananas and told me that if I drank a glass of milk fresh from the nanny goat he would give me one. I didn't like milk, but I loved bananas so in order to have the banana I had to make the sacrifice and drink the milk. That was just when he went to town because we had no bananas on the *rancho*. So it was usually only once a month that I drank milk,

Susana

after my grandfather brought bananas from town and until there were no more left. By the end of the week they were pretty black on the outside, but to me they tasted wonderful.

He was always so supportive of me. I gave all the goats names. I remember one we called "Miel" [Honey] very well. She always gave two bottles of milk that were honey-colored and that's why I named her that. There was another one who I called "Pedrita", because I thought she looked like the singer Pedrito Fernández. Of course, that was only my opinion. Another was "Chispita" [Sparky]. She didn't grow very big and had a small white star on her forehead. The last one was "Chichischurris" because her *chichis* [teats] were very small. I remember that the goats would walk in a line. If one started then they would all line up behind.

One thing that was hard was that women were very restricted and weren't allowed to do many things. My grandfather was very liberal. He gave me wings to do more things. Riding a horse— well, forget that. I was allowed to ride a burro, but always side saddle, never with open legs, he told me. There was a bony black mare that he would help me put the reins on, and she was so gentle I could ride her. I always wore a dress when I was riding because women couldn't wear pants. My grandmother was always shouting at me and asking if I wasn't ashamed of everyone seeing my filthy legs. My grandfather encouraged me to be more liberal. I think I am what I am today thanks to the fact that when everyone else scolded me for all the bad things I did, my grandfather didn't. He gave me the courage to go on. Maybe that's why I'm so crazy, so free-spirited. I hardly ever speak to him nowadays and I hardly ever see him, but I know that whatever I do, good or bad, I can count on his support. I know he wasn't mad at me like the rest of the family because I married the man I did. He understood that I did what all of us have to do—choose our own husband or wife. He told me he was very glad that it was my childhood sweetheart because they had known him well since he was a little boy and knew what he was like.

Shattered Dreams

I had an aunt named Juana, and I got along with her very well. She was so funny! My grandfather's name, by the way, was Juan. Anyway, I would follow her around a lot because she would make me dresses out of the left-over material from making her own. But the bigger reason that I hung around her was that she cleaned the church. And then, because I didn't have any dolls, while she cleaned she let me carry around the baby Jesus. For me it was like being in heaven. And she always combed my hair and gave me baths. Even today I get along very, very well with her.

My aunt and my maternal grandmother are always so shocked by the things I say and how I say them. They say, "*Ay*, who would have thought that dirty, skinny-legged little girl was going to say the things she says today, and do the things she does."

They never let my aunt get married. Two men asked for her hand in marriage, but her father said no. Now that she's forty years old she has married a man who is as old as my grandfather, and he treats her badly.

My husband Ricardo and I have known each other since we were little. We went to catechism together and saw each other every day. We were about seven years old and would play a lot of games like hide and seek, *toro escondido* and *corretizas* before the doctrinal lessons started.

I knew that he was the person I wanted to marry. I loved him from way back when we were just kids. When my parents brought us to the United States I didn't see him again for a long time. I came to the States in 1995 and didn't see him again until 1999 when I went back to Mexico for a visit. I realized that I still liked him, or rather that we liked each other. And then I didn't see him again until 2004 when I was studying at the University of Northern Iowa and had an internship in San Miguel Allende, Guanajuato. The reason I asked to be sent there was because I knew that I would be able to see him more often. I told myself that if there was ever going

Susana

to be something between the two of us it would happen during the time I was in Mexico. If he didn't ask me to become his *novia* then, I decided I would come back to the U.S. and look for a boyfriend, for a serious relationship.

In fact, I had left a boyfriend in the States who had asked me if I wanted to get engaged, but I asked him to wait until I came back from Mexico and told him that if I returned still unmarried and with no other commitments then we could become *novios*, but if not, then it was over. So when Ricardo finally decided to ask me to be his fiancée, I called the other boy that I had left waiting and told him to go on with his life and that I wasn't going to be able to marry him.

When my internship was over I had to go back to the United States. We made plans to continue our relationship. Ricardo crossed the border without papers to come here. He arrived in California and was working there for several months, and then he went to Kansas and from there it was easier to get together. He would travel to Iowa to see me. I continued to study and was about to finish college when my father found out that he was here in the U.S. and that we were seeing each other. He couldn't believe that I was in love with a man who came from the same *rancho* as we did and who had no college education. I didn't care what he thought or anything about his prejudices.

When my father found out that Ricardo and I were engaged he was furious. He gave me every earthly reason why I couldn't be with him. I don't know exactly why he didn't want Ricardo to be my boyfriend. He went from telling me that he was "illegal," that he had no education, that he would bring me bad luck, that he was my mother's half-brother, that he had a bad "aura," and a bunch of other ridiculous things. None of his excuses mattered to me, and least of all that he might be my mother's half-brother because he looked a lot like his father and it made no sense that he was my grandfather's son. My father was so worked up over this that he threatened to turn my boyfriend in to I.C.E. as an undocumented worker unless we broke up. Finally he threatened to kill me and then kill Ricardo if we stayed together. He said that he would kill me with his own hands before allowing his blood to be mixed with the blood of that "illegal alien." Of course he didn't use those exact words; he called Ricardo every horrible name in the book.

As that disaster was unfolding it seemed so ridiculous to me because when my father said those things we had been married for six months. Yes, we married secretly, and we didn't tell anyone. The family realized we were married after we had been [married] for all those months.

We got married because I was afraid that my father would send *la migra* after Ricardo and he would be deported. We decided to get married in case anything like that happened, and if they caught him we would already be married and it would be easier for him to come back to the United States.

It was before I graduated that we got married. By the time my father found out, I had finished college and become independent enough to make my own life. He had never supported me while I was studying. He didn't help financially nor did he give me any moral support. He always underestimated me but he would say to his friends that I was going to college thanks to him because he was paying for my studies, but that wasn't true.

Because of what my father was like I always said I wanted a man who was completely different from him. I didn't want a man who would control me and who I had to depend on 100%. I wanted a man who would support me, who wouldn't cut my wings but would help me to fly, a man who would respect me and accept my professional career.

Susana

When I went to the university I went out with a lot of guys as friends. At first I treated them as just friends, and if they wanted to control me or dominate then I never considered having a serious relationship with any of them. I always had in mind that Ricardo was the only man who had what I was looking for and that's why I married him. After all of his unconditional support after the raid and now that I'm applying to law school, I realize that I couldn't have found a better husband than him. I thank God for the husband I have. I'm very proud of him because he earned his GED and is studying English. Our goal is for him to continue his studies, learn English well, and then get a technical degree to become a professional.

Shattered Dreams

Carmen

Hello, my name is Carmen, and I'm from Mexico. I was born in a small village in San Luis Potosí and that's where I lived as a child. I went to school and finished high school but I didn't have the means to continue my studies. I had just enough money for food but not for studying. I worked in the fields harvesting chilies and beans, and that's all I did. When I was 13 years old, I would usually work two days a week because there was only full-time work for the men. Sometimes I would work cleaning houses, and I began to do that when I was 13.

I lived with my mother and a brother and sister because my father was in the United States working to send us money. With what he sent we only had enough to buy food and not enough for my mother to buy us toys or clothes. My life in Mexico was pretty bad. There weren't things like toys or things to wear, just food, and some clothes and shoes. I wanted a bicycle and I liked dolls, but I couldn't have things like that. It was sad because we were by ourselves with just our mother. When my father came to the United States, it took him a long time to cross the border and to find work. Then he started to send money, but it was only enough to buy food and finish building our house. We have a little house in our village.

After a time, my Dad decided to bring us to the United States to give us a better life. First he brought my 12-year-old brother, and then he brought my mother. My sister and I stayed in Mexico with my grandmother. For the two of us it was very hard when our mother left us because we weren't used to being without her. We were by ourselves with our grandmother. It wasn't the same as being with our mother. I was used to being with my mother all the time and to going with her wherever she went. After she left I was

Carmen

always alone, and I felt there was no one I could depend on. After seven months of waiting to join her, they sent for us. They sacrificed a lot to do it because only my father was working, and they had to get a lot of money because my parents had to pay $1600 for each of us to make the trip. Our parents gave up everything to save enough money to bring us. But at last we were coming to the United States, my older sister and I.

Thank God we didn't have a problem crossing. We had to walk all night. I was fifteen and my sister eighteen. We came through Nogales, Arizona. My father had hired a *coyote* to get us across the border. My uncle took us to Nogales and delivered us to the man who was going to take us all the way to Phoenix. We walked from 4:00 in the morning until 8:00. We were running, too, and sometimes we fell. It was just my sister and I with that man. He was running, and if we fell he just left us there and we had to get up ourselves. Sometimes we had to get through barbed-wire and we would fall, and sometimes we would get stuck with cactus spines, but he just went on because he was afraid immigration would catch him. I don't exactly know why, but he just kept on. We had to run after him. He didn't seem to care that he was leaving us behind.

We crossed at about 7:00 or 8:00 in the morning, and some other people picked us up. They were waiting for us in a house that looked abandoned. And then soon a lady arrived, and she took us to a hotel, and from the hotel they took us in a van. We were hidden under the seats so that people couldn't see us. Then we had to wait two days in the hotel with another man for my father to pick us up. He finally came to get us in Phoenix and took us to Las Vegas.

Thank God we reached our parents safely. I was fifteen years old when we got to Las Vegas where we stayed for five months. Then my father decided to move to Postville, Iowa, because an uncle who lived there said there was a meat packing plant that hired people who were not legal. That's the reason he came to Postville. In Las

Shattered Dreams

Vegas my father had worked mowing lawns. He was the only one who was working, the rest of us stayed at home. No one worked, not even my mother. My brother was the only one going to school. I didn't because we were planning to move to Postville.

It didn't go well for us in Postville because just after we got here my father had an accident. Two days after we arrived, he found a job on a farm. He started work at 2:00 and that day was the second day he went to work. Just after he left someone called us and said he had had an accident. The car was destroyed, and they don't know how my father survived. They had to take him in a helicopter, and they said he probably wouldn't live. He was in a coma for three days. They were going to take him to a rehab center because he had a brain injury. He couldn't think very well. They did some other tests, and he did better. He broke his foot and his arm, but they operated on them. He had something done to his brain, too. We were very sad, and we didn't know what was going to happen because he was the only one who was working, but God helped us. My sister and I went to work at Agriprocessors because people said you could get a job there, and my father couldn't work. I had to help my mother. My older sister and I started to work on the same day. I was only fifteen years old but seeing that my father couldn't work, I had to get a job.

At that time there was a man who came to Postville to get documents for people, and he sold them to us for $120. With these papers we could get jobs. He looked like a Mexican to me. The day we asked for our papers was the only time I ever saw him. I began to work in October of 2005, at 15 years of age. My job was to package the meat. I also removed the bones from beef. Sometimes I used a knife to cut the meat. Other times there was one of those machines that cuts up bones, like a saw, and they had me putting the bones in the machine or removing them from the barrels. I would pick up the bones and someone else would cut them, or they had me taking out the bone and putting it on the conveyor belt. I always did that job. Sometimes I worked 21 hours a day. I would start at 7:00 in the morning and leave at 2:30 or 3:00 the following morning. I would sleep maybe 4 hours and then return to work at 9:00 a.m. They wouldn't let me start any later than that. This went on for a year. I always felt very tired because it was a lot of work, standing all day. It was always very cold, and I was on my feet all the time. There were times we didn't want to stay any longer but the "yellow hardhat" [supervisor] told us that if we didn't stay we would lose our jobs or that we had to ask an "orange hardhat" [manager] for permission to leave. All of the supervisors wore hard hats, and the different colors showed who was higher up.

These "hardhats" were Mexican and they were really nasty, they would yell at us a lot. Sometimes the conveyor belt would be very full of meat, and we would be working as fast as we could and even so a "green hardhat" [department leader] would shout at us and tell us we were *huevonas*, that we should speed up, that if we didn't want to push ourselves as hard as we could we should leave. They always said that the door was wide open and told us that in that company people came to work and not to gossip.

I needed the job to help my father, and that's why I continued to work there, but after a time I stopped because I wanted to go to school. I didn't go to work for about a week, but a "yellow hardhat" from the plant sent me a message that it was urgent for me to go back to work because they couldn't get more workers. They said they didn't have permission to hire more people and that I had to come to work because they couldn't replace me. They called me at home from the office. I told the woman at the office that I couldn't work because I was going to go to school, but she said it was urgent for me to work because they weren't accepting more people. So, I went back to Agri and about three months later immigration arrived.

Everything was okay until that day when everything changed—

Shattered Dreams

May 12, 2008. Immigration came to Agriprocessors and on that day my dreams and those of many other people ended. The day Immigration arrived they treated us as if we were animals, as if we had committed some terrible crime, and that's just not true. They accused us of identity theft. They tied our hands, our feet and our waists, and they yelled at us. They physically abused us because they tied us so tight that we couldn't even move our feet. They wouldn't even untie us so we could eat, and we could only eat by bending over. They tied my feet so tight that I couldn't stand it. It felt like that thing that they tied me with was cutting into me so I told one of the policemen that I needed it loosened on my foot a little because I couldn't take it. He told me no he wouldn't because that's the way it fit. He said I should put my thumb underneath it and if my thumb fit then it was fine. Later, when I couldn't stand the pain anymore they had to use pincers to cut it off me, and they risked cutting me on the foot.

I felt so...so worthless and humiliated because they put me in places I could never have imagined. They put us in cells with other people that...well, I had never seen sexual things, and they put me in the most degrading situation and I watched the couples who were having...who were doing their things there, and you couldn't do anything about it because you had to be in the same room with all the other women. Sometimes they humiliated us, and there were some women who would yell at me. Sometimes they would make fun of me because I didn't speak English. I don't know what they were thinking and why they picked on me. It was very ugly.

Sometimes they would shut everyone in a cell block, two to a room. They always left me alone in one room when they did that. Sometimes we were shut up like that for 24 hours in a room like this one only smaller. I would be all alone all day; they would just bring me food. They locked us up because they were bringing through high-risk prisoners, people who had killed someone. They shut us up alone for 24 hours with just a little window. In there I felt like

Carmen

I just couldn't, that I could no longer...I said to myself that I was not going to be able to get out of there, I felt so bad, I felt in such despair. They would always put me in a cell alone. They would put the others in groups of two. I think they put me by myself because I looked younger.

It was hard being far from my family because I was used to being with them. My Mom always took care of me and talked with me. But in those jails I felt alone, with no one to look after me. They treated everyone the same there. They yelled at us to make our beds because they said our moms weren't going to do it for us. We had to get up at 5:00 or 6:00 in the morning. Sometimes they gave us food or bananas that had gone bad, or if we left food, they would bring it back and give it to us the next day.

It was hard for me to imagine being deported, that I was going to be all by myself at the border. I didn't know what I was going to have to do or if I was going to be alone. I worried that something would happen to me, and I was afraid because of the uncertainty. Sometimes I communicated with my family by letter, and sometimes I had money to use the phone and I could call them.

I was so desperate that I was always asking the officials when they were going to let me out. They told me they would let me out "when hens had teeth," in other words, they were laughing at me. They didn't say anything true like "when a flight is ready" or "wait a bit," they would just say "when hens have teeth." *Ay*, I was so angry and sad, but I didn't say anything to them. I just went back to my room and hoped that one day they would let me out of there.

All of this has affected my life a lot because it isn't the same as it was before. Sometimes you dream that it's happening all over again. Now I have to take antidepressants because I've been seeing a psychologist and I'm not right in the head. There's a lot of anxiety and sadness in my body, and they told me I had to take the pills for six months, but no, I now have to take them all year. Now I'm seeing a counselor, and I feel a little better.

Shattered Dreams

When Immigration came to Agriprocessors all my dreams ended, and many other people lost their dreams, too. I had hopes of working hard, of being with my family, of returning to my own country one day, of doing well in life, enjoying my youth. I never imagined I would go through what I went through. But I no longer feel the way I used to. I feel sad, and even though people say a long time has passed and I have to forget, sometimes I find it difficult to forget how they treated us. At times, when you're asleep, you dream that Immigration has come back again.

The day of the raid, when Immigration arrived, I was working and all of a sudden people started to yell that Immigration had come. The workers from other areas had begun to run. I just stood there as if I was paralyzed and tried to think of what to do. I don't know how but I got the strength to run upstairs. I was very, very frightened. I didn't know what was going to happen to us. In about ten minutes Immigration came to get us.

When Immigration showed up there were about fifteen people up there, and the agents shouted at us, "Come out of there. Come out. There's nothing you can do. You're completely surrounded. Don't try to run away. Don't do anything."

They had us take off our aprons, our hard hats, and everything. They had us form a line, and they took us downstairs where I saw a lot of American police officers. Some people had tried to run away, and the police tied them up in an awful way with their hands behind their backs. There were even people who were bloody because they had hidden, and their arms were bleeding. The agents took us down, and they made us sit at some table where they were asking information about where we were from. Then they chained our feet and our waists, and they put us on a bus and took us to Waterloo. From 1:00 in the afternoon until 3:00 a.m. they had us sitting there, and they were questioning us. We went all day without eating, and we were very cold because they didn't even give us sweaters. They

Carmen

didn't care if we were cold. We were freezing to death. After that they took us to different jails.

I was in four different jails. I was in Eldora (in Iowa), in Georgia, in Kansas and in Florida. It was very sad and ugly and in every prison there were people I knew from Postville. In every prison they had to check everything, search us to see that we weren't bringing in anything. Then we had to change into used clothing that was from each jail. They took us in vans, all chained together with our hair down. They wouldn't even let us use a scrunchie or a hair band. And sometimes it was very cold and other times it was hot because they turned the heat on so high. And sometimes we would fall on top of each other; there was no way to balance because we were chained. We were very thirsty because they never gave us water. There were times we spent all day in a bus or van and we'd get so tired because we were tied up and there was no way to get comfortable and rest a little. Sometimes we travelled all day, six or eight hours, without anything to drink. Other times they gave us a little bottle of water.

The hardest place was Georgia because it was so disgusting. That prison was horrible. It was dirty, and the bathrooms were filthy. To go to eat we had to keep our hands behind our backs waist high with our palms facing backward. We had to be very careful not to turn in another direction. We had to look straight ahead, and if you turned at all they would take you out of the line and put you at the end and then you wouldn't get any food. They would count the minutes and sometimes we had only 5 or 10 minutes to eat. We had to eat really fast, and sometimes we just didn't have time to eat anything, just enough time to be checked by the police who would tell us not to move so quickly. When they said the meal was over you had to go back to the cells, whether or not you had eaten anything. And that was the hardest part. If you didn't do exactly what they said, they would put you in the hole. I never had to go there. In Tallahassee, Florida, it wasn't as difficult. They gave us more to eat, we could go outside a little, and there was a church we could go to. It was better.

They put us in prison where we were kept for six months. They treated us like criminals, and I think what they did to us was very cruel. They told us it was going to be five months, and after five months I didn't know anything about them bringing us back here to Iowa. I talked to my mother, and she said it was possible that they would bring me back but it wasn't certain. She said they wouldn't bring back the other women from Postville, just me. I would be alone at some other place. I was glad, but at the same time I thought they might just move me to another jail by myself and I would be there for more time because they told me it would take three weeks to get the papers done so I was in prison for six months. I was in Tallahassee, Florida, for two months.

After five months of my imprisonment, they took us out of the jail we were in to another place that was like a detention center for deportation. A lawyer came to see me there and told me they were going to bring me back here to Postville, but that I had to wait a while for the proper documents and so that someone could come and get me. I felt glad that I was going to see my family. My mother was very sad when I arrived, but now she's calmed down a little. My father sometimes starts thinking about what happened, and it's hard for him to get over it. Sometimes he starts to say, "Why did this happen to you? Why?" And I tell him that it's over now. Now that I have papers I feel more at ease because I'm not running the same risks as before and because now it's possible for me to get a good job, one that pays well.

I think the government should give us work permits because Americans don't do the jobs that we do. We deserve work permits. There's a lot of injustice. If they're going to arrest us, then they should deport us. But it is so unfair that they treat us like they do, that they lock us up. It's not right the way they treat us because we

Carmen

haven't come to take anything away from anybody. Sometimes in jail the American or black women would say to us that we came to take away their jobs or their food, that it was a good thing that we were in prison. Sometimes that would bother us, but other times we just let them say whatever they wanted.

The raid changed my life because it will never be the same. They took us from one place to another. They shamed us in the worst way. In prison it's hard to live with people you don't know, and they humiliate you a lot. I would tell someone who wanted to come to the United States not to come, because hopefully in your own country no one will abuse or imprison you. You come here just to suffer and if that's the case, then you should struggle to get ahead in your own country.

Shattered Dreams

Teresa

I was born in Zacatecas in 1978. The *rancho* we lived on was very poor. The streets weren't paved, they were dirt, and the animals just walked all over them. People got around on bicycles. There was no pavement. When I came to the U.S. they were just starting to dig ditches for the sewers because at that time we didn't have plumbing. Nobody had bathrooms. There weren't any phones either.

Well, actually, there was a public phone booth where people went to talk. It was in a little store where everyone from the *rancho* would go and wait in line for phone calls from their relatives in the U.S. My family never had people in the U.S. All of our relatives lived in Aguas Calientes and Monterrey, in Mexico. And I often thought to myself—when we hear that someone received a message saying they had to go to the phone—what could it be like waiting for a call from another place? And the first time I talked on the phone, I asked myself, how does this contraption work? How am I going to be able to hear someone from so far away? I looked at the receiver and thought, "Why am I hearing her?" But I really was hearing her! It seemed so incredible to me. Even now I still can't explain it. It just seems so strange.

There has been a lot of progress in my town lately. Even my mother has her own phone in the house. She now has a bathroom, running water, and electricity for lights. She tells me that the school is bigger. Before, there were only four tiny rooms, and those were the classrooms. It was surrounded by a wire fence. *Mamá* said that there is a lot progress with instruction because there are more teachers now. Before, there were just two.

Teresa

The *rancho* was very small in the beginning, but later on more people started coming because they started to plant more crops. Those of us who had lived there for a long time didn't have money or farming equipment or anything, so new people showed up with the means to use the land. Those people stayed and married into the town. Now there are a lot more people, and my mother says that if I saw them I wouldn't know a lot of them. I probably would know quite a few who are my age and many of the older folks that I used to meet when my mother would send me out to borrow a little bit of milk, or sugar or a couple of eggs.

Life on the *rancho* consists of getting up early, tending the hens, milking the cows, and sweeping off the patio. Then you work in the fields, growing corn and beans. Life in a larger village is different. You have businesses like pharmacies, butcher shops, tortilla stores, and the streets are paved. There are doctors, and there's more progress. On a *rancho* you are much more isolated, but you know everyone and people always greet each other on the street. For us, a *rancho* is a very small, rural place where everyone shares in a life together. It's a lot different from a town that's bigger, where people are more prepared because there are more opportunities and possibilities.

I had a very happy childhood because my mother and father were very loving and affectionate. Even though we basically had nothing, we were a close-knit family. The only problems we had were economic. My *papá* didn't earn enough to buy us shoes. My older sister would make us sandals out of heavy cardboard and bits of thread. We used them at home. We avoided going outside a lot so that people wouldn't see us. I remember once when we went out to the fields with my *papá* and it was raining. I was crying because my shoes had fallen apart. My parents and older brothers and sisters walked, and we little ones rode on the burro. I felt terrible about my shoes being ruined by the water. My sister told me not to worry, that as soon as we got home, we would find another cardboard box and make new ones.

Shattered Dreams

Not having shoes was a big trauma for me, and I was so jealous of the kids who did have them because right in front of my house there was a store and the little girl who lived there had shoes. I asked my father why I didn't have shoes like she had, and he would just hang his head and say that maybe I would get a pair for Christmas.

I remember being a very good student at school. When I started classes I really wanted to be something in life. Right now I still have that desire to move ahead and make something of myself. But money has always been the barrier to my dreams. The teachers said I was very intelligent. They chose me to participate in a poetry contest. I was so excited and thought I could win because they had picked me, but my mother said I couldn't go because the family couldn't buy what I needed for the competition. There were eight kids in the family and a lot of expenses.

I also dreamed of being part of the school's honor guard, and I worked hard to get good grades. One day a teacher told me I was going to receive a scholarship because of my grades, and I felt like the doors of heaven had opened up for me because I wanted to be a teacher. The dream never became reality because my father didn't have money to pay for my schooling. The scholarship I got was small and only for a short time.

When I got to sixth grade and always was first in my classes, they named me to be part of the honor guard, and I was so excited. The honor guard is a group of students who carry the flag when there is some patriotic holiday or official act and you march in front of the whole student body. I told myself that one day I would carry the flag. But like always, money was the barrier between dreams and reality. The uniform was expensive. The truth is there wasn't any money. My mother told me it wasn't important to be part of the honor guard, but it really was important to me because I wanted to stand out, to be someone exceptional. I wanted everyone to see me

Teresa

carrying the flag and to feel important. Money was always the door I couldn't open. Money, money, money. Always money.

When I finished grade school I went to work in the fields with my father. That was my graduation—planting corn and beans. Instead of carrying my school backpack, even if it was handmade from an old red t-shirt, I was now just working the land. I always imagined that when things got better and I could study, I would have a backpack like the girl who lived across the street. I've always been jealous of that girl—even now—because she has her car, her daughter, her husband, her store; and all I have is this electronic shackle that I.C.E. put on my ankle.

In my teens all I did was work. In my small town there are only pigs, chickens and burros. One day my father decided we should go visit my godmother, who lived in Zacatecas, so that I could get to know her. I hadn't seen my godmother since my baptism. I was about 15 or 16 years old, and after the visit I stayed behind to work for her. *Ay*, she turned out to be a real witch. I seemed to have so much bad luck! I wondered why she couldn't see the good in other people. She had taught her daughters that those of us who grew up on the *ranchos* were inferior. When my father was around, everything was just fine. He brought them bags of beans and a hog. My godmother always pretended to be very affectionate when he was around. As soon as he turned his back she would say, "Get out of here, you *rancho trash*, you filthy Indian, running around dressed in rags." They never took me out in public with them.

I asked myself, "Why do they treat me so badly? My father always brings bags of food so that I'm not a burden and they have enough to feed me. Why do they abuse me and refuse to give me food?"

While I was there I took care of my godmother's little girl who was kind of crazy. They would shut the two of us up in a little room. I don't know what was wrong with her, but it wasn't Down's syndrome. She wasn't able to talk or go to the bathroom. She was like a baby; you had to do everything for her. She got used to me and was always hugging me. At night she slept in my bedroom. I think my godmother got a little jealous of me because her daughter always wanted to be wherever I was.

She would say, "You're an Indian! You stink. Don't go near my daughter. You're so ugly." She was always insulting me. "When you got here you were starving and scrawny because all you ever ate was beans." My godmother was so nasty.

My godmother's father was a legal U.S. resident, but he lived in Zacatecas because he was old and sick. He said that he would like me to always do the cleaning in his house. I knew how to do a lot of things because my mother had taught me. I knew how to prepare dishes from *chile en molcajete* to *tortillas*.

He said to me, "I want you and no one else to clean my house."

At that time he paid me 90 Mexican pesos which now are worth about 10 American dollars. I liked doing chores for him because he paid a lot of money. But my godmother didn't like me working for her father.

She said, "How can it be that an Indian, a *ranchera*, is earning more money than my own daughters who have studied in the best schools!"

My godmother was always trying to make me go back to the *rancho* and saying that she didn't want me and that I was taking food from her daughters. She said that when I came to them I looked like a starving alley cat. Her daughters made fun of me saying that I was getting chubby.

Living in that house was my Calvary. Even so, I was willing to make the sacrifice to leave the *rancho* behind and get ahead in life. I wanted to be like the others who had left the village and then came

Teresa

back in better circumstances. Another thing I wanted was to buy a television for my mother and sisters and brothers because I wanted my siblings to watch what I had never been able to see—cartoons. My father, working the fields his whole life, was never able to earn enough to buy a TV. When I got to my godmother's house, I saw that she had a very big television, and I said to myself, if I stay here I'm going to be able to buy one, too. I think that seeing that TV made me envious. That envy made me put up with everything and do whatever—to wash and clean—whatever. I worked there about a year until I was so fed up I just about exploded.

I began to feel angry all the time and to close myself off from the world. For example, I didn't know how to use the phone, and I would get frightened when it rang. Like I said earlier, I just couldn't explain to myself how a person could be talking through those wires. I couldn't wrap my mind around the idea that another person was at the other end. I learned about phones and refrigerators in my godmother's house. In my own house we never had those things; they were just a fantasy.

I wanted to phone my father to tell him to come and get me, but even though there were a lot of phones in the house I couldn't get them to work. Then I figured out that my godmother was unplugging them all so that I couldn't use them. I wanted to tell my father that they were mistreating me, but I thought he wouldn't believe me anyway. So I had to stay and just take all the abuse, over and over again.

Finally, all their abuse, name-calling and insults managed to force me out of their house. Of course, they were very white skinned, tall and beautiful. They had no idea what it is to plant, to harvest, to work in the fields. What they did know was how to eat the food that my father brought. Why did they refuse to give me enough food?

Another girl who worked in the same house told me that she

was going to help me get out. She gave me a phone card. In Mexico you can use a prepaid card to call from public phone booths.

It's different here. I didn't even know how to do that so the girl taught me how.

At about that time, my godmother's father died and I decided I didn't want to take a step backwards and go to the *rancho* to work among the burros. My godmother had a sister who was an optometrist and she wanted me to work for her. I thought that if I agreed to do that, life would change because I would have many different opportunities to move forward, to have some money, and to know and understand more. My dream was to work and be able to send money home to help feed my brothers and sisters so that my father wouldn't have to be worried about them not having enough to eat. I wanted him to be able to buy them shoes. I believed I could provide the solution to everyone's problems, that I could help them all.

So, I went to work with my godmother's sister-in-law. I cleaned house for her. I cleaned everything, even that old woman's butt. People like her have no compassion. They are so proud, so high and mighty; such tyrants and so mistrustful.

During the several years I was working for her, I always took out the garbage. She lived in downtown Zacatecas, so when I went out I would see girls of my age with backpacks and I thought there had to be a school somewhere nearby.

And then, one of those days, a young girl stopped and asked me, "Where are you from?"

"I'm from a *rancho*."

"Don't you want to go to the *escuela abierta*?"

I was flabbergasted. I'd been living right there and had no idea

Teresa

there was a school nearby for adults to help them catch up on grade school and get a high school diploma. I practically had to beg on bended knee to get permission to go to school for three hours. When I told the *Señora* I wanted to take classes, she made an awful fuss, but I insisted that I wanted to finish high school.

Her husband told her, "It's okay, Chilo, let her go and have a little free time." He convinced her to let me go to school.

When I started to study, I felt so small and insignificant compared to the other young women who were taking classes. They had nice book bags and pretty clothes, and there I was dressed in rags.

My work schedule at the *Señora*'s house started at 6:00 a.m. and ended whenever she felt like it. I also had to do things for her friends and just whatever she said. She had her own business—an eye clinic. I helped her by taking the lenses to the lab and picking them up. I cleaned, and I went to pick up her prescriptions. Her house was a very large house. That was my job, and there was nothing I could do but abide by whatever she wanted. When I started to study, I worked from 6 a.m. to 6 p.m. and then started class at 7:00 p.m. and finished at 11:00 or 11:30. After school, I had to return home, do my homework, clean the kitchen, and straighten up the house.

I spent three years like that with the goal of finishing high school. And then the family accused me of stealing, but I was able to account for the missing money. I left right after that incident. This is what happened. They had so much money that once the husband put 500 pesos inside the pages of a book.

Since I cleaned everything, I was in the library dusting and shaking out each book, and I had seen the money. I had never had any desire to steal anything because I always remembered my parents' words: "Never steal anything from anyone. That's what evil people do. You must always respect others and be humble like we are in our home."

So, even though I saw the money and needed it, I left it in the book. When I finished cleaning the library, the man went in and then started shouting to his wife, "Chilo, Chilo, come here."

She came down the stairs like a lion. And then they were whispering and pointing.

And then she said to me, "Tell me where you have the money."

And he shouted like an ogre, "I had 500 pesos in this book."

It turned out that the *Señor* had so much money that he forgot what book he had put it in.

Just before that incident I had finished my studies. I hardly slept while I was studying. The only thing that mattered to me was to get my diploma. I wanted to show it to everyone and tell them I had earned it washing clothes and cleaning houses in the city. So I had graduated, had my diploma, and was getting my clothes packed to go back to the *rancho* and my father. I never showed them my grades nor told them I graduated. Why should I? They didn't care what I did.

The *Señora* was so angry that I had finished my schooling that when I finally showed her my diploma she said, "But what is that? What is that?"

"It's my diploma," I said with tears in my eyes.

She couldn't get into her head the idea that a scrawny cat like me could have finished in only two years—record time! She was so upset because her children, who went to the best schools, were lazy and never did graduate. Still today, they haven't amounted to anything.

Teresa

When they accused me of stealing the 500 pesos I didn't care if they threw me out or I had to leave. I had my high school diploma. So I said, "I'm going to show you right now where that money is. Come with me."

I knew the book with the money in it was in the youngest son's bedroom. And I knew that if I just told them that the boy had stolen the money they wouldn't believe me because I was pretty much a nobody in their house. I just did as I was told. But the kid was 16 years old then, and I was furious. I felt so sad and helpless because I never thought they would accuse me of being a thief. And I just didn't care anymore and was glad that even though I was a servant I had continued my studies.

I said to *Señor* Arturo, "I am very poor and my family needs help. My mother doesn't even have shoes. But go search my room, and then I'll tell you where the money is. I don't want you accusing me of stealing ever again. All these years I've worked for you I've shown you how honest I am."

And then I took the two of them, with the broom still in my hands, to their son's room, and said, "Omar, I want you to give your father the money you took from the book right now. You tell your Mom and Dad the truth, that you don't like me, that you want them to throw me out, and that you took the money so that I would get the blame."

I said to them, "Up until today I've been grateful to you for giving me a job, but I'm leaving and never coming back to this house."

I thought I knew how to handle myself in the city. I felt all grown up and ready to take care of myself. I knew how to get back to my *rancho*. I thought I could just start cleaning in other houses and be successful and send money to my mother. And I said to myself that I could work and study for a profession.

The couple, weeping, asked me to forgive them. In three years

Shattered Dreams

I had never failed them. They had often given me packets of bills to deposit. I wasn't about to sell my reputation for 500 pesos. The *Señora* said I could stay with them until I completed my studies. I told them no, because their children were devils. They were never again going to lay eyes on this "*ranchera*, Indian, mustache-face, *pañienta, burro.*"

When I arrived at my *rancho* everyone was happy. My sisters and brothers had grown up, and I knew a lot more about life, and I knew I could earn money. But at that point the man who was to be my husband crossed my path. He brainwashed me and convinced me to marry him. The first three months were fine. He's divorced and has a daughter from his first wife. My mother-in-law was the fly in the ointment, always saying, "Son, there goes your daughter," always harping on the fact that he had a daughter and making me feel bad.

Because of our poverty, we ended up going to Monterrey. I felt liberated there because we were no longer in his mother's house. I started working in a toy factory to help with the expenses. My sister showed up and moved into our house. This caused a lot of friction because he wanted all the attention for himself. If he sat down on the bed he wanted me to come right over and sit next to him and not even look at me sister.

And my husband always had this fantasy of going north. He would say "I'll go first, and then I'll send for you." I think I knew early on that he would end up coming to the United States. I heard the words *El Norte* as if they meant the salvation of the world. My husband was always saying, "Things are better there. You never go hungry. With what you earn you can pay for food and clothes."

He convinced me. He came here and left me there, but first he took me back to live on the *rancho*. He thought that if he left me in Monterrey I would find another man. He took me home so that his mother could watch me and tell him how I behaved. The good

Teresa

thing was that he left me at my mother's house, but even so my viper of a mother-in-law was always spying to see what I did and didn't do.

Maybe eight months went by when one day I got the news that my "salvation" had arrived. I was going north, and the *coyote* had already been paid. My husband had paid for my brother, too, so that I wouldn't have to go alone and so that nothing bad would happen to me. My brother was so happy because as far as he was concerned my husband sat at the right hand of God.

We went to Nogales, Sonora. My brother walked across the border. The *coyotes* told me that because I'm a woman they were going to have me cross at a checkpoint. But one night I experienced more anguish than I had ever felt in my life because my brother disappeared. I had stayed behind in a flea-ridden hotel while the *coyotes* took my brother across. The *coyotes* were always telling so many lies, and we were from just a small *rancho*, totally ignorant and unsophisticated. Our minds were just blank.

The *coyotes* said that my brother had made it across just fine. "Tomorrow, you're going."

But I needed to hear my brother's voice telling me he was on the other side of the border or I wouldn't believe them.

The *coyotes* said "He's in Nogales, Arizona," but I was uneasy and suspicious.

I spoke with my husband, and he told me my brother hadn't been in touch at all.

So I said to the men, "Where's my brother?"

"He's fine. He's in a house where they are taking very good care of him."

Shattered Dreams

They continued to keep information from me, and I started yelling that I wasn't going to leave. Then they took me to a woman who was going to disguise me. They were going to dye my hair blond. I was afraid that at the border the agents would say I didn't look like the photo on my ID or that they would ask questions I couldn't answer. I was so afraid that I refused to go. Three days went by, and they couldn't tell me where my brother was. Finally they said to me, you know, your brother got lost in the desert. It wasn't true. It just wasn't true. The *coyotes* themselves had kidnapped him, and they were keeping him in an abandoned house.

My brother told me that a bunch of gang members had caught up with them on the other side of the border. He said, "They took our clothes. They took our shoelaces. They knew where we were going to cross. Of course, they didn't take anything from the *coyotes*; they were all in on it."

They held my brother on the other side of the border for three days in a house with 50 other people. There was nothing to drink. The *coyotes* only gave them dirty water and chicken bones. My brother had five dollars. He told one of the men he needed to eat. There was a man with a gun guarding the door. Finally, he escaped by crawling though the bathroom window. The only thought that occurred to him was to find a store where he could get juice or milk. The immigration officers got him, and though some might have considered this a disaster, for him it was a blessing, because he wanted to get back to Mexico to find me.

So from jail he contacted me in the hotel and said "I'm in jail. Don't believe the *coyotes*, I'm going to be deported." And I was so scared and so was he.

"How am I going to be able to find you when you're deported?"

I ran out of the hotel really frightened. He had told me to take

Teresa

a bus that said "Zacatecas." I said, "God, you have to help me." I didn't want to leave until I met up with my brother in Nogales.

He was so defenseless and vulnerable. For me, it was like traveling with a young son who doesn't know anything. But God is great. The only thing I took was a bottle of water, the money I had, and my mother's phone number so that I could contact her back home on the *rancho*. I walked around searching for a phone from 9:00 in the morning until 6:00 p.m. Everyone looked at me as if I were some strange creature. The streets were full of ugly, drunk people.

I wondered what I would do at nightfall. I knew they could do to me what they had done to my brother. I started to scream at God—"You must hear me!" I turned around and saw two men coming towards me. I stared at them and recognized my brother. "*Ay, Dios de mi vida*, here you are in person! How could this happen in such a large city?"

Because my husband is as stubborn as a donkey, we had to go to Ciudad Juárez. He wanted us to cross no matter what. We went to my sister-in-law's house. My brother and I had a tremendous argument there.

My brother told me, "I know you're my baby sister, but I have my children and my wife here in Mexico. And our mother is here, too. I'm devastated. If you go, you'll take half my heart with you, but you have to do it."

I hadn't understood until then how traumatic his experience had been. So I stayed and waited to cross over in Juárez because my husband insisted that he had already paid and didn't want to lose that money.

When the time came for me to cross with a group of people, I had to be ready at 3:00 in the morning. I crossed the river and got to a corral full of chickens and pigs. They had told me to wait there for half an hour and a van would come to pick me up. They took me to a hotel, gave me clothes, breakfast, and a plane ticket.

"A plane? How am I going to get on a plane? I'll die!" I never thought I would ever be inside an airport. They disguised me again at the hotel. They tried to dress me up and make me look like a tourist. I asked the *Señora* to write down where I was supposed to go on a piece of paper. She said she couldn't and I wondered why.

They took me to the airport, and they told me to show my ID and go up the stairs, then turn right and that's where the plane will be. Once there you'll be all set. But I was afraid of getting on the plane, and I never went up the stairs. I missed the plane and the ticket was lost.

When I was waiting in line, a voice said, "Will the woman in the orange blouse please come out of the line?" They asked to see my visa and passport. They asked me where I was heading. They thought I was a "wetback," of course.

A female immigration agent told me, "don't be nervous. Who else is with you? Give me your bag."

They searched me. "Where are you from?"

"Mexico."

"We're going to take a picture of you and fingerprint you. You'll be held just a few hours. Where did you cross? What is your *coyote*'s name?"

I told them his name because I remembered what he did to my brother.

"Thank you for cooperating with us."

They deported me to Juárez. I went back to the house that

Teresa

belonged to some relatives of my brother. Three days later the *coyotes* talked to me and said we were going to try again. I didn't want to lose my husband's money. He had paid $5,800 for me and my brother.

I realized that all the *coyotes* are connected. I decided to give up on the ones in Nogales and work with *Doña* Rafaela in Juárez. The *coyotes* are like one big family distributed all along the border. They charged us a lot because they said we were going to cross at the check-point. They were going to dye my hair blond and give me jewelry and fine clothing to wear as if I were a true American.

When they said I was going to cross at a check-point I said no, that they needed to find some other place to get across. I didn't want to try there because I had already been caught and they knew me. Then the *coyote* told me I was going to go with him because he had promised my husband that he would deliver me. He patted my face and said, "Let's try one more time."

I felt very suspicious and thought that if I went with him by myself something bad could happen to me. Then their boss arrived. The men were her *achichincles*, her accomplices. I was telling all the other people waiting there how I had been caught the first time I tried. They were all nervous and scared and wanted to go back home. The old lady got furious and grabbed me by the hair and shut me in the bathroom. She told me I was despicable and worthless because I had frightened all her clients and I shouldn't have told them anything.

I decided to ask them to give me the money back. They only gave me $2,800. With that money I looked for another *coyote*. He got me across the border for $400. He helped me cross the river at 8:00 in the morning, in full sight of Immigration. I was very close to the van with the agents. I remember it was white with green lettering. The *coyotes* told me not to get nervous and to keep on walking because "right now they won't see a thing." I think the

Shattered Dreams

coyotes gave them money to look the other way and leave us alone. I was pretty nervous because I was all muddy. Right in front of where we came out of the river was a highway, we crossed it and came to a group of trailers and one of the doors opened.

They told me, "Take off your sneakers, wash off the mud, and pretty soon a van will be here to pick you up."

The van showed up fifteen minutes later. There were two men who told me all the information the *coyote* had given them, and they knew who I was, so I trusted them. They took me to the *coyote*'s house in Las Cruces. Another man who had been with me stayed at the same place. I spent a night there.

That morning the *coyote* told me, "We're going to take you to a semi and you're going to wait there about half an hour. Then two men will arrive and you go with them to Denver.

He took me and put me in the semi-trailer with a bunch of storage boxes. It was freezing cold. When I got in I was amazed to see there were more people inside—Cubans, Guatemalans, and Brazilians. There were about 25 of us. The two men arrived, and they drove us to Denver. We passed through two checkpoints and we couldn't make a sound. Before we got to the checkpoints, the men knocked on the trailer to let us know a checkpoint was up ahead.

I arrived at a hotel. Two enormous men got me off the semi; they weren't the same ones who had put me inside. When they took me into the hotel, the owner already had all my information. That's where I opened my eyes and saw more and understood what life is all about.

I couldn't sleep at all that night because I was scared that the Cuban or the other woman I was sharing a room with would strangle me during the night. I was also wondering how it was possible that all the women traveling with me were pregnant! But to my surprise

Teresa

they weren't. When they went into the bathroom they took off their clothes, piece by piece, and under all those clothes that had money, documents, and who knows what else. I was amazed to see how much they could carry in their supposed pregnant bellies.

The following morning a rich-looking man took me to the bus station and from Denver I came to Waterloo, where my husband picked me up.

Soon I was working at Agri. While I worked there, there was a supervisor who was the devil in person. By that time I was pregnant, and I had to ask to go to the bathroom. She would say to the other supervisor, "That fat old lady wants to go to the bathroom to look at herself." That's the way she would talk to me. "Don't let her go because she's a good-for-nothing and will get spoiled. That's quite a belly that she's got there."

I was sure she had never had a baby—that her stomach had never looked like that. Every woman goes through the same thing. I remember one day that I asked another supervisor if I could go to the bathroom, and he told me, "Sure, *Señora*, go ahead." Of all the supervisors, he was the only one who was noble and treated the workers well. The other supervisors would get on his back because he was nice to us. If someone had to go to the bathroom, he would take their place in line and cover the work until the person got back. He did everything.

On one occasion I went to the bathroom and the woman supervisor didn't know, and when she realized, she charged into the bathroom to look for me. She kicked open the door and said to me, "You're fired."

"Fired? Why?"

"Because there's nothing in the toilet. You didn't go."

Shattered Dreams

But I was feeling sick. I was absolutely green around the gills. I felt like I was going to faint. The reason I went to the bathroom was not because I needed to do *pipí* or *popó*; I needed to wash my face.

I said, "So I have to show you what I'm doing for you to believe it? People don't come to the bathroom for just one reason. I'm feeling bad and I came to the bathroom to wash my face."

"Tomorrow there's no more work for you. You took three minutes."

I thought I had lost my job, and I left the bathroom. Outside there was a "yellow hardhat" [supervisor] named Casam. I tried to tell him that she had fired me for going to the bathroom. He said, "No, get back to work. Don't pay attention to her. I'm the one who's in charge here." Then she got real mad because she thought I was going over her head.

She loved to play practical jokes on people and to swear and be vulgar. If she walked behind you she would grab your butt. Or she would grab a breast as she walked by. Sometimes she would sneak up and plant a kiss on your neck or ear. It got to a point where I couldn't take it any longer. All the women were complaining about the same thing. I said that this wasn't normal. How is it that one woman treats all the other women like that and no one says a thing? So once, when I was upset over something, I went to the bathroom and she was in there with two other women. I had a little bit of hair coming out from under my hair net. I almost never spoke to her because I was trying to keep my distance. I was afraid of her. She liked to bite the ears of the other women. And she would say, "You'll pay big time if you tell your husband." I thought she was so strange.

Anyway, I went into the bathroom, and there were those two other women with her. She had made one of them cry because she hadn't let her go to the bathroom. When I went in she started to

Teresa

say that she's the one who gives the orders, that she's the boss, that she was going to screw over everyone. And I got so mad that I turned around, and she looked at me and said, "And you Teresa! Fix yourself up. Look at that friggin' hair. You look like a witch."

Two days earlier there had been an inspection at Agri. Those were the days when the supervisors would run around saying, "don't you have steel gloves? Wait a minute and I'll bring you a pair." How were we going to be using gloves if they never gave us any? Safety measures were really lax. They'd give us the gloves for five minutes while the inspectors were there and then they'd take them away. They also gave us ear plugs, goggles, and new knives and knife sharpeners. And everyone was so happy with all that safety equipment. But when we got our checks they had taken out all the money spent on those things. Why? They hadn't give them to us for safety, but just to pass the inspection, but we had to pay for all the equipment even though we didn't use it. It seems odd, but that's what they always did.

A few days before every inspection the female supervisor I've been telling you about would say to us, "We don't want any women with straggly hair coming out of the hair net, or colored hair, or lots of make-up, or painted nails, nothing like that." But she always looked like a clown. She always wore thick lipstick, eye-liner, fake nails, and lots of jewelry.

I told her, "Look, Filomena, if you're criticizing me because I have a few locks of hair out of the hair net, then you should be an example. You should follow the rules. When you start following the rules in this plant, then so will I. If you teach me and show me how, I'll follow."

"Why are you talking to me that way? You're trash, just a stupid Indian, a bitch, you are—I don't even know what you are."

"Why? Because you're always wearing rings and earrings. You

never come without make-up. You paint your lips all the time and are always putting on perfume and jewelry. And nobody says anything to you because you are you. Well, if you think I'm committing the biggest crime because I have a teeny tiny bit of hair out of the net...You run around all day with your clown face. The day you don't put on mascara is the day I'll tuck in every bit of hair. Don't bother me. Oh, and be very careful about touching me again."

"What are you saying? Why are you saying that I touch you?"

"Because you've done it enough times. The next time I'll complain to my husband because I'm tired of letting you get away with your little games. You say it's to prevent me from slipping and falling, that I smell nice, that I took a bath today, or you say, 'what a pretty blouse,' and you use that as justification for touching me and the others all over our bodies. I don't like women like you."

I puffed up like a lion. I had already told my husband. A few days after that incident Filomena began giving me more work. And she yelled and swore at me more.

She said, "I'm going to put you in a section with all men. Then you'll know what it means to work."

"I'm not afraid of hard work."

"Be very careful about telling anyone what is happening."

I felt so much pressure at work and felt so afraid that whenever I saw Filomena I would start to shake. I knew that I shouldn't let her see my fear or she would bother me more. Then a few days later she molested me again. I was working with the men from the USDA. Near my work space was a staircase that people used to go down to another office. I was right next to it, and she came and grabbed my breast. But she put her hand under the apron. We wore long aprons that went down to our knees. She came by and

Teresa

stuck her hand inside.

"*Ay*, Teresa, how firm your breasts are. Does your husband play with them?"

I was beside myself. I felt myself get red from rage and shame. What she said to me just wasn't normal. It's a lot for a person to take. It was strange because she did the same thing to all the women. There were times when I would go into the bathroom and find one or another of the women crying because of what she had done to her.

I would ask, "What's wrong?"

"Filomena grabbed me and kissed me on the neck. I was so afraid."

She was always a different kind of woman. Finally I had told my husband that I couldn't stand it because this and that had happened at work. I said I couldn't stand her for another week. She terrified me. My biggest fear was that no one could tell me that when I left work at 3:00 in the morning and was alone in the parking lot that she wouldn't do something to me. That woman was way over the top. But I thought that if I quit my job we wouldn't have enough money to pay the rent. We wouldn't have money for food. I thought about it a thousand times. Should I say something or should I keep silent? What was going to happen? In the end, I knew I had faced greater dangers than that, so the next time she touched my rear end, I turned to her and said, "You know Filomena I want to talk to you because I'm going to the office right away."

She laughed and answered, "Ha, ha...so you want to go to the office! What for?"

"Because I don't like you going around touching me. Maybe some people like to be touched and pawed at, but I don't." I had every intention of going to the office to complain.

Shattered Dreams

"Look, Teresa, I tripped and fell, that's all."

"This is the third time you've had so-called 'accidents' right next to me. The first time it was a breast, the next time a kiss, and now my butt. Tell me, where are you going to 'fall' next time?"

And she laughed and started making fun of me. "Look, stupid, they're not going to believe you because I've been working and supervising more than seven years and you're just a *pinche* worker. They'll never believe you over me, Teresa. I've been working here a long time. I'm at a much higher level than you are."

"Listen, Filomena, It doesn't matter if you're the strongest and have the deepest roots. Do you remember the Twin Towers in New York? They looked very strong and safe, and they fell in spite of that."

"The only thing I'm going to say to you, Teresa, is that you had better think it over. Be very careful."

"Why do I need to think it over? I'm tired of you. I'm fed up. I'm not going to put up with any more of your touching."

I was very upset and determined. Then she realized I was, in fact, going to accuse her. I'm sure she thought I was going to get her kicked out. I didn't go to the office right away because the old witch got scared and backed down. I think I look pretty furious when I get mad. I was fed up. The old snake turned into a rabbit.

Later on she began to molest me again to the point of almost making me quit. The tactic she used was to overburden me with work and then joke around and tease me. Finally I went to the office and told them what was happening to me. What they told me was, "We're sorry, but we can't get involved in production issues. We can only help with other kinds of things in the plant."

Teresa

I spoke with the head of human resources. That day my husband went with me.

The woman asked, "Who is he?" "This is my husband."

"Why did you bring him along?"

"Because I would never hide something like this from him."

Then another blond woman with bangs said, "We can't do anything against that supervisor because she is the kind of woman Casam likes. She's his woman. If we have to choose between her and you, well..."

I was amazed. Then my husband said, "We're not going to be able to solve anything here. They're never going to fire Casam's lover."

Ay, but what was this? It was pure crap. Everybody knew everything but covered it up. Everyone knew that if you didn't go along with what Filomena and Casam wanted, they had ways of getting back at you. They always came out on top.

I went to talk to Casam. Even though they treated us like dirt, I was never disrespectful towards anyone at work. I asked him to change my work schedule and give me the morning shift. And he made up a lot of excuses for not doing it. I pushed and pushed. And then one day he asked me to come see him in his office. It seemed odd to me. A week earlier my husband had had an accident at the plant and because there had been no one who could substitute for me, they wouldn't let me leave to see him in the hospital. After my husband had the accident, Casam harassed me even more. So he asked me to go to his office, and when I got there he said he was going to give me the morning shift. That was in December or January because Immigration came in May.

Then he asked, "What's your reason for wanting to change shifts?"

"Because I have headaches." I sure wasn't going to tell him that my headaches were caused by Filomena. "I can't stand it any longer. It's a migraine. I can't sleep because I have my son. I need to change my schedule."

"But, *Señora*, you're so attractive. Wouldn't you like to have good jewelry, nice clothes and a good car?"

I wondered why he was asking me those things.

"Teresa, how long have you been married? Is that man really your husband?"

"Yes, he is."

"Well, you're not wearing a wedding ring."

"We're not supposed to wear jewelry while we're working. Besides, I don't need a ring to know that I'm married."

"Yes, but your husband may not be able to earn as much anymore. Maybe he'll lose his job." That felt like a threat to me.

"You're still a very young woman. If I change you to the day shift…"

"What?"

"Just answer me one question. Do you like sex a lot? Do you have a lot of sex with your husband?"

I just froze and couldn't answer. I understood what he was asking me.

"Are you hot? How hot are you?"

The only thing I could say was, "If you think I'm going to answer that sort of question, you're mistaken. Would you like my husband

Teresa

to ask your wife those questions?"

He got red in the face and yelled at me, "don't you bring my wife into this. She's a lady."

"So am I. And nobody is going to say those things to me. If you don't like people bothering your wife then you shouldn't bother me."

"But you have nothing, nothing. I'm offering you jewelry, and nice clothes, and a car. I'm even offering you freedom from work."

"You can offer me all the gold in the world, I don't need those things. If you want to give me a job, give it to me in a proper manner, without asking for anything in return. I know that I no longer have my job after this, I know it. And I'm going to tell my husband what is happening.

But he was a real coward when it came to handling problems like this with men like my husband. And my husband was well known for being hot-tempered.

"No, don't say anything to your husband. This is a secret."

"My husband and I don't keep secrets from each other. You thought it was a good idea to talk to me and proposition me this way? Well, I'm going to tell my husband exactly what you said."

"No, look, your husband is not fired. You aren't fired, either. Just go on working. I'm just saying that one of these days you and I can go out for dinner."

"No, I'm never going out with you. I'm never going to ask you for jewels, or nice clothes. All I want is to work."

About two weeks after this conversation he started insisting again: "You're so beautiful. You have such a pretty butt." He wanted to see if I would weaken. Finally, seeing that I was never going to go along with his propositions, he got tired of trying. And then we discussed changing me to the morning shift. Nevertheless, he told me, "We can't make a change like this overnight. We need people on the late shift."

I think he knew what was going to happen, that Immigration was going to come. I'm convinced he knew. They were trying to be sure production could continue. Thinking back I can see that they were changing the most productive day shift workers to the night shift, and those who weren't so productive at night to the day shift. They were putting those with more experience at night, too. Those of us who were paid less and were worth less at the job were put on the day shift to be handed over to Immigration. That's what they were doing. That is exactly what they were doing. By now I finally realize what was up. Even with my limited intelligence I've been catching on. That was their strategy.

So, the last three months before the raid, I continued working. Casam even had the audacity to show up at my door after the raid and tell me to go back to work. There I was with the GPS shackle on my ankle and all the legal problems to solve, and without my husband because he had disappeared. Casam was so cynical as to knock on my door on May 14th and say to me, "Oh no, there's no problem with you, María. There's work for you. Come back to the plant!" Sometimes he called all of us "María."

I couldn't imagine what he was thinking that he didn't realize the seriousness of the situation. He even went to the church the day after the raid and asked the people there to go back to work, maybe to help him pick-up the pieces of chicken that had fallen on the floor! The company didn't want to lose a cent, of course. That Casam spoke a lot of Spanish, though not fluently, just words. Anyway, he wanted the workers to go back to the plant as if nothing had happened.

The day Immigration came I was working with some of the

Teresa

men of the USDA. A few weeks earlier, we had received notices from the management that our Social Security numbers were no longer any good and that we had to get new ones and also change our names. The supervisors handed out the notices. Filomena gave me mine.

The supervisors joked about the change in our names. Casam laughed and said, "So, how you name now?" [Teresa affects his flawed Spanish.]

I never changed my name. I've always been Teresa. I've always had that name. And when Casam would hassle me he would always ask for my real name because he thought we always changed them. I told him Teresa was my name and that was that. He would tease everyone: "How you name now? You name Guadalupe. You name María. Okay? You use name you want."

Even though the plant may deny it now, they know they gave us fliers with that information. It was stupid of me not to keep that paper because it could be important proof to show the judge so that he knew what we were ordered to do. I asked Casam why I should change my name. My name is Teresa and I don't want to change it and can't. Anyway, how was I going to understand if they started calling me by another name?

Then he said, "Understand, woman. You number no work no more. No good. No good."

I always asked him why, but he never explained. The bosses at the plant were always protecting themselves and doing everything for their own benefit. A few days after Casam had told me about the new number, I wasn't able to continue working because I couldn't get into the plant. The way they invented to fire people without explanation is that the ID chip [access card] you had to use to get into the plant wouldn't work. When that happened we knew that if the door didn't open with our plant ID then there was no more work for us. And who were you supposed to talk to or complain to? Nobody!

That's what happened to me on about May 4th, 2008. So that very same day, my husband spoke with Casam to ask him why I had been fired. He said that there was nothing wrong, it was just better for us. My husband insisted, and Casam said that he should bring a new ID and Social Security number in three days. I went back to the plant without papers and Casam let me in. Security let me in because Casam had told them to. And that's how I started working again three days before the raid.

On Friday, May 9th, one of the supervisors told me he wanted the papers with the new ID and Social Security number by Sunday. On Sunday he asked for them, but I had forgotten them at home. I lied to him and told him that I didn't have them yet. This little voice in my head was saying, "don't hand in those papers." The supervisor kept insisting that I give him the documents. Again I lied and said that I had sent the money for them the week before, but they hadn't arrived yet. That little voice kept saying, "don't give them those papers. They're not yours."

Later that day, Casam told me that if I didn't give him the papers there would be no work for me the next day. There was no getting out of it so I gave them the papers and Casam made copies and gave me back the originals. It was the following morning that Immigration raided the plant.

It was such a strange and ugly thing, and I had never been so terrified or panic-stricken by guns. It's probably because I never had one right in front of me. That day was like the end of the world to me. When you come from a ranch and see only chickens, pigs, fields and ordinary people you don't know anything about handcuffs and pistols. And even less about guns pointed at your head! I thought, "Dear God, are there people in the world so evil that they want to kill other people? The only one who can take life is You."

Teresa

At the same time, I wondered why these men were so heavily armed if all we were doing was working? They were wearing black vests like the ones I've seen on television that maybe have iron or steel inside. They had guns attached to their legs, and I don't know what else.

That day there was a stairwell just in front of where I was working. One of the women from the USDA came up, and she was sobbing. She said something in English to the man beside me. The only thing I understood was "Immigration." As she turned away, I asked the man what she was saying.

"What's wrong?" I asked.

"Teresa, Immigration."

His eyes filled with tears. He was always kidding around, so I didn't believe him at first.

He said, "Immigration is right outside the door. I'm sorry, I'm so sorry."

That man was always really nice to us. Then I started to cry, too. There are Americans who are really good people. I can't say they all are bad. He was a good guy, and he said to me, "Teresa, take care of yourself, and may God help you."

The only thing I did was to throw off my work apron. I tossed aside the knife for fear of slipping and falling with it. I didn't scream. I went and hid in the freezer. It was very big, but you couldn't hide there for long because it was so cold. There were just two women there and the rest were men. We went up some stairs. Then we heard those terrible echoing shouts, so full of hate and vulgarity. Those sounds paralyzed us like rabbits cornered by an immense boa constrictor.

Shattered Dreams

I thought, "What is that?" I still couldn't believe it. Why do they have so many guns? Are they going to kill us? Are they going to kidnap so many people? I couldn't find a reason for that many weapons. They were so safe and protected and there we were, filthy, covered in animal fat, with no way to resist. They opened the door of the freezer, and the insults started.

One official shouted, "Dogs, sons of bitches. You're really fucked now. Get down here, you *cabrones*."

They shined a big flashlight on us. I remember all the many chains that were fastened to the ceiling that were used to hang the chicken carcasses, and I remember the despair I felt hearing those voices and coming out from among the chains. There were two men in front of me, and then the *migra* officer, who was enormous, a tremendous gorilla of a man. Just seeing him made my legs tremble. He aimed his gun at us and said, "Come on, you pile of shit. Get on out of there."

They spoke Spanish. It's strange that they spoke Spanish so well, with perfect accents, as if they were just like us. They used the same vulgar swear words that sometimes come out of our mouths. I wondered what that was all about.

The officer took out his pistol and put it to the head of one of the Guatemalan men. The man froze and started to beg, "Please don't do it, I have a family."

My heart was in my mouth and I don't know why, but I started to see a vision of my mother. Like I said before, I couldn't imagine that there were people who would want to take the lives of others. I prayed to God to make the officer pause and not kill that poor man. But I thought, "If he wants to, he'll shoot." The Guatemalan was caught just as if he was another chicken hanging from the chains, and the officer began to curse and taunt him. Then two other men from Immigration showed up, and they forced us down the steps.

Teresa

Since I had my boots and other work equipment on, I went to the bathroom to take them off. We were freezing and could hardly move. When they led us from the freezer and took us someplace else, I could finally grasp the reality of what was happening. I can still see the face of one of the women officers. She was looking at us with so much disdain, disgust and horror. When they took us out of the freezer, she immediately put on a pair of rubber gloves and a face mask. She was dark-skinned, tall and fat, and she kept looking at us with such revulsion. I've always said that in Mexico we view Americans as something really special. We say with admiration, "Look at that gringo." But they despise us.

They took me for questioning. They wanted to find out if I had any children, but for fear they would go to my house and take my husband I said I didn't have any. But in one corner a saw a large group of women who had plastic wrist bands of a different color. I began to wonder why. The female agent asked me a lot of astute questions.

"Where's the rest of your family? Who else is with you here?"

For me they were all the same question. I told her that no one was with me in Postville. Then they put me in plastic handcuffs, and I went over to the group of women who were in the corner. I asked them why their cuffs were a different color from mine. They said they had told the agents they had children and the agents said they were going to be allowed to see them. *Ay*! So I went back to the female officer.

"*Señorita*, excuse me. I do have a son."

She turned around and shoved me really hard. "Why the fuck didn't you tell me? Why did you lie to me?"

"You never asked me if I had a baby. You just asked who came here with me. But I do have my son."

283

Shattered Dreams

"Yeah, and where was he born?"

"My son is from here. He was born here."

"And exactly where was he born? Did you give birth here among the chickens? Was he born here in the plant?"

"No."

"Give me all the correct information about your son."

"My son was born here."

"And who's the father?"

"He has a father, but I don't know where he is."

"How can you not know where he is?"

"With all the people you have arrested here, I don't know what has happened to my husband."

"Well, okay. Go on now."

They never told me they were going to let me go. I only knew that they were going to fit me with an electronic shackle. I thought they were going to let me leave to pick up my son and then be deported. I didn't care about anything except taking my son with me.

Then they took us to a bus. They held us there for many hours. We were shut inside. From there we could see how the agents were opening up the cars that were in the parking lot. They took the papers out. One official came on to the bus, and one of the señoras asked him why they were breaking into her husband's car.

The agent ridiculed her saying, "What have you got in there? Drugs? Cocaine? That's why you don't want us to open the trunk."

Teresa

And then I said to the officer, "You think that we're going to be selling drugs? If we had drugs, we wouldn't be working like animals twelve to fourteen hours a day. People who deal drugs don't have to come here to work. Those people are running around loose and in nice cars. They don't have their hands full of chicken shit like we do."

The agent just gave me an angry look because I had answered him back. That was at maybe about 3:00 in the afternoon. It wasn't until 6:00 p.m. that it was my turn to get out of the bus to answer more questions.

"What's your name? Where are you from? What is your father's name?"

They knew everything. I was surprised by what they knew that I had not told them. It really was amazing how all sorts of information about me came out of the computer.

Then they took me to another bus. They asked me how many times and how I had tried to cross into the United States. I also told them how much I had paid. I think the fact that when I had crossed the border in El Paso I gave them the *coyote*'s name helped me. All of that information that I gave them was on the computer. And then they pushed a button and my picture appeared. My God! That's me!

A very sly officer asked me, "How many times did you cross over? Just once?"

"No, I tried three times and on the third I was successful."

"Aha, you're a smart one."

I kept my mouth shut. They had a lot of information against me. They also knew about the time I went to the U.S. consulate to request a visa because I wanted to come with proper documents. Then they started to ask for my visa.

"You came here with a visa. So where is it? What did you do with it? What's your address?"

"I don't have a visa."

"You came into the country with a visa. Here's the date they gave it to you."

"No, I don't have one. They turned me down. Do you know why? Because I didn't have any money and the only thing they care about is money. Whether or not I could get a visa depended on whether I had good clothes or not."

"Yes, you're telling the truth. Here is where they say you were denied a visa."

The man who was at the computer wrote something and then gave me several sheets of paper. I never threw those documents away. After awhile, I sent them to my lawyer. I had no clue what was on them, what they were about.

Then they put the electronic shackle on my ankle. I remembered right away that I had seen those but only in movies. I wondered why they were putting that metal band on me and what I was going to be able to do or say. Can I walk with that thing on my ankle? What's going to happen to my leg?

"Can I shower with that on?" I asked the officer.

He answered in an ironic tone, "Look, sweetie, you can even go swimming with it and nothing will happen to you. Ah, but don't leave this area because we'll go looking for you and then you'll be really screwed."

I thought to myself that this was really bad. When I was leaving the enclosure where they had the computers, I thought to myself, "Oh, my God. Will I be able to stand this weight on my leg for very long?"

Teresa

When I was leaving an agent asked me, "Where do you live?"

I thought for a moment. If I tell them where, they're going to go and get my husband. Out of pure fright, I didn't say a word and started walking faster. The house where my son's babysitter lived was right across the street from the plant's exit, like three blocks away from the railroad tracks. I thought, if I go for him they're going to see me. They're going to follow me, and then they're going to get the people in that house, especially the woman who was caring for five children. "What can I do," I thought. Finally I decided I had to go get my son.

I was knocking on the door when one of the men with USDA who worked with me said, "Teresa, your son isn't there." But how could he know that? Then he repeated, "Your son isn't there. Come with me. Get in the car, and we'll go to the church."

"No. Why?"

"Because all of the children are at the church. Let's go."

I got into his car. Even as we were driving, Casam caught up to us in his car and said, "*Señora*, you come my car."

I said, "Casam, not even God can forgive you."

And the USDA man turned to him and said, "Get the Hell away."

I thought to myself that Casam had neither soul nor feelings.

Casam said, "It's not my fault. It's the Cuban's fault."

Three months before the raid a new supervisor arrived. He was from Cuba. He was a very strange man, always watching everything. That Cuban was an Immigration agent because the day of the raid he was with the other agents. When that wretched Cuban started to work at the plant he was a "yellow hardhat." He was weird, and he stared at you as if he wanted to strip you naked. He was always spying, wanting to see and hear everything. The jerk would do whatever he wanted. When his socks got wet he would even dry them in the same microwave that we used to heat our food.

We knew he was Cuban because of his accent and everyone at the plant said so. He was pretty light-skinned, stocky, had a round face, and light brown hair. When Immigration was at the plant and they took us out to the buses, he was sitting with the agent in charge of everything, joking, drinking water and pointing out all the people as if to say, "Look at all the people I got for you." It was strange to see him there, but I understood he must be with Immigration. I recognized him.

After the raid we found out that he had made maps of the plant. He always stayed around roaming the plant and mapping when everyone else was leaving. Some say he had a tape recorder, tiny as a pen, which he carried around with him all the time.

At the plant they always told us that Immigration had been paid off, and that there were people who were watching the highways to warn us if the agents were on their way. The owners of the plant must have known that Immigration was coming. Like I said, there were maps they got from inside the plant so that not even a mouse could escape.

That day when I arrived at the church I found my son with only one shoe on, hungry, and crying. I hugged him and thought that even with this shackle I can have my son with me. It was such an awful day. I don't think I'll ever forget it until the day I die. I'm never going to forget.

So many things happen in this country. When you come you don't weigh the dangers you face both crossing the border and getting a job. You don't even know what Social Security means. When you come from a small *rancho* in Mexico, you are so innocent, with a pure mind. When you arrive you have no evil or viciousness in you, and you don't want to hurt anyone. If someone says to you, go and do this or that, you do it because you think it's right. You don't realize it isn't like home. I would see the Social Security card and ask myself what those numbers meant. In Mexico they give work to people who have studied. It's always that way. Why do they ask for that card with my photo here? I never understood the seriousness of having that ID. I had to go through this nightmare to understand.

The trauma that I suffered during the raid means that I can't stand to see tall men with dark glasses. It's worse if they have baseball caps because that's how the agents looked. Even nowadays, if I see a man like that I freeze and I stare at him even though I know that I haven't done anything wrong. The emotional damage that was done to me on that day was enormous.

Since the raid, everything has been so hard. I have suffered blow after blow. But, I pick myself up and keep going.

Epilogue

In February 2009, on nearly the same day she received news of receiving a US visa that would allow her to stay in the country, Teresa was diagnosed with thyroid cancer. In April of 2009 her thyroid was removed. Two months later she received her first chemotherapy treatment, and in December 2010 she had her second treatment. The results have been favorable and her level of cancerous cells has diminished. She has received no other treatments but continues to see an oncologist every three months. Her greatest concern is her five-year-old son because she fears that the cancer will come back more aggressively and may kill her.

The supervisor "Casam" was arrested in Israel in March

2011. He was finally extradited to the United States in 2013 to face criminal charges for harboring undocumented workers and document fraud. Another supervisor sought by the F.B.I. is still at large and thought to be in Israel.

Glossary

Achichincles	accomplices, hangers on
Atole	a drink made from corn flour, water, sugar, and cinnamon
Batidor	a clay pot to heat liquids
Barranco	a deep ravine
Brazalete	A GPS device or electronic shackle that is fitted on the ankle
Brujos	traditional healers, healers
Cabrón	dude, bastard, jerk, son-of-a-bitch
Caimito	plum-like fruit
Caite	sandal
Canasta	woven basket
"*Carup*"	the place in Agriprocessors where the chickens are "cut up"
Centavos	cents, one-hundredth of a quetzal
Chaparra	short girl, little one
Chicharrines	flour fritters
Chichis	breasts
Chile en molcajete	chilies ground in a mortar
Chiles rellenos	peppers stuffed with filling
Chocobananos	frozen bananas dipped in chocolate
Comal	a disk of clay or metal used to cook or heat tortillas
Compañero	buddy, companion
Con permiso	"with your permission" or "excuse me"

Shattered Dreams

Conejo	rabbit
Corretizas	a children's game like tag
Corrida De Toros	bullfight
Coyote	a smuggler who is paid to take people illegally across a border
Dios de mi vida!	Oh, good God!
Don/Doña	courtesy titles, Mr./Mrs.
Escuela abierta	an evening school for adults, similar to GED classes
Feria	a fair or festival
Fiesta	party
Frijoles	beans
"Hardhats"	Agriprocessors had a system of colored hard hats worn by employees to designate the position of each worker. Blue - worker (chicken area); gold - line leader; green - department leader; orange - manager; red - Quality Control; white - worker (beef area); yellow - supervisor.
Hija/hijo	child (female/male)
Híjole	an exclamation conveying surprise or emotion
Huevón/huevona	bum, lazy person (male/female)
Huicoy	a chayote, a green fruit used in soups, resembling a pear and tasting somewhere between a cucumber and a summer squash

Glossary

Huipil	a richly embroidered cotton blouse worn by women in Central America, very often very wide and low-cut
M'ijo/a	"mi hijo/a", my (boy/girl) child
Macapal	a forehead harness
Maestro	teacher
Mamá	Mom
Migra	the agents of the U.S. Immigration and Naturalization Service (INS) or Immigration and Customs Enforcement (ICE)
Mojado	wetback
Mucho Gusto	"Glad to meet you."
Novios	boyfriend and girlfriend
Pan pirujo	home-made bread
Pañienta	a word used to diminish a woman, a reference to brown spots that form on the face due to pregnancy
Papá	Dad, Papa
Patera	a pod that contains a cotton-like substance inside to suck on.
Pepián	meat cooked in a thick brown sauce
Pinche	lousy, horrible

Shattered Dreams

Pipí	to urinate or pee
Popó	to defecate or poop
Quetzales	units of Guatemalan money, each worth about 13 cents
Rancho	a small village or farm, an agricultural "company town"
Ranchero/a	someone who comes from a rural village
Refacción	merienda, a snack with soda pop
Río Bravo [Norte]	the Rio Grande, the river on the northern border of Mexico
Señora	woman
Tapiscar	to harvest
Típico	refers to traditional products, especially woven articles, made in Guatemalan indigenous communities for sale to tourists
Toalla	a towel
Toro escondido	a children's game like hide-and-seek
Tostadas	a fried tortilla with beans and lettuce on top
Tzute	a dress or kilt, traditionally worn by indigenous Guatemalans

Glossary

Mujer de vida alegre   a loose woman

¡Vámonos!   "Let's go!"

Vieja   "old lady"

Bibliography

Amnesty International Report 2009 - Guatemala, May 28, 2009. http://www.refworld.org/docid/4a1fade8c.html

Amnesty International Annual Report 2012: Guatemala. http://www.amnesty.org/en/region/guatemala/report-2012

Bacon, David. *Illegal People*: How Globalization Creates and Criminalizes Immigrants. Beacon Press, Boston, 2008.

BBC News, Head of UN anti-impunity panel in Guatemala resigns, June 8, 2010. http://news.bbc.co.uk/2/hi/world/latin_america/10263494.stm

CNN.com, Guatemala Declares Calamity as Food Crisis Grows, Sept. 9, 2009. http://edition.cnn.com/2009/WORLD/americas/09/09/guatemala.calamity/

CNN.com, Mexican Drug Lord Makes Forbes' Billionaire List, March 13, 2009. http://us.cnn.com/2009/WORLD/americas/03/13/mexico.forbes.list/index.html

Elias, Paul. The Associated Press, Fed. Court Opens Door for Guatemalan Asylum Claim, July 13, 2010. http://www.huffingtonpost.com/huff-wires/20100712/us-asylum-guatemalan-women/

Encyclopedia of Nations, Mexico - Poverty and Wealth, 2010. http://www.nationsencyclopedia.com/economies/Americas/Mexico-POVERTY-AND-WEALTH.html

Bibliography

Fieser, Ezra. Correspondent, *Christian Science Monitor*. Guatemala Slowly Confronts Widespread Rape of Women, November 20, 2009. http://www.csmonitor.com/World/Americas/2009/ 1120/p90s01-woam.html

McCleskey, Clair O'Neill. Homicides Fall For Third Consecutive Year In Guatemala. *Insight Crime*, January 3, 2013 http://www.insightcrime.org/news-briefs/homicides-fall-third-consecutive-year-guatemala.

McKinley, James C. The New York Times, U.S. Is Arms Bazaar for Mexican Cartels, February 5, 2009.

Molzahn, Cory Et Al. Drug Violence In Mexico Data And Analysis Through 2011. Special Report Trans-Border Institute, John B. Kroc School of Peace Studies, University of San Diego, March 2012. http://justiceinmexico.files.wordpress.com/2012/03/2012-tbi-drugviolence.pdf

Nissen, Julia. Guatemala's Eternally Woeful Tale: The country's problematic fight against impunity. Council on Hemispheric Affairs, July 7, 2010.

Overseas Advisory Council; Global Security and News Reports. Guatemala 2010 Crime and Safety Report, May 4, 2010. https://www.osac.gov/Pages/ContentReportPDF.aspx?cid=9323

Salgado, César. Más de 5 mil indígenas, víctimas de explotación en ranchos de Chihuahua. *La Jornada*, September 23, 2001 http://www.cesarsalgado.net/200109/010923g.htm

Taylor, Jerome. How the Rising Price of Corn Made Mexicans Take to the Streets, The Independent (London), June 23, 2007. http://www.questia.com/library/1P2-7481473/how-the-rising-price-of-corn-made-mexicans-take-to

Villarreal, M. Angeles and Cid, Marisabel, NAFTA and the Mexican Economy, Congressional Research Service Report for

Congress, November 4, 2008. http://www.fas.org/sgp/crs/row/RL34733.pdf

Youderian, Annie. Asylum Victory for Guatemalan Women, Courthouse News Service, July 13, 2010. http://www.courthousenews.com/2010/07/13/28785.htm

Biographies of the Compilers and Editors

Luz Hernández, Ph. D. candidate in Hispanic Linguistics at the University of Minnesota, received her B.A. in Hispanic Literature and Linguistics from the Universidad Autónoma de Puebla, Mexico, in 1999, and an M. A. in General Linguistics at the Universidad Autónoma de Puebla in 2002. She worked as an instructor of Spanish at Luther College, in Decorah, Iowa, 2004-2010. Luz has presented in English and Spanish at recent conferences in the United States, Paris, Cuba, and Spain on linguistics and immigration. Shortly after the 2008 Postville raid, she became a member of the St. Bridget Church Hispanic Ministry's Postville Response team, serving as press liaison, and as an interpreter and translator. She has also been a member of the Decorah Human Rights Commission, a team member for the Material Witness Support Group of the Decorah Faith Coalition, and Community and Media Liaison for Luis Argueta's documentary film *Abused - The Postville Raid*. In addition to several articles on linguistics in Spanish, she published in Guatemala (F & G Editores, 2009) a translation of Erik Camayd-Freixas's important essay *Interpreting After the Largest I.C.E. Raid in U.S. History: A Personal Account*. She co-authored with Dr. Gerardo Sandoval the article "Gender, Transnationalism and Empowerment in Postville, Iowa: Women with Electronic Shackles," which is about to appear in *Transborder Latin Americanisms: Liminal Places, Cultures, and Power (T)here*, editor Clara Irazabal, Routledge Press, New York, (2013). In September of 2011, she began her Ph.D. studies in Hispanic linguistics at the University of Minnesota, having been awarded a DOVE Fellowship.

Virginia Gibbs (Professor Emeritus of Spanish, Luther College), earned her B.A. at the University of Wisconsin-Madison in 1965; an M.A. from New York University (Madrid Program), 1976; and a Ph. D. in Hispanic Language and Culture, University of Minnesota, 1988. She lived in Madrid, Spain, from 1965-1976. She has published *Las Sonatas de Valle-Inclán*, Editorial Pliegos, Madrid, Spain, 1992; and *Latin America: Curriculum Materials for the Middle Grades*, Center For Latin America, University of Wisconsin-Milwaukee, 1985, Revised edition, 1988. She is the author of articles in a variety of academic journals. She is a past-president of the North Central Council of Latin Americanists. Soon after the 2008 Postville raid, Virginia became active in the relief efforts, interpreting for attorneys, government agencies, and doctors. She also helped some of the women form a co-op for the sale if their traditional Guatemalan weaving and jewelry. Her volunteer work interviewing 30 women, for approximately 2 hours each, to document the psychological impact of the raid on their families was key in planting the seed for this project and forming the personal connections that enabled it. Now retired and living on the Oregon coast, she is on the Board of Directors and serves as a volunteer at the Newport Centro de Ayuda. She is also a member of the Immigration Information Response Team of Lincoln County.

Made in the USA
San Bernardino, CA
29 May 2014